Coaching Pitchers

Third Edition

Joe "Spanky" McFarland

Human Kinetics

Library of Congress Cataloging-in-Publication Data

McFarland, Joe, 1954-
    Coaching pitchers / Joe "Spanky" McFarland.— 3rd ed.
        p. cm.
    ISBN 0-7360-4509-0 (Soft cover)
    1. Pitching (Baseball)   2. Baseball—Coaching.   I. Title.
    GV871 .M27 2003
    796.357'22—dc21

                            2002014980

ISBN-10: 0-7360-4509-0
ISBN-13: 978-0-7360-4509-4

Developmental Editor: Leigh LaHood; **Copyeditor:** Jan Feeney; **Proofreader:** Coree Clark; **Graphic Designer:** Nancy Rasmus; **Graphic Artist:** Sandra Meier; **Photo Manager:** Dan Wendt; **Cover Designer:** Jack W. Davis; **Photographer (cover):** Cathy Kushner; **Art Manager:** Dan Wendt; **Illustrator:** Tim Offenstein; **Printer:** Versa Press

Human Kinetics books are available at special discounts for bulk purchase. Special editions or book excerpts can also be created to specification. For details, contact the Special Sales Manager at Human Kinetics.

Printed in the United States of America   10   9

Human Kinetics
Web site: www.HumanKinetics.com

United States: Human Kinetics, P.O. Box 5076, Champaign, IL 61825-5076
800-747-4457
e-mail: humank@hkusa.com

Canada: Human Kinetics, 475 Devonshire Road, Unit 100, Windsor, ON N8Y 2L5
800-465-7301 (in Canada only)
e-mail: info@hkcanada.com

Europe: Human Kinetics, 107 Bradford Road, Stanningley
Leeds LS28 6AT, United Kingdom
+44 (0) 113 255 5665
e-mail: hk@hkeurope.com

Australia: Human Kinetics, 57A Price Avenue, Lower Mitcham, South Australia 5062
08 8372 0999
e-mail: info@hkaustralia.com

New Zealand: Human Kinetics, Division of Sports Distributors NZ Ltd.
P.O. Box 300 226 Albany, North Shore City, Auckland
0064 9 448 1207
e-mail: info@humankinetics.co.nz

To all those who truly enjoy a swing and a miss,
a broken bat, shutouts, knockdowns,
and 6-4-3 double plays.

contents

foreword

In the fall of 1984 Joe "Spanky" McFarland took a look at a lanky kid from rural Georgia and saw something that no one else had seen—a big-league pitcher. The kid was me, and thanks in large part to the things that Spanky taught me, his vision—and my dream—came true.

Spanky faced quite a task in trying to turn a raw country thrower into a smooth and fundamentally sound pitcher. With his help I was exposed for the first time to two of the keys to good pitching: mechanics and strength training. Both are vital to any successful and prolonged career. Hand in hand with this development of a solid physical base, Spanky taught me drills to help improve both velocity and control. The combination allowed me to progress from throwing 87 mph in my freshman season to throwing 96 mph in my junior year. Although not everyone can improve so dramatically, Spanky's drills can help almost any pitcher reach his potential. His control and speed drills, coupled with the techniques he uses to develop pitching strength and low-wear-and-tear mechanics, can be of great help to pitchers regardless of age or level of competition.

Spanky's teachings went beyond those of physical development. He also instilled in me a confident and aggressive mental approach to pitching, a true necessity in developing a pitcher's physical talents to his fullest.

It's impossible for me to say enough about Spanky's contribution to me and my career, and I'm not the only one he's helped. Now Spanky is sharing his ideas and practices in *Coaching Pitchers*. Along with the information designed to help individual pitchers develop both mechanically and mentally, there are tips gained through years of experience that can help coaches better utilize their pitching staff. This will ultimately help in avoiding injuries to pitchers and, of course, in winning.

Coaching Pitchers is a great learning tool for both pitchers and coaches, from Little League to college ball. If you pitch or coach pitchers, try the ideas of a truly dedicated pitching coach who has worked long and hard at his job and his love.

Kevin Brown
Pitcher, L.A. Dodgers

preface

Lots of people know pitching. But not every pitching expert is an expert coach. Coaching pitchers requires much more than knowledge alone. Good coaches must add to the vast quantities of pitching information the ability to teach and apply that information to athletes.

To become better coaches, we must continually search for new ways of communicating pitching knowledge to different pitchers. Each time we hear a new way to explain a skill or concept or we learn a new teaching drill, we grow. It may even be that the more we learn, the less we coach, because when we have mastered our trade we will know what works for every pitcher we encounter.

Knowing the principles of psychology is a crucial difference between pitching experts and pitching coaches. A coach needs to understand direction, motivation, and stress in making daily decisions about pitchers' welfare.

Pitching coaches must also be effective managers, directing, developing, and satisfying as many as a dozen pitchers who can only work one at a time. And the coach must know the physical effects of pitching to intelligently decide who can and cannot pitch on a given day. Games and careers can be saved or lost based on such decisions.

Taking the path from pitching expert to pitching coach means learning how to apply pitching knowledge, and all that it involves, to real people. My intent in this book is to help you move along that path. I'll break down the facts of pitching and combine them with effective ways to teach, motivate, and develop pitchers to reach their individual potential.

acknowledgments

I'd like to thank those athletic directors and head coaches who gave me a chance to help kids through baseball. I would also like to thank all the pitchers, young and old, whom I have had the pleasure of working with over the years in our quest to get hitters out.

I thank my family, Deb, Tara, and Ty, for putting up with me and my obsession—baseball. I would also like to thank God for all of the above and everything else in my life.

chapter 1

Developing Proper Mechanics

When a pitcher develops good pitching mechanics for the delivery, he is apt to have good control and to throw in a loose, injury-free way. Good mechanics can also lead to greater arm strength; many pitchers have increased fastball velocity by working religiously on mechanics. Keep in mind that it takes a lot of time and many repetitions to break existing habits.

In this chapter we break down the full-windup delivery into its many phases and show you how to teach each phase in progression. We begin with the lower-body mechanics, progress into upper-body mechanics, and finish with a look at the entire delivery.

Lower-Body Mechanics

Lower-body mechanics are important for both control and power. The mechanics begin with the feet—the pivot foot and stride foot—and progress up through the legs to the hips. *Lower-body mechanics should be altered to match the pitcher's natural arm slot. The pitcher's natu-* *ral arm slot should never be adjusted to match the lower-body mechanics.* To create a good overall pitching delivery, a pitcher must develop a solid mechanical base.

Foot Placement on the Pitching Rubber

Contrary to popular belief, there is no preferred foot placement on the rubber; it is a matter of individual preference. Conventional thinking has the right-handed pitcher on the right side and the left-handed pitcher on the left side of the rubber.

Instead of making a steadfast rule about which side is best for either right- or left-handers, let's think about how a pitcher can get the best results from his pitches. A pitcher with a low three-quarter or a side-arm pitch may prefer to use the opposite side of the rubber to take advantage of his natural movement.

A right-handed pitcher who starts on the right side of the rubber and throws slightly across his body may benefit from being on the left side of the rubber. From this angle he goes in a more direct line to the target, which

Developing proper technique not only ensures effective pitches, but it also strengthens the arm and helps prevent injuries.

enables him to use his hips more and doesn't cause him to lock himself out.

Experimentation and observation will provide the answers to where a pitcher should place his pivot foot on the rubber. Once a pitcher establishes a position, he must work from that position on a regular basis to create consistency.

Footwork Initiating the Windup

A pitcher can use three different techniques in the beginning of the windup as he shifts weight from the back foot to the pivot foot: the rocker step, the step back, and the step to the side. All three techniques are effective when executed correctly, and each pitcher should choose the technique that works best for him.

In all three techniques, the pitcher should keep his head over his pivot foot to ensure that he does not transfer too much weight backward away from the target (figure 1.1). The rocker step and the step back start momentum and develop rhythm for the windup.

Figure 1.1 Head over pivot foot.

Rocker Step

The pitcher places the pivot foot on the appropriate side of the rubber, with the front section of cleats hanging over the front of the rubber and the back section of cleats on top of the rubber. The stride foot should be behind the rubber at shoulder-width distance from the pivot foot (figure 1.2). When the pitcher takes the sign, his weight should be over the pivot foot. He should have very little weight on the stride foot, and he should be up on the toe of the foot.

Once the pitcher has the signal and begins the windup, he simply shifts his weight and rocks back. Keeping his head over his pivot foot, he shifts his weight from the pivot foot to the stride foot. The stride foot starts up on the toe and, with the weight shift, goes back on the heel (figure 1.3). As the stride foot goes onto the heel, the pivot foot begins to pivot. When the weight starts to shift back to the pivot foot, the stride foot goes back up on the toe before beginning to lift into the gathered position (figure 1.4).

The rocker step has two advantages. First, most pitching mounds in high school, and

Figure 1.4 Pivot foot action.

some in college, are not constructed correctly and drop off behind the rubber. A rocker step, rather than a step back, is helpful on an incorrect mound. Second, when a runner is on third base, there is less chance of a balk should the runner start toward home. The rules state that the pitcher must clear the rubber with his pivot foot when stepping off to deter the runner. This is somewhat confusing to the pitcher if both feet are starting on the rubber as in the step-back technique.

Step Back

Many pitchers like to use the step back when starting the windup because it gives them a better rhythm than the rocker step. The step back is fine as long as the pitcher keeps his head over his pivot foot when stepping back—this will keep him from stepping too far (figure 1.5). Also, the pitcher must try to step within the boundaries of the rubber and not off to the side—the momentum of a step to the side would cause him to go toward first or third base rather than second base before going toward the plate.

When using the step back, the pitcher starts with both feet on the rubber while getting his sign. With a runner on third base, the pitcher's weight should be on the stride foot when he gets the signal—this weight shift helps him get off the rubber if the runner breaks for home. After getting the signal, the pitcher starts the windup by stepping back with the stride foot or stepping off with the pivot foot.

Figure 1.2 Proper position for taking the sign.

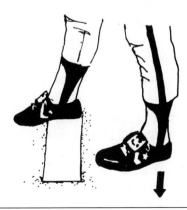

Figure 1.3 Weight shift on the windup.

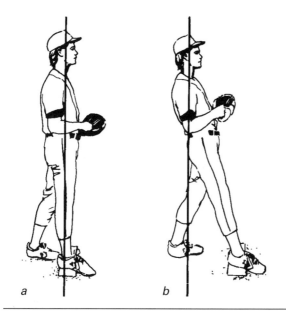

Figure 1.5 *(a)* Correct and *(b)* incorrect step back.

Step to the Side

When a pitcher's arm slot drops down to low three-quarter or side arm, it makes mechanical sense to step to the side instead of back toward second base (figure 1.6). The pitcher with the low arm slot will use more rotation and coil in his delivery, and stepping to the side seems to make the pivot leg lift and hip rotation movements a more fluid motion.

Figure 1.6 Stepping to the side.

Pivot

When the pitcher begins to step or rock back, the pivot foot lifts slightly (although the foot does not appear to lose contact with the rubber). The pitcher then rotates the foot exter-

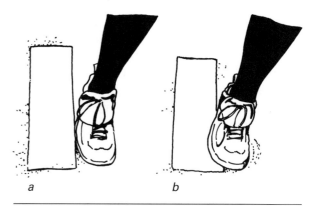

Figure 1.7 During the pivot, only the outside of the foot touches the rubber, as shown in *a*.

nally and places it in front of the rubber with only the outside of the foot making contact with the rubber (figure 1.7).

Young pitchers commonly make the mistake of pitching with the foot half on and half off the rubber, thinking that this will give them a greater push. Later in this chapter we will see that a push or drive isn't nearly as important as balance. With the pivot foot half on and half off, it is impossible to gather momentum; a pitcher cannot balance with his pivot foot in this position. Without this pause for balance to gather momentum, the pitcher will rush, causing control problems and possible injury.

The pivot foot should always be placed in front of the rubber with the toe slightly lower than the heel. The level of the heel is important for many reasons:

- If the heel of the pivot foot is lower than the toe, the pitcher tends to lean back during the delivery (toward first base for a right-handed pitcher). This may cause loss of control or injury.
- It is difficult to balance for the gathering phase when the heel is lower than the toe.
- The primary movement in any leg activity requiring a push is plantar flexion, in which the ball of the foot pushes down and the heel comes up. So when starting off the plate, the pitcher gets greater push by starting with the ball of the foot slightly lower than the heel.

- Placing the toe lower than the heel may help the pitcher lean in a bit (toward third base for a right-handed pitcher). This may help keep shoulders and hips closed until the proper sequence.

Gathered Position

The gathered position is that point when all momentum from the windup comes together for a change of direction before the pitcher goes toward the plate. The stride leg lifts and rotates back to load the hips, which are preparing for the stride to the target (figure 1.8). In this phase the body is getting lined up, loaded up, and ready to explode to the plate.

The technique, timing, and tempo of getting to the gathered position will vary from pitcher to pitcher, but each pitcher must have a consistent gathered position. When the gathered position is consistent from pitch to pitch, the release point will become consistent, which correlates to better control.

Figure 1.8 The gathered position.

Back Leg in the Gathered Position

As the stride leg is lifted and rotated, the back leg must remain tall and only slightly bent. A slightly bent back leg will provide good balance; and by staying tall, the pitcher will keep the advantage of pitching on a downhill plane.

Many pitchers will want to bend the back leg too much and collapse the back. When collapsing occurs, the pitcher's release point will be much lower and the baseball will travel at a much lower angle. A pitch with a higher release point is much harder to hit than a pitch with a lower release point.

Stride Leg in the Gathered Position

Each pitcher has his own delivery, so there is no prescribed movement of the stride leg in the gathered position. The stride leg movement varies according to the arm slot of the pitcher. The gathered position and the movements leading to the gathered position should be adjusted to work with the pitcher's existing arm slot. Changing arm slots to match lower-body mechanics is a major contributor to arm injuries.

It is important to understand that the pitcher *lifts* his leg into the gathered position. Many refer to this action as a *leg kick*, which is not accurate at all. The pitcher's arm slot determines the height of the leg lift. When the arm slot is high, the pitcher should lift the leg high with little hip rotation. The lower the arm slot, the lower the leg lift and the more hip rotation involved.

The pitcher with the high arm slot should work up and down in his delivery. The stride leg will go up and slightly back before going to the target (figure 1.9). The pitcher with a high three-quarter arm slot will require less height in his lift, but he needs more hip rotation. The low three-quarter or side arm slot will not need as much height in the leg lift but will require even more hip rotation in the gathered position (figure 1.10).

Getting the pitcher into the proper gathered position according to his arm slot is crucial for development of control and velocity. For ultimate power, control, and arm health, the pitcher should combine the proper height of the leg lift with the proper amount of hip rotation. In the quest for more velocity, a pitcher will often go to extremes with the leg lift and either go too high or get too much rotation for his particular arm slot.

Figure 1.9 Vertical (high) leg lift (overhand pitcher).

Figure 1.10 Horizontal leg lift (low three-quarters).

Common Leg Lift Problems

Lifting the stride leg into the gathered position is one of the first and most important movements a pitcher makes. When the beginning of a movement is off, the rest of the movement will follow, and the result is a poor delivery. The majority of leg lift problems can be corrected with repetition of the correct movements.

Leg Swing

A leg swing occurs when the pitcher swings his leg up and back to the gathered position. A small leg swing may be beneficial to a pitcher's rhythm, and as long as he maintains balance, he should not tamper with it. When a pitcher has too much leg swing, the foot will go too far back behind the rubber, causing him to lean toward the plate with his upper body (figure 1.11). When the upper body begins to lean forward, the pitcher will begin to rush forward ahead of his legs, which will result in high pitches. Too much leg swing sometimes causes the pitcher to get too much hip rotation, or coil, in his delivery, which will create problems depending on his arm slot.

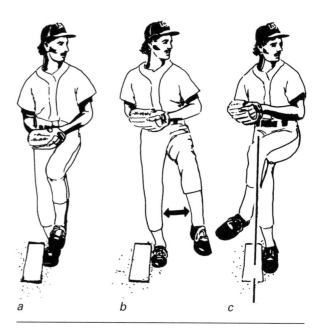

Figure 1.11 *(a)* Proper hip rotation in the gathered position; *(b)* too open; *(c)* too closed.

Kick Instead of Lift

The foot should be under the knee during the leg lift (figure 1.12a). When a pitcher kicks his foot out away from his center of gravity, as shown in figure 1.12b, his body will compensate in balance by tilting back in the opposite direction of the kick. A small kick with the foot may not be a problem; however, when a pitcher has an exaggerated kick, his torso will tilt backward and not stay in a line with

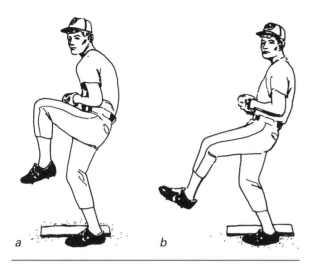

Figure 1.12 *(a)* The foot must be below the knee in the gathered position. *(b)* Incorrect foot position.

the target. *The body will follow the head as it goes off line. The head should remain over the pivot foot before going to the plate.*

Flexed Stride Foot

The stride foot in the gathered position should be relaxed and hanging down at a slight angle. When a pitcher flexes his foot in this position, he will be in a heel-down position instead of a toe-down position (figure 1.13). The heel-down position will cause the pitcher to land on the heel during the stride and create problems later on in the delivery. The stride foot should be under the knee in a relaxed position before going to the plate.

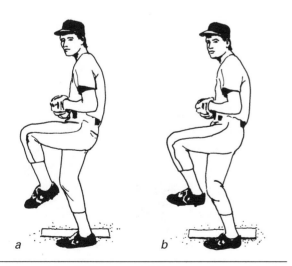

Figure 1.13 *(a)* Proper and *(b)* improper foot position for the gathered position.

Stride

The stride is the major contributor of poor control and will also limit or enhance a pitcher's velocity. The direction of a pitcher's stride is a big factor in determining location, and the degree to which a pitcher uses his hips will determine his velocity. Pitchers should work daily on the proper stride to have a solid, repeatable delivery, which includes both power and control.

Direction of the Stride

The pitcher should step or stride directly toward the target. The target in this case is the catcher's mitt, which will move according to the pitch. A catcher may set up 6 inches inside, 6 inches outside, or anywhere in between. The plate is 17 inches wide plus 6 inches on either side, so the pitcher will be throwing to a spot somewhere in a 29-inch area. (Should the target move in archery, the archer would adjust his arm, as would the free-throw shooter if the basket moved between shots.)

Upon locating his target, the pitcher makes the appropriate leg lift and strides on a straight line to the target (figure 1.14). Pitchers should make every effort to land on or near the line to the target. Many pitchers will insist on

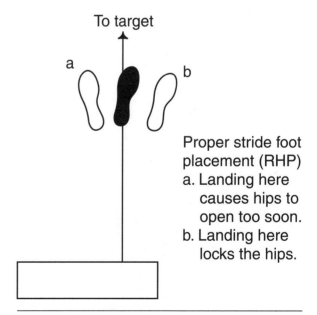

Figure 1.14 Stepping directly toward the target is the most efficient stride.

stepping in the same spot for every pitch; however, it is much easier to make a two- or three-inch adjustment with the stride than to change release points with the throwing hand. Simply said, the pitcher will line up with the target, step toward the target, and throw to the target.

Using the Hips to Create Power in the Stride

Once the leg is loaded up and back, the stride leg will travel down to an area slightly in front of the rubber. When the stride foot is an inch or two above the ground, the foot will then follow the slope of the mound until it reaches the landing spot in line with the target. Simply put, the pitcher's stride leg will go up, down, and skim the ground (figures 1.15, 1.16, and 1.17).

As the stride begins, the pitcher must keep the hips closed until the stride foot hits the ground. This action is similar to the stride of a good hitter. In both cases the hips do not open until after the foot lands for optimum power. When the hips start to open before the foot lands, the pitcher loses power; this is similar to the hitter who opens up too soon and swings the bat using only his upper body. The right-handed pitcher will face third base as he delivers the pitch, and the hips will pop as the foot lands. The hips then cause the

upper body to rotate as the pitch is made. Leading with closed hips is the key to throwing for velocity; at the same time it produces less stress on the throwing arm.

The foot should remain under the knee until the pitcher begins to go to the plate. At this time the foot should go first, followed by the knee, and finally the front hip. When the foot and knee go together, the hips open too soon and the pitcher loses power. The stride foot should also stay on line to the target and not stray left or right of the line. When the stride foot of the right-handed pitcher lands

Figure 1.16 Stride leg goes down.

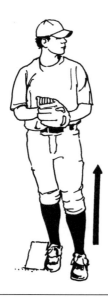

Figure 1.15 Stride leg goes up.

Figure 1.17 Stride leg skims the ground.

too far left of the line, the hips will open too soon. When a right-handed pitcher's foot lands too far right of the line, the pitcher's hips will not open, and the pitcher will lose the power from the hips and must make the adjustment with his upper body to hit his target. This is not only physically tough to do but also puts added stress on the throwing arm.

Landing

The stride foot should land on the line to the target with a slightly closed foot (figure 1.18). Should the foot be too open upon landing, the hips will open too soon and the upper body will begin rotation too soon, causing a loss of power and stress on the throwing arm.

When the stride foot lands too closed (for a right-handed pitcher toward third base), the pitcher will lock his hips, lose power, and add stress to the arm. (Think again of the hitter and his stride foot. When he opens up his foot, he loses power; if his foot is closed off, he completely locks his hips.)

The pitcher should land on the inside of the stride foot. As he transfers the weight to the

stride leg, the foot will spin slightly to position pointing to the target. This action will occur naturally and should not be forced. Landing on the inside of the foot will help to keep the knee inside the foot and help the hips to stay closed until the proper time to unlock.

Stride Leg Bent but Firm

The stride leg should be bent but firm upon landing. The stride is used to stop the body's forward momentum and transfer it to the throwing arm. The stride leg cannot do this if it collapses on landing. Instead the leg should straighten slightly *after release*. The momentum created in the windup will be sustained if the stride leg angle is approximately 90 to 105 degrees. (When the stride leg angle is less than 90 degrees, there is a tendency to collapse the stride leg, which will kill momentum for the throwing arm.)

Stride Length

The length of the stride varies from pitcher to pitcher and should be the result of proper use of the hips, proper stride direction, and a proper landing. A pitcher does not benefit from trying to jump at the target or increase the length of the stride. Many young pitchers associate a longer, more powerful stride with more velocity and create many problems with overstriding. *Stride length is a result, not an action.*

When a pitcher focuses on using his hips correctly, staying closed, floating his hips toward the target, and keeping the knee of his stride leg inside, he will establish the length of the stride. When the pitcher deliberately tries to reach out with his stride foot, the back leg will collapse so that he can drive at the target, the hips will open up, and the stride foot will often land on the heel instead of on the inside ball of the foot (figure 1.19). As a result of this drive to the plate, the throwing arm will not get set up high in the back, which will create high pitches and extra strain on the throwing arm. The pitcher will then throw behind his front leg instead of over the front leg. In essence, the back side is fighting the front side instead of the two sides working together.

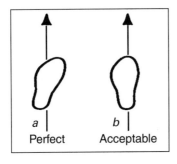

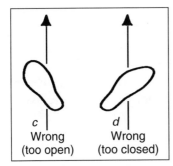

Figure 1.18 The foot should *(a)* land slightly closed, or *(b)* point straight to the plate. In *(c)* the hips open too soon, and in *(d)* the hips are locked out and cannot open.

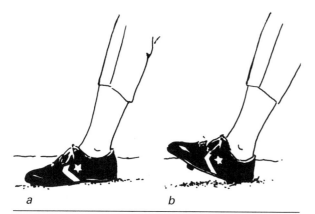

Figure 1.19 *(a)* Proper and *(b)* improper landing.

A stride that is too long shows some observable signs. The stride foot landing on the heel is an obvious indication. The pitcher who overstrides will sometimes lock his leg before the upper body is over the stride leg, causing the pitcher to stop forward momentum and start to spin out to the side. The lower body pushing back against the upper body will create a lack of velocity and control as well as place extra strain on the arm.

At the conclusion of a solid delivery, the pitcher will finish his pitch with his nose out over his toes, and the arm will be free to follow through and decelerate on its own (figure 1.20). When a pitcher overstrides or locks his front leg before the pitch, the throwing arm will recoil and not take its natural path of deceleration. A sudden change of direction or recoil of the pitching arm will lead to arm injuries.

Figure 1.20 Nose in front of the toes.

Measuring Stride Length and Direction

When a pitcher is having a good day in the bullpen and he is using his legs for optimal control and velocity, he should measure his stride length as a reference on those days when he is not performing up to his standards. For a quick reference, the pitcher can measure his stride by walking heel to toe back to his position in front of the rubber. In a practice setting, the coach may want to use a tape measure to record the optimal stride length.

During preseason or winter work, if the pitcher is throwing on a wooden or fiberglass indoor mound, he can mark the mound with tape or marker much as a pole vaulter or long jumper does in track for quick reference.

Stride length and stride direction are the keys to control of the baseball. Stride length affects the pitcher's release point and will determine whether the pitch is up or down (vertical). Stride direction will affect the pitcher's ability to control the baseball side to side (horizontal). A pitcher must work hard to have a consistent stride to the plate for optimum performance.

Back Leg

When the pitcher has started forward in the delivery, he rides the inside of his pivot-leg knee. His center of gravity should be over the inside of that knee. This will keep his hips closed and his momentum back until right before the landing, when the foot turns, the hips open, and the forward momentum is transferred. All of these actions, of course, generate power to whip the arm (figure 1.21).

After the ball is released, the back foot begins to rise. The back foot rotates internally, and the knee should remain close to the body. The back foot must not drag—it must leave the rubber immediately. Any time the back foot drags, it kills a lot of the forward momentum that has been built up, diminishing velocity.

After the pivot foot rolls, the proper action is for the foot to go up in back as far as is natural. The pivot-leg knee should stay in as

Figure 1.21   Riding the inside of the back leg.

close as possible to the stride leg. This action promotes good control because it keeps the body in the strike zone (figure 1.22). A common mistake pitchers make is to lift the back knee up and out toward third base (for a right-handed pitcher) as if getting on a horse.

Figure 1.22   When the back foot rolls, the knee stays in.

Importance of a Free Back Leg

For every action, there is an equal and opposite reaction. When a pitcher is balanced on his stride leg during the actual throwing of the ball, the hand whips toward the plate and down in front of the body. To compensate for this whip, the back leg should be free to come up in back as high as is needed. It is not uncommon for a hard-throwing pitcher's back foot to be higher than the pitcher's head during the follow-through (figure 1.23).

Figure 1.23   The back foot may be higher than the head during follow-through.

Fielder's Stance

After the foot is rolled, with the knee staying in close to the body, the foot should fall naturally to a spot approximately 18 to 24 inches from the stride foot. From this position, it should be easy for the pitcher to field his position (figure 1.24).

Upper-Body Mechanics

Upper-body mechanics begin simultaneously with lower-body mechanics. The hands actually initiate upper-body movement when starting the windup. This preliminary action

Figure 1.24 Pitcher's fielding stance.

during the delivery will be discussed only briefly; the most important aspects of upper-body mechanics start when the pitcher gets to the gathered position. At this point, the shoulders and head play a big role in the delivery. The arms, working opposite each other, turn all the power generated from the legs into the final act of generating speed when the ball is pitched. Upper-body mechanics don't end after the ball is released, however. The follow-through, or finish, of the pitch is important to performance and injury-free pitching.

Handwork for Taking the Signal

A pitcher can use two distinct styles when taking the signal from the catcher. Pitchers may prefer one or the other, but neither style is superior.

Ball in Glove

Before taking the signal, the pitcher places the ball in the glove in such a way that, when he is ready to take the ball out of the glove to make the pitch, he can easily grip it properly. His pitching arm then dangles down by his side or stays with the ball in the glove. The advantage of having the ball in the glove is that the pitcher can change grips and the opposing team won't be able to figure out what the pitch will be.

Ball in Hand

When using the ball-in-hand style, the pitcher should place his hand at his side or behind

his back. The advantage of this style is that if the pitcher needs to make a throw to another base, he already has the ball in his hand. The disadvantage of this style is that a pitcher must be sure not to take his grip on the ball before he starts his windup. When the ball is not in the glove, opponents may be able to see the grip and foresee what the pitch will be.

Handwork Initiating the Windup

Simultaneously with the footwork of the windup, the hands start a preliminary movement to gain momentum. Pitchers all have their own ways of getting into a gathered position; the type of preliminary action a pitcher takes in the windup is not important in terms of mechanics. Many pitchers prefer to go over the head with the hands, others like to start with the hands in the gathered position, and still others like to start with the hands lower than the gathered position and bring them up to the breaking point (figure 1.25).

Comfort and rhythm often determine hand placement in the preliminary phase of the windup. *As long as the pitcher keeps his head over his pivot foot and gets to the gathered position with good balance, his windup style is acceptable.*

Figure 1.25 Different handworks for initiating the windup.

Hands in the Gathered Position

When the pitcher is in the gathered position, his hands should be at rest next to his body at his center of gravity. (To find the center of gravity, hang the arms straight down at the sides and fold them at the elbows across the body. Where the hands meet is the approximate center of gravity.) See figure 1.8 on page 5.

There are several reasons to place the hands in the gathered position. Resting the hands on the body at the center of gravity creates a constant breaking point—that is, the ensuing actions of the glove side and ball side will always be constant. It is impossible to break the hands in the same place every time when they are away from the body. When hands break away from the body, it is usually caused by late-inning tiredness. When the hands break at different locations with each pitch, the pitcher's timing will be thrown off. A one-inch difference in the break point may mean six inches' difference in the pitch, a loss of a few miles per hour, or a greater chance of injury.

When the pitcher holds the hands away from the body, the throwing arm has a tendency to go *behind* the pitcher, creating too much arm swing. When the pitcher holds the hands next to the body, the arm cannot go behind him but only straight back, giving the pitcher extension but not wasted motion (figure 1.26). The hands should break at the precise moment when the stride leg and the body start forward. Any deviation from this will create improper timing.

When the stride leg starts forward before the hands break, rushing occurs. The leg and body are out in front of the throwing arm, so the tendency is to try to rush and catch up to the leg. The delivery is not synchronized, and the pitcher is more apt to throw a high pitch and open the door to injury.

The desired position before the throw is the T-position, with the front shoulder closed and the fingers on top of the ball. To get to this position, the pitcher must rotate the thumb of each hand down when the hands break. This ensures that the pitching arm takes the de-

sired swing with the fingers on top of the baseball. At the same time, rotating the glove hand thumbs-down keeps the front-side shoulder closed until the proper time (figure 1.27).

Lead-Arm Action

Think of the lead-arm action as a one–two punch. In the first step, the lead arm reaches toward the plate. At the same time, the stride leg starts forward (figure 1.28). At the conclusion of this segment, the lead arm is straight or almost straight toward the plate. The throwing

Figure 1.26 The ball hand should go back toward second base, not toward first or third base.

Figure 1.27 The glove hand and the ball hand should rotate thumbs down.

Figure 1.28 The stride leg starts forward as the lead arm reaches toward the plate.

Figure 1.29 The T-position.

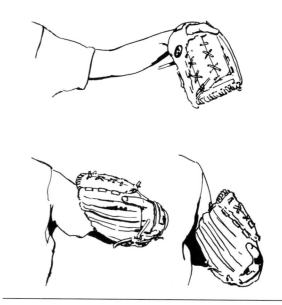

Figure 1.30 Pulling the glove low and to the side.

arm is also set up and ready to start acceleration. This is called the T-position (figure 1.29).

In the second step, the lead arm comes back in to the hip in a tuck position. (Imagine reaching out with the lead arm and grabbing the top of a fence and then pulling yourself over the fence during the tuck.) The athlete should try pulling the glove as low to the side as possible for a better follow-through (figure 1.30). Simultaneously with the tuck, the throwing arm accelerates toward the plate.

When the shoulders are lined up and the lead elbow is pointing at the target, the next sequence of moves will be determined by the pitcher's arm slot. The lead-arm elbow of a pitcher who has an overhand arm slot will come down by his side. The lower the arm slot, the farther away from the body the lead elbow should travel. The elbows of the lead arm and the throwing arm should mirror each other in the delivery for optimum performance.

Many pitchers have what is called a "dead" front side—they don't use their front side to create power. To see how the lead arm can create power, think about the martial arts punch. One arm is tucked and one is straight toward the target. The key to this punch is that the opposite side is pulling in while the punching side is extending toward the target. Similarly, in pitching the lead arm is pulling in while the throwing arm is starting acceleration.

The glove should never travel behind the pitcher's body but should stay in front and slightly to the side. The lead elbow will travel back behind the pitcher and can be seen sticking up in the follow-through, but the glove should remain in a position to catch a ball hit back up the middle. (With the aluminum bat and the strength of today's hitters, a pitcher must be able to protect himself.)

Flying open occurs when the lead arm "flies" away from the pitcher toward first base (for a right-handed pitcher) or third base (for a left-handed pitcher). When the lead arm goes astray, the lead shoulder follows (figure 1.31).

Flying open causes several problems for the pitcher. When the lead shoulder creates horizontal momentum and the throwing shoulder attempts vertical momentum (high three-quarter to overhand delivery), the result is strain on the throwing shoulder. Flying open also causes control problems. For a pitcher to have good, consistent control, all

Figure 1.31 Flying open creates horizontal momentum.

Figure 1.32 In the T-position, the fingers should be on top of the ball.

body parts must work together in proper sequence.

Throwing-Arm Action

When the hands break from the gathered position, the throwing hand's first movement is down and back. The palm of the hand faces down while the arm extends back toward second base. Many pitchers take the throwing hand down and back toward first base (for right-handed pitchers), and this is acceptable if the throwing arm can still catch up to the body in the delivery. The problem arises when the arm swing is too big and the body starts to the plate before the arm is in the correct position. The throwing hand should try to go down and back and up toward second base for the most efficient delivery.

The throwing arm should be back and up toward second base, but full extension is not necessary. (Extension out front during release is important.) The fingers should be on top of the ball, and the wrist should be loose but should not flop (see figure 1.32).

The overhand pitcher should take his throwing hand back toward second base; however, the lower the arm slot, the more rotation occurs, and the throwing hand may travel toward first base (right-handed pitcher) or third base (left-handed pitcher). As the stride foot lands, the pitcher's throwing hand

should be set up in the back and ready to go to the target.

A common mistake some young pitchers make is to turn the ball over (palm up) before they get to the top of the backswing. Turning the hand over too soon leads to flinging the ball with a stiff arm. The correct method of turning the hand over at the top results in a more efficient throw as well as less strain on the rotator muscles.

As the stride foot lands, the arm starts forward in the throwing phase with the elbow automatically leading. The elbow should be at least as high as the shoulder when it comes by the pitcher's head. (A low elbow is not mechanically efficient and will cause elbow injury.) The hand follows the elbow forward, on an inside-out path that starts at the point where the hand goes from on top to behind the ball. When the hand is behind the body, it should be inside the elbow and moving outward. As the hand gets closer to the release point, it moves farther away from the head toward full extension. By the time the arm is fully extended, the ball has been released and the hand is out in front of the body. The hand now pronates and starts to come back inside the elbow during the follow-through. The ball is released at a point even with the bill of the cap when the arm is still bent but on the way to full extension. After the ball is released, the arm pronates as a reaction to the rigorous throwing action. This pronation is one of the arm's protective mechanisms (figure 1.33).

Figure 1.33   The arm pronates after release.

The path the arm takes during the delivery—whether it be side-arm, three-quarter, or overhand—should be the same in relationship to the head and elbow. The differences in these pitching styles are due to the degree of flexion in the torso. A side-arm pitcher bends a great deal at the waist, but the elbow is still as high as the shoulder (figure 1.34). The three-quarter delivery also requires some flexion of the torso. Only the overhand pitcher should keep his torso straight during delivery.

Hooking occurs when the pitcher's wrist is flexed (cocked) when the arm is extended down and behind the pitcher. The palm

Figure 1.34   The torso should flex during delivery.

should be facing first base (right-handed pitcher) and not facing up. Hooking is another habit that pitchers need to break early—it is almost impossible to correct after a pitcher gets to high school or college (figure 1.35).

Hooking causes too much action in the wrist and creates control problems. Because the wrist goes from full flexion to hyperextension in the backswing, it prevents the development of consistency. Pitchers who hook will also have a tough time being drafted into professional baseball.

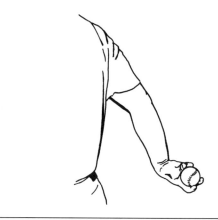

Figure 1.35   Hooking the wrist creates control problems.

T-Position

The T-position, like the gathered position, is a checkpoint in the delivery. The arms should be extended and level with the plane of the mound so that the upper body resembles the letter T.

The T-position is the last position the body takes before the throwing arm starts forward. As the stride leg approaches landing, the throwing arm sets up and prepares to start forward with acceleration (figure 1.36). Simultaneously, the lead arm prepares to come back into the center of gravity. As the stride leg lands, the lead arm comes back toward the center of gravity, and the throwing arm starts forward.

Timing is the key to a good delivery. If this sequence is off for some reason, the pitch will not be mechanically efficient, which will result in less accuracy, less velocity, and a greater chance of injury.

Figure 1.36 The T-position is the last position before the forward throwing motion begins.

Figure 1.38 Shoulders that aren't level cause control problems.

Shoulder Action

The shoulders should remain horizontal to the mound throughout the delivery until the throwing arm has been set up and is coming forward (figure 1.37). (The exception might be the straight overhand pitcher who drops his back shoulder back to some degree to allow for the overhand release.) When the throwing arm is coming through with the pitch, the shoulders will tilt depending on how much pull the lead arm is contributing.

Figure 1.37 The shoulders should remain horizontal during delivery.

A common problem among pitchers is aiming the front shoulder up in the air. The front shoulder should be pointed toward the target. To throw a great distance, the pitcher must drop the back shoulder and elevate the front shoulder, but when throwing from a mound, he must aim the lead shoulder toward the plate. When the back shoulder is down and the lead shoulder is up, the pitcher

will usually have a control problem (figure 1.38).

The shoulders should rotate, or coil, depending on the arm slot of the pitcher. The overhand pitcher's shoulders should remain in a line from home plate to second base throughout the gather phase of the delivery. The high three-quarter pitcher will have a little bit of rotation, or coil, and the low three-quarter or side-armer will rotate even more before going to the plate.

Follow-Through

A pitcher's follow-through is important for injury-free pitching. Theoretically, the follow-through does not affect the pitch because the ball has left the hand. A good follow-through can gently slow down the tremendous arm speed built up during the throw and reinforce good pitching mechanics.

A sound delivery features a nice follow-through, just as an inefficient delivery prohibits a good follow-through. For this reason coaches have gotten by with saying that to get a pitcher to follow through is to make him throw the ball lower.

The path the follow-through takes is unique to each pitcher. The follow-through should continue the path the pitcher's arm took to release the ball. An overhand pitcher finishes with his elbow just to the outside of his stride-leg knee. A three-quarter-arm pitcher gets more horizontal momentum and therefore finishes farther away and up from the knee. A side-arm pitcher finishes closer to the waist on his opposite side. A follow-through should not be forced; the arm should just go along its intended path (figure 1.39).

Figure 1.39 The arm should follow its natural path during the follow-through: *(a)* overhand; *(b)* side-arm.

Recoiling the Throwing Arm

A common error of many pitchers is to recoil the throwing arm after ball release. Instead of letting the arm take its natural course after release, the pitcher snaps the hand back up, causing tremendous pressure on the shoulder and elbow. The pitcher's back also straightens up instead of bending during follow-through to allow the whole body to gradually slow the arm, preventing injury.

Recoiling, whether with the arm, back, or both, is dangerous, and pitchers should prevent it or eliminate it for injury-free pitching. For help in correcting recoiling, see the chair drill, page 64.

Combining Upper- and Lower-Body Mechanics

Perfect pitching mechanics require not only perfect upper- and lower-body mechanics but also a perfect synchronization of the two. When his two body halves aren't working together, the pitcher loses control and velocity and increases the odds of being injured.

In the ideal delivery, the pitcher has balance before and after he releases the ball. Balance before the pitch refers to the gath-

ered position in which the pitcher momentarily balances on one leg before he pitches the ball. Balance after the pitch refers to when the pitcher is again balanced on one leg in the finished position (figure 1.40). A good balance point after release leads to a good fielding position to protect the pitcher from the ball hit up the middle.

An extremely hard thrower sometimes has such arm speed that it forces him to fall off during the follow-through. As long as the pitcher reaches to the plate and falls toward the plate, this is acceptable. When the pitcher falls off to the side, there is a problem earlier in the delivery. Too much rotation in the gathered position can cause the pitcher to fall off as well as fly open with the front side, which causes the head to travel away from the target, taking the body along. Occasionally, something simple such as landing on the outside of his stride foot will cause an extreme fall off the mound.

Figure 1.40 Balance *(a)* before and *(b)* after the pitch.

Sequence, Timing, and Rhythm

A pitcher can work hard to perfect his delivery and have each segment in good working order, but unless he has the proper sequence and timing as well as some rhythm in his delivery he will not realize his potential. As the pitcher lifts the leg to the gathered position, he should also lift the hands. The hands will rise slightly as the knee comes up; and as the knee starts down to begin the stride, the hands will also go down and prepare to separate (figure 1.41, a and b). As the stride foot begins to go toward the target, the hands separate (figure 1.41c). The hands separate exactly at the time the stride leg begins to move toward the target. When the hands break too early, the upper body will arrive in the throwing position before the legs. When the hands separate too late, the legs will be in the throwing position before the arms. *When the stride foot lands, the shoulders must be aligned with the target and the throwing hand must be at its apex in the back.*

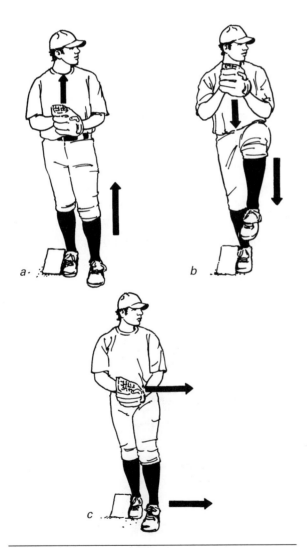

Figure 1.41 A rhythm is created when the hands bounce with the stride leg knee: hands bouncing *(a)* up and *(b)* down, and *(c)* breaking as knee goes forward.

When the hands bounce up with the stride-leg knee, it creates a rhythm to get all the parts working together for proper timing. The size of the bounce is an individual preference but should not travel higher than the chin and should only go up and down and not travel away from the body. Too much movement in the bounce may work to create a loss of rhythm and an inconsistent break of the hands.

Alignment During Delivery

Imagine a line drawn from second base through the rubber to home plate. In the ideal pitching delivery, all of the pitcher's movements, weight shifts, and momentum should stay on or close to this imaginary line. Any movement, weight shift, or momentum that takes the pitcher toward first or third base is not only wasted but also forces the pitcher to constantly try to correct this misalignment—creating extra movement, weight shifts, and momentum. The end result is too much side-to-side action and not enough action to the plate. The ultimate result is less control and more injury.

Let's examine the different components of the delivery and the alignment of their movements.

Pivot Step

The nonpivot foot starts the pitching delivery; to maximize efficiency in the windup, the pitcher should step according to his own arm slot. The overhand pitcher steps more in a line toward second base; the lower the arm slot, the more the step should move toward first base (right-handed pitcher) or third base (left-handed pitcher). The initial step starts the pitcher with the proper amount of rotation in his delivery. Regardless of where the pitcher steps, the head must remain over the pivot foot.

Leg Lift

Often a pitcher will kick his foot toward third base (right-handed pitcher) when he gets into the gathered position. When the foot goes away from the body, the upper torso counters this weight shift by leaning back.

The foot should stay under the stride-leg knee, and the head should stay over the pivot foot in the gathered position.

Hands

The hands should remain close to the center of gravity in the gathered position. When they get away from the body, the first reaction is for the throwing hand to go back in the opposite direction when the hands break. A right-handed pitcher's hands, when held away from his body toward third base, will cause the throwing hand to go back toward first base before getting extended in the T-position. This extra movement toward first base can cause too large an arm swing, and ultimately it can cause the pitcher to drag his arm through delivery. A big arm swing makes the body start toward the plate before the arm sets up.

Stride Leg

When a pitcher steps to either side of the line to the plate, he is cheating himself mechanically. A pitcher who throws across the body (a right-handed pitcher steps to the third-base side of the line) blocks out his hips and cannot create nearly as much power as he would if he used his hips. When a pitcher opens up the hips too much (a right-handed pitcher steps to the first-base side of the line), he also cheats himself of power.

Front Shoulder

The front shoulder also should follow the line between second base and the plate. When the front shoulder opens up (for a right-handed pitcher, the shoulder goes toward first base), the throwing shoulder tends to drag through the delivery (which can cause injury); and the rest of the body tends to go with the front shoulder, causing the pitcher to fall off the mound toward first base.

Lead Arm

The lead arm should extend toward the plate when the pitcher is in the T-position. When the throwing arm starts forward, the lead arm should come in to the center of gravity. If it were to fly open (toward first base for a right-handed pitcher), it would take the front shoulder with it.

Head

The head may be the most important component of the pitching delivery. Wherever the head goes, the body follows. When the head goes toward the first-base side of the plate, the body will follow. When a pitcher falls off toward first base, it is often because his head pulled him in that direction. The head should always go directly at the target.

90-Degree Rule

Five instances in a pitcher's delivery require an angle of approximately 90 degrees between two body parts. A coach should be able to measure these angles with the naked eye, and by doing so he can determine whether a pitcher is mechanically sound.

- *Gathered position.* In the gathered position, the angle of the stride-leg knee should be no greater than 90 degrees (figure 1.42). With the foot under the knee, the leg lift will be at 90 degrees when the stride leg is at the waist; but should the pitcher lift his leg higher, the angle will go to less than 90 degrees.

- *Landing of the stride leg.* When the stride leg lands to stop the forward momentum, the

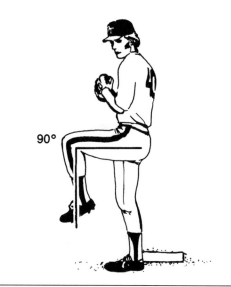

Figure 1.42 The stride-leg knee should be at 90 degrees at the waist and decrease in degrees as the leg rises.

angle of the knee should be at least 90 degrees (figure 1.43). At anything less than 90 degrees, the stride leg will collapse. (An angle of up to 105 degrees is acceptable.)

• *Throwing-arm elbow.* When the elbow starts forward in the acceleration phase, it should be at least as high as the shoulder. This requires a 90-degree angle with the torso and the upper arm (figure 1.44). (This angle can be greater than 90 degrees but never less than 90 degrees.)

• *Lead-arm elbow.* As the throwing arm goes toward the plate, the lead-arm elbow should be approximately as high as the lead shoulder (figure 1.45). (This angle can be less than 90 degrees but never greater.)

• *Throwing-arm acceleration phase (external rotation).* When the elbow is lined up with the torso and is leading the hand into the release area, the goal is a 90-degree angle of the elbow (figure 1.46). Generally speaking, the

90° or higher

Figure 1.43 On landing, the stride leg should be at least 90 degrees.

90°

Figure 1.44 When the elbow starts forward, the angle between the body and the arm should never be less than 90 degrees.

Figure 1.45 The lead arm should never be more than 90 degrees.

Figure 1.46 During external rotation the elbow is at 90 degrees.

more velocity a pitcher has, the more external rotation in the arm. Many pitchers who have shoulder injuries lose the flexibility in the shoulder joint and cannot get back to 90 degrees, and they lose velocity as a result. *Do not force the elbow ahead of the hand. This happens naturally when the torso starts forward.*

Matching Arm Slot to Delivery

Once the pitcher establishes a natural arm slot, he should tailor the delivery to that particular arm slot. A coach can determine a pitcher's natural arm slot by watching him play long toss.

The lower the arm slot, the more rotation, or coil, in the delivery. The lower the arm slot, the more bend in the pitcher's torso. The higher the arm slot, the lower the finish and the lower the arm slot the higher the finish.

The front-side elbow must take the opposite path of the throwing arm during delivery. The path of the front-side elbow will determine how high the back leg will travel and how close it will land to the stride leg during the follow-through.

Overhand Arm Slot

The overhand pitcher will use an up–down delivery to take advantage of his arm slot. The overhand delivery will feature a higher leg lift than lower arm slots use and will have little if any hip rotation when getting to the gathered position. Even though the knee will come up higher, the foot must remain under the knee in the gathered position and when going to the plate in the stride.

Every effort must be made to keep the body lined up between home plate and second base because the overhand delivery is an up–down delivery and uses very little side-to-side rotation. The lead arm and shoulders may have a little tilt but must be pointed at the target during delivery. The front-side elbow must stay close to the body throughout the delivery.

During the follow-through, the throwing arm must finish outside of but close to the stride-leg knee. The back leg in the overhand delivery should be high in the back before finishing in the fielding position.

High Three-Quarter Arm Slot

The high three-quarter pitcher will use a little more side-to-side rotation in his delivery than the overhand pitcher to take advantage of his arm slot. The high three-quarter delivery leg lift will not be as high as the overhand's leg lift but should include a little more rotation of the hips. In the gathered position the knee of the lift leg should rotate back to the back side of the rubber to load the hips before going to the plate.

The shoulders will rotate slightly on the high three-quarter delivery, which will cause the throwing arm to go toward the first-base side of second base for the right-handed pitcher and the shortstop side of second base for the left-handed pitcher. The front side will

also rotate slightly in the gathered position but will point to the target when the stride foot lands.

During the follow-through the throwing arm will finish outside the stride-leg knee at a greater distance away from the knee than the overhand delivery uses. *The farther the throwing hand is away from the head during delivery, the farther outside the stride-leg knee the throwing arm will finish.* The back leg will not finish as high in the back, and the back foot will land farther away from the stride leg in the fielding position.

Low Three-Quarter Arm Slot

The low three-quarter pitcher will use more rotation, or coil, in his delivery to take advantage of his arm slot. The lift-leg knee will not be as high as the lift for the high three-quarter arm slot but will rotate more toward second base. The lift-leg knee will rotate to the back of the pitching rubber or even slightly behind. The shoulders will also rotate more in the low three-quarter delivery, causing the throwing arm to swing more toward the second baseman for the right-handed pitcher and toward the shortstop for the left-handed pitcher.

The torso will bend slightly at the waist during the delivery of the low three-quarter arm slot to keep the throwing-arm elbow at shoulder height. The lead-arm elbow will point to the plate when the stride foot lands, but it will travel away from the body opposite of the throwing arm.

The path of the throwing arm in the follow-through will be outside the knee at a proportionate distance. The pitcher's back leg will land farther away from the stride leg in the fielding position.

Side-Arm Slot

The side-arm pitcher will use more rotation in his delivery than other arm slots require, to take advantage of his arm slot. The leg-lift knee will coil back behind the pitching rubber. The shoulders and throwing arm will also rotate more than in any other delivery. The throwing hand of the right-handed side-armer may rotate as far as the second baseman before lining up again as the stride foot hits the ground.

To keep his elbow at shoulder height, the side-arm pitcher will bend his torso at the waist even more than the low three-quarter pitcher. The side-arm slot lead elbow will take the opposite path as the throwing arm and appear to be flying open.

The throwing arm in the follow-through will reach to the plate and then follow the lead elbow across the knee. The back leg will not get high in the back and will land farther yet from the stride foot in the fielding position.

chapter 2

Teaching Grips and Techniques for Pitches

Several kinds of pitches are appropriate for the young pitcher's repertoire, including the fastball, curveball, slider, and several types of change-ups. Knuckleballs, knuckle curves, slip pitches, and spitballs will not be discussed—these gimmick pitches are not good for young pitchers because they either injure the arm or do not help develop the arm.

First and foremost, a pitcher needs to develop his fastball. This is his staple, and he will throw it 50 to 100 percent of the time. A pitcher also needs a pitch that changes speeds, such as a change-up or a curveball (the curveball also adds movement). When the pitcher masters the fastball and change-up, then—and only then—should he work on a breaking ball.

Once he has mastered the fastball, change-up, and curveball and can throw them with control, these should be all the pitches a young pitcher needs. He can add a slider at a later time, depending on the success of the curveball. It is very difficult to throw both the curveball and the slider because of the different mechanics, so a pitcher should choose one or the other.

In this chapter we discuss the various pitches. *A pitcher should use the same arm slot and the same arm speed for all of his pitches.*

Fastball

The fastball is the first pitch learned and should be used more than any other pitch in the repertoire. Obviously velocity, control, and movement of the fastball dictate how often and in what situations the fastball will be used. When a pitcher is learning to throw the fastball, he should make a conscious effort to learn control and movement first, then add velocity later. This principle applies even more for the higher-level baseball pitchers.

By slightly changing the basic fastball grips, a pitcher can get various results. Variations of the fastball are four-seam, two-seam, cut, and sinker. The first fastball to master is the four-seam fastball. The pitcher should prove that he has good control of this pitch before he attempts to throw any of the others.

Four-Seam Fastball

The four-seam fastball is the easiest pitch to control. The four-seamer usually doesn't have much movement, so it is an ideal pitch for young pitchers to use to master the strike zone. Because it lacks movement, this pitch is less important to the older pitcher who has good control but needs a fastball with movement. The exception to that rule is the pitcher with the great arm who can throw at or around 90 miles per hour. He should use the four-seamer because the ball will have good movement at that speed—and obviously a pitcher who can throw 90 miles per hour with good control will win.

The four-seam fastball is held with the index and middle finger across the horseshoe of the baseball. The end joints of the fingers should be over the seam to ensure a good grip. The thumb should be on the bottom of the ball on an imaginary line between the two fingers on the top (figure 2.1).

The pitcher should hold the ball loosely in the hand, and he should have at least a finger-width space between the ball and the palm of the hand. Ideally the enclosed end of the horseshoe seam should be closest to the middle finger; this helps with the feel of the seams, given that the index finger is shorter (figure 2.2).

Regardless of how a pitcher usually grips his fastball, certain situations always require a four-seamer.

- *Brushback pitch.* Any time a pitcher goes inside at the hands to brush back the batter, he should throw a four-seam fastball. Because this pitch has less movement than the two-seam fastball, there is less danger that the ball will tail into the batter.

- *Moving the feet.* A pitcher sometimes will try to make the hitter move his feet if the hitter stands too close to the plate or steps in

toward the plate when he strides. A hitter will step in when he has trouble hitting the low-and-away pitch. Moving the feet will keep the batter from adjusting to the outside pitch. When learning how to make the hitter move his feet, the pitcher should use a four-seam fastball. An older, experienced pitcher who has great command of his two-seam fastball may want to run the ball inside at the hitter's feet.

- *Pitchout.* When a pitchout is to be thrown, the pitcher should use a four-seam grip on the fastball. Good control and lack of movement help the pitcher give the catcher a pitchout he can handle easily to throw out the stealing runner.

- *Fielding chance.* Any time a pitcher fields a batted ball, he should attempt a four-seam grip. This helps him make an accurate throw.

Two-Seam Fastball

The two-seam fastball has more movement because of the grip and therefore is harder to control than the four-seam fastball. The pitcher should throw the four-seam fastball until he has proven that he has mastered the strike zone. The two-seam fastball becomes more important to the older pitcher who does not have an outstanding arm and must rely more on movement than on speed. The two-seam fastball moves to the pitching-arm side of the plate. Often it will also sink, producing a pitch that tails away and down.

The pitcher can grip the two-seam fastball in two ways. The fingers can go either with

Figure 2.1 For the four-seam fastball, the fingers should be on the top of the ball with the thumb directly underneath the ball.

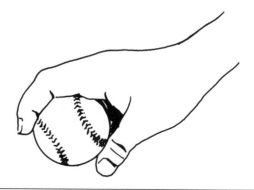

Figure 2.2 The enclosed end of the horseshoe seam should be closest to the middle finger.

the seams or across the seams. When the fingers go across the seams, the pitcher can hook the end joints of the index and middle finger on a seam and get a good feel for the pitch. However, many pitchers prefer to lay their entire fingers lengthwise on a seam. Both grips are effective (figure 2.3).

The two-seam and four-seam fastballs are thrown the same way except for the grip. For either pitch, the pitcher should keep his fingers behind the baseball for ultimate velocity. Putting the fingers off center decreases velocity and control but enhances movement.

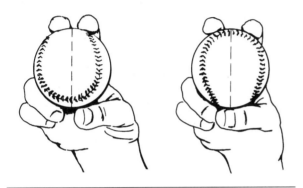

Figure 2.3 Two-seam fastball grips.

Cut Fastball

The cut fastball moves away from the pitcher's throwing side. A right-handed pitcher's cut fastball moves from right to left with approximately 95 percent of the velocity of the ultimate fastball. In the cut fastball grip, the thumb slides to the outside of the center line of the baseball (figure 2.4). With the thumb slid over, the baseball is held slightly off center and therefore does not have a regular

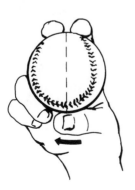

Figure 2.4 The cut fastball grip.

top-to-bottom fastball rotation. Instead, the ball has slightly more sidespin and runs away from the pitcher's throwing side.

The cut fastball and the slider are similar in that both balls are held off center. The slider, however, is held more off center and therefore breaks down as well as away. The cut fastball is excellent training for the slider.

Sinker

The sinker moves down and to the throwing-arm side. A right-handed pitcher's sinker moves from left to right and has some down movement with approximately 95 percent of the velocity of the ultimate fastball. In the sinker grip variation, the thumb slides to the inside of the baseball's center line. Sliding the thumb up the inside of the baseball causes the ball to be held off center, giving it a sidespin that causes sinking movement (figure 2.5). The higher the thumb goes up the side of the baseball, the more sinking movement but less velocity it has. Many pitchers slide the thumb up top and use this pitch as a change-up.

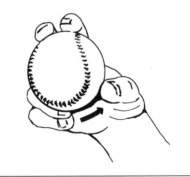

Figure 2.5 The sinker grip.

Finger Pressure and Wrist Angle

A pitcher may want to experiment with finger pressure to add more movement to the fastball. With more index-finger pressure, the baseball moves more to the throwing-arm side. Extra pressure on the middle finger causes more movement away from the throwing arm. *Remember, one inch of movement of the ball to one side or another when it goes toward the batter is worth two miles per hour.*

For maximum velocity and minimum risk of injury, the ball should extend straight out from the wrist. Regardless of arm angle (overhand, three-quarter, or side-arm), the hand and ball should line up with the wrist to ensure total mobility of the wrist in the release (figure 2.6). Correct alignment of the wrist allows greater range of movement in both hyperextension and flexion. The greater the range of movement, the greater the velocity.

Comfortable Speed With the Fastball

With the introduction of the speed gun into the baseball world, many pitchers are becoming obsessed with velocity. Throwing as hard as one can for as long as one can is becoming the norm for young pitchers as they search for more velocity. Velocity has become more important than both winning and the health of the throwing arm.

Comfortable speed is the most effective speed for the pitcher. Sometimes this is referred to as the 95 percent fastball. When throwing at a comfortable speed, the pitcher will have his best control and, at the same time, his greatest movement. Overthrowing, or throwing with maximum effort, leads to

poor control, and the baseball has a tendency to straighten out. The analogy of the golf swing puts this concept into perspective. In an effort to drive the ball 300 yards, a golfer will overswing, causing him to gain a few yards but lose accuracy in the process. A comfortable swing will yield a playable distance as well as keep the ball in the fairway.

Pitching at a comfortable speed gives the pitcher another weapon in his pitching arsenal: the ability to change speeds up. Old-time pitchers refer to this as reaching back to get a little extra on the baseball. The majority of major league starters will throw 85 to 90 percent of their fastballs at a comfortable speed but will reach back for a little extra on occasion when necessary.

Overthrowing (using maximum effort on every fastball) will also create health problems. An engine run on full throttle will invariably wear out before an engine that is backed off somewhat. Mechanical flaws in the delivery are magnified when a pitcher uses maximum effort on every pitch.

Maximum-effort pitchers will take much longer to recover than pitchers who use a comfortable speed. For starting pitchers this means more time between starts, which inevitably leads to fewer starts in a season. Maximum-effort relief pitchers will have

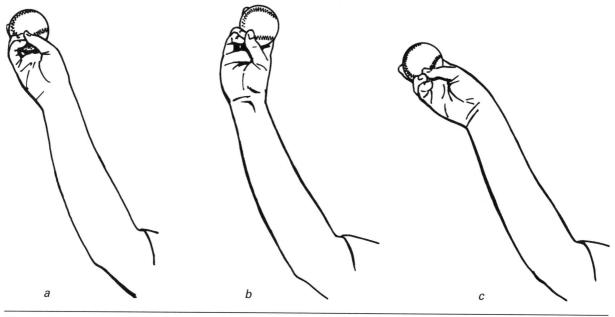

Figure 2.6 *(a)* The ball should extend straight out from the wrist; *(b)* and *(c)* are incorrect positions.

fewer opportunities for saves than pitchers who use comfortable speeds.

All pitchers want to gain velocity and improve their arm strength; however, the pitching mound is not the place to work on gaining strength. Throwing long in the outfield (long toss) is the place for development of velocity. The pitcher's mound is the place the pitcher goes to work on getting batters out.

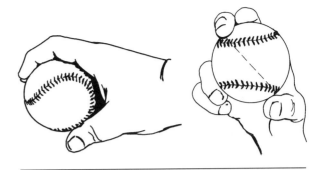

Figure 2.7 The curveball grip.

Curveball

Except for the release, the curveball is thrown with the same mechanics as the fastball. Once a pitcher understands that important fact, he will easily learn the proper way to throw a good curveball.

First we will look at proper technique for the curveball. Then we will look at some improper methods and myths, and we will discuss how to correct some of these improper methods.

A good curve breaks both vertically and horizontally and also changes speeds. For young pitchers, a flat curve will work because the hitter will bail out. However, the older a pitcher gets, the more he needs to develop downward movement, because older hitters have learned to adjust and stay in to hit the ball. (The curve that breaks down is obviously more difficult to hit; the bat is narrower than it is long.)

Curveball Grip

The middle finger is the primary source of pressure and is placed against the inside of a seam. The curve can be gripped several ways, but the most common is the four-seam grip. In this grip, the fingers go in the open end of a horseshoe and are placed against the seam (right side for a right-handed pitcher, left side for a left-handed pitcher). The curve uses a lot of the finger, unlike the fastball, which holds the ball on the fingertips. The index finger simply lies next to the middle finger in the curve grip (figure 2.7).

As a general rule, the more the ball is choked back in the hand (also, the more finger that is on the ball), the slower the curve

will be. Each pitcher must experiment with ball placement in the hand, grip tightness, and pitch speed. Pitchers will have many small adjustments to make before they find the best curve.

The thumb plays a big role in throwing a curve. It can be either bent or straight (figure 2.8). Either way, the thumb is on the seam directly opposite that of the middle finger—the thumb and middle finger should be bisecting the ball. (The bent thumb can give more flip than the straight thumb, which may cause more rotation.)

The thumb's actions are exactly the opposite of the middle finger's actions. When the middle finger pulls, the thumb pushes. The result is the spin that makes the curveball break.

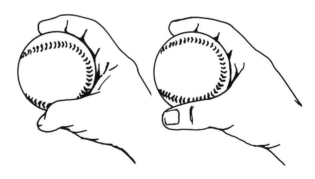

Figure 2.8 The thumb can be held either bent or straight.

Curveball Release

The release point of a curveball is slightly later than that of the fastball. In other words, the pitcher holds onto the ball a little longer. Adjusting the height of a curveball is very simple. If the pitch is consistently high, simply hold onto the ball a little longer. If the pitch is too low, reverse the process and let the ball go sooner. Pitchers will need to throw countless curves to develop the touch needed to be a good curveball pitcher. (This is one good reason young pitchers shouldn't throw the curve. It takes many pitches to master—pitches that could be used to strengthen and develop the arm.) The release point of the curve should be almost identical to that of the fastball; the only difference is that the curve is held slightly longer. The grip and wrist action are different, but all else remains the same. Remember, *fastball mechanics until the release!*

The pitcher releases the curve by twisting the hand with the thumb rotating from under the ball to behind the ball, going upward to the top of the ball. The thumb will point toward the plate after the release (figure 2.9). Simultaneously, the two fingers take the opposite path, going from top, to front side, to the bottom of the ball. The top-to-bottom rotation of the fingers is what causes the ball to spin and move in a downward path. Should the ball break more horizontally, the pitcher is throwing on the side of the ball, and the two fingers and thumb are rotating from side to side.

When the pitcher's arm is coming into the release area, he rotates the hand a quarter turn. The palm faces the batter until it gets into the release area, when the hand turns so that the palm now faces the pitcher. The fingers should run along the side and hook over the top of the ball (figure 2.10). When the fingers don't stay on top, it is impossible for the pitcher to get any downward break on the curveball. By placing the hand in this position before release, the pitcher adds con-

Figure 2.10 Place the hand in the correct position before the release.

sistency to his curveball delivery. From this position it is much easier to stay on top of the curve and throw a consistent curveball with a consistent break, which of course leads to better control.

12-to-6 Curveball

Imagine a big clock in front of the target area with the number 12 on top and the number 6 on the bottom (figure 2.11). When the pitcher stays on top of the curveball by keeping his fingers on top of the ball, the baseball breaks from 12 o'clock to 6 o'clock. This is the ideal curveball—it breaks straight down and is therefore hardest to hit. When a pitcher cannot get his fingers on top of the ball, the

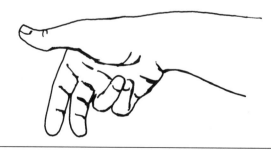

Figure 2.9 The fingers go in front of the ball and the thumb points toward the plate.

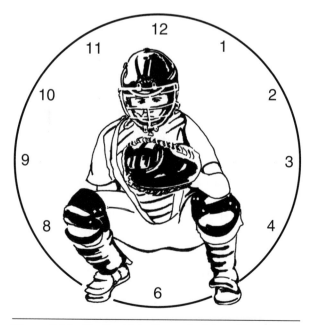

Figure 2.11 For the 12-to-6 curveball, imagine a clock in front of the target area.

curveball will break not from 12 o'clock to 6 o'clock but rather 1 o'clock to 7 o'clock or even 2 o'clock to 8 o'clock (for a right-handed pitcher). These can be effective pitches, but the pitcher should strive for more downward break.

A three-quarter or side-arm pitcher will have to settle for more side-to-side break. It would be very tough to get a 12-to-6 break with these arm slots. A three-quarter or side-arm pitcher will have more movement in on the fastball, so sidespin movement away with the curveball may even be better for these types of pitchers.

Curveball Follow-Through

When throwing the curveball, the pitcher must change the follow-through slightly to guarantee a sharp curveball break rather than a looping curveball. In the fastball follow-through, the pitcher wants good arm extension toward the plate before the arm finishes elbow to knee. After release of the curveball, the pitcher's arm should remain bent so that it does not extend toward the plate. This type of bent-arm follow-through is good for two reasons: First, elbow injuries occur when a curveball pitcher extends the arm as in the fastball; the elbow has a tendency to hyperextend, which over time will cause bone spurs and bone chips. Second, an extended arm causes the pitcher to throw a looping curveball rather than a sharp-breaking curveball.

Teaching the Curve

It is important to communicate to young pitchers that the fastball and the curve are very similar. The curve is 95 percent fastball and 5 percent turn and bend. When learning a curve, a pitcher must understand that a curve is not a wholesale set of changes in mechanics. A curve is simply a fastball with a little turn and bend.

The pitcher learns the curveball by holding the ball out in front, simulating the release point. He should flip fastballs and notice the direction his fingers take and then begin to turn the hand during release and bend the elbow (or pull the hand back) after release.

When the pitcher understands the release, he can start the process by starting with the ball back by the head going to release. Many pitchers turn the ball back by the head instead of during release. The result is a big, loopy curve, and the pitch resembles a karate chop. The proper sequence is to reach to release point, turn the hand during release, and then bend the elbow and pull the hand back.

When the pitcher can execute the release, then—and only then—should he actually throw a curve, using the same arm slot as he uses in his fastball. The pitcher should master the curveball release and follow-through at slower speeds, increasing the speed of the pitch only after proper execution.

Pitchers should wait as long as possible to learn the curve; they should first learn how to hit spots with the fastball and change speeds with the change-up. Coaches need to monitor all curveball work because mistakes in release and follow-through with the curve can cause considerable damage to the arm. Young pitchers who have initial success with the curve can become addicted to using curveballs. The fastball should always be the dominant pitch until the pitcher reaches physical maturity.

Curveball Myths

Many coaches believe myths that cause them to teach improper techniques for throwing the curve. Some of these myths are harmful to a young pitcher's arm, and some techniques are improper because the mechanics allow the batter to easily pick up the pitch. These myths are mentioned here in an attempt to put them to rest.

Shortening the Stride

Coaches for years have taught pitchers to shorten their stride when throwing the curve, in an effort to keep the pitch down in the strike zone. But in fact, the pitcher should land in the same place on every pitch for consistent mechanics. A pitcher who lands in different locations on different pitches risks injury because of what that does to the condition of the mound. And the batter can pick up on changing stride length, which can tip him off to the pitch. Instead of shortening his stride, a pitcher should concentrate on getting his head out in front of his stride leg; the coach should encourage him to stay on top of the ball with the bent-arm follow-through.

Wrapping the Curve

In an effort to make a pitcher throw a 12-to-6 curveball, many coaches have the pitcher get the fingers and hand on top of the ball before the release area. Not only is this mechanically wrong, but the batter can also then see a curveball coming before the pitcher releases the pitch.

Wrapping the curve causes the elbow to be down below the shoulder, which can lead to elbow damage. And when the wrist is wrapped so close to the head (no extension), the elbow and shoulder both have much more strain placed on them during the twist of the release (figure 2.12). When the arm is extended out away from the body, as in fastball mechanics, there is very little strain on the arm.

The wrapped curve is easy to pick up because the wrist begins to wrap on the way up. Also, even though many pitchers do have some luck with this pitch, it is not easily thrown past a good hitter; it has a big break and is slower than a curve delivered with proper fastball mechanics.

Many pitchers are taught, wrongly, to bring the ball in closer to the head for more vertical

Figure 2.12 Wrapping the curveball leads to arm injury.

break. Instead, for best results the arm should use the same path as the fastball.

Leading With the Elbow

Many coaches still teach pitchers to lead with the elbow when throwing the curveball, for a greater break. The arm naturally leads with the elbow, so this action should not be forced. The pitcher should use fastball mechanics until the release.

Slider

When thrown correctly, a slider will break approximately six inches away and six inches down at a velocity as close as possible to that of the fastball. A good slider causes a groundball. An excellent slider is a strikeout pitch.

The slider is a dangerous pitch for two reasons. First, the pitcher can injure his elbow if he has a mechanical problem, because a slider is thrown as hard as a fastball. Second, the slider that isn't delivered properly (high in the strike zone) usually gets hit very hard. (This may be the main reason so many coaches don't like the slider. If thrown high, at a speed close to that of the fastball, the slider looks very much like a fat fastball. The curveball at least has the change of speeds and may alter the batter's timing.) A low slider breaks downward much more than a high slider because of the later release point.

Slider Grip

Just as the curve is thrown off the middle finger, the slider is thrown off the index finger and middle finger. The pitcher should find a place on the ball where both the index and middle fingers are on the same seam. The next step is to slide the thumb counterclockwise (right-handed pitcher) (figure 2.13). The distance the thumb moves varies according to hand and finger size as well as grip strength. On release, the hand pronates slightly (turns clockwise).

The ball is thrown as a fastball is thrown. The key to the slider is to throw *through* the ball, not around it. This is the difference

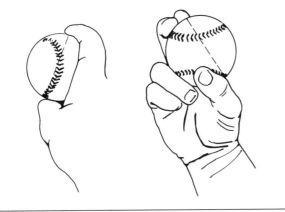

Figure 2.13 The slider grip.

between the slider and the curve. If the fingers go around the ball, the result is a hard curve, or what is sometimes called a "slurve." (The slurve is what hurts the most pitchers' arms. Throwing around the ball at fastball velocity can ruin the elbow. High school pitchers can throw the slider if they throw it *through* the ball.) The fingers should separate from the ball at a spot behind the ball, only in the lower right quadrant instead of in the lower middle as with the fastball.

Some coaches teach pitchers to throw the slider using the middle finger and the thumb to pinch the ball, creating the slider spin. The ball is held slightly off center with the thumb moved toward the middle finger. On release of the ball, the middle finger and thumb pinch the ball, creating the slider spin.

Teaching the Slider

The same process is used for teaching the slider as for teaching the curve. The process should start with the release out front and work backward. The slider is only a fastball with a smaller turn and less pull than the curve. The hand turns slightly at release and is followed by a slight bend of the elbow. The majority of injuries to the elbow are caused by hyperextension of the elbow after release that results from trying to throw the slider as hard as the fastball. The same arm slot and arm speed as the fastball are required but, because of the slight turn of the hand, the slider should be six to eight miles per hour slower than the fastball.

Slider or Curveball?

A pitcher should not try the slider until he has tried to throw the curveball and is unsuccessful. A good curveball is a better pitch than the slider, and it is easier on the arm. The curveball not only has a bigger break, but it is also slower, which gives the pitcher a change of speeds. Most Hall of Fame pitchers threw a curveball and, because the curveball is easier on the arm, also pitched without injuries long enough to win up to 300 games.

Relief pitchers are often successful with the slider because they usually have to face each batter only once a game. Relief pitchers also pitch far fewer innings than a starter pitches, so they are less likely to be injured when including the slider among their pitches.

Change

In an era when hitters are stronger than ever, aluminum bats are several ounces lighter, and the major emphasis is on hitting for power, the change has developed into a valuable pitch. The change is a feel pitch and takes many repetitions to master and maintain, so it must be practiced on a daily basis. (For extra repetitions of the change, the pitcher can throw the change during flat-ground work and long toss.)

When thrown with the same arm speed and the same arm slot as the fastball, the change will look like the fastball in every way except that it will be thrown 10 to 15 miles per hour slower. This change of speeds will upset the hitter's timing and cause him to swing early. Consequently, the batter will either hit the ball on his front foot (therefore losing power) or perhaps miss the ball altogether for a swinging strike.

The ideal change is a pitch that can be thrown consistently for a low strike, at a lower speed, that looks exactly like the fastball. The change, when thrown correctly, is a great pitch to complement the fastball and can be used in fastball counts to retire aggressive hitters. There are as many ways to throw a change as there are pitchers, and as long as it gets the desired results of appearing to be a fastball, control low in the zone, and reduced speed, it is a quality change.

The farther back in the hand the baseball is held, the slower its velocity. Also, the farther apart the fingers are spread on the baseball, the slower the ball's velocity. All pitchers should understand these principles and experiment with them at a young age to learn how to change speeds and at the same time appear to throw a regular fastball.

Circle Change

The circle change is gaining popularity because, except for its strange grip, it is thrown with fastball mechanics. The two middle fingers grip the ball in the circle change. (The regular fastball is gripped with the first two fingers.) The index finger lies along the inside of the ball, forming the letter O with the thumb. (Some pitchers prefer to put the index finger on the thumbnail.) The ball is also held off center. The thumb and the middle finger are much closer together than they are for the normal fastball. The thumb starts on the line bisecting the two middle fingers and then slides around toward the middle finger. The ball should be held out on the tips of the fingers and thumb to allow maximum movement (figure 2.14).

When throwing the circle change, the hand automatically comes over the ball, creating a screwball-type movement. This movement should just happen naturally and not be forced. The pitcher should use the same mechanics and, most important, the same arm speed as for the fastball.

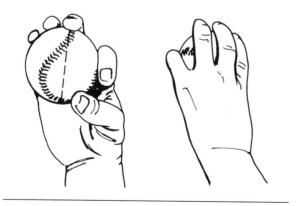

Figure 2.14 The circle change-up grip.

The advantages of the circle change are that the pitch breaks down and away and that the tendency when learning this pitch is to throw the ball low. The circle change can also be used as a strikeout pitch if thrown correctly. The disadvantage of this pitch is that it is difficult to master. Pitchers who choose the circle change will have to work on it in the bullpen as much as they work on the curveball.

The circle change must be thrown out in front to be effective. It should be thrown just as a fastball is thrown, but it should reach out front during release. Remember, the circle change is a fingertip pitch and, to be effective, it has to be thrown and not pushed.

The change overall is a feel pitch, but the circle change takes a lot of repetitions to maintain the feel and to throw the pitch effectively. These repetitions cannot all be from the mound because of pitch limitations and general arm care, so the alternatives are to play catch or do flat-ground work, drills, and even long toss with the circle change.

To generate movement both down and toward the arm side, the pitcher must keep his fingers on top of the baseball. When the ring finger and pinky finger start to spread out and go around the side of the baseball, it makes it impossible to get arm-side spin. This is still a good pitch because it will have all the change requirements and downward movement. Young pitchers with small fingers may have to grip the ball in this manner and, as they get older, may want to get on top of the change. A good beginning exercise when experimenting with the circle change is to place a rubber band around the last three fingers to keep them together and on top of the ball.

Pitchfork Change

Another change grip that is gaining popularity is the pitchfork change. Because of the simplicity of the grip, it can be mastered in a short amount of time and still meet all of the change requirements.

The middle finger is placed on top of the baseball, and the thumb is placed directly under the ball opposite of the middle finger.

The index finger will then be placed on one side and the ring finger on the other so that they are directly opposite each other. The little finger is completely off the ball in the pitchfork change grip (figure 2.15).

As long as the fingers are lined up opposite their partners, the decisions about seams and finger pressure are completely up to the pitcher. This pitch should be thrown with the ball out on the fingertips to begin with, but individual adjustments can be made as long as the change requirements remain (same arm slot, same arm speed, controllable low in the zone, and 8 to 12 miles per hour slower than the fastball). A pitch held this way and thrown out front like a fastball will sink somewhat but will have little side spin unless adjustments are made in the grip and release. To get more of a tumbling effect from the baseball, the pitcher can lift the middle fingertip off of the ball and apply pressure on the inside of the first and third fingers, thus creating a split-finger tumbling action that will dive in the last six to eight feet.

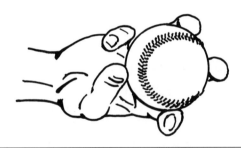

Figure 2.15 The pitchfork change grip.

Slide-Step Change

Combining the slide step with the change adds another option to the pitcher's repertoire. Hitters must load a little sooner when the pitcher uses the slide step, and adding the change with this delivery creates problems in the hitter's timing. Many hitters will load and start their swings prematurely, assuming that the standard slide-step fastball is on the way.

Unless the pitcher has a change that has serious movement, it is not good practice to throw back-to-back changes; however, with a slide-step change in his arsenal, a pitcher

can throw the change and immediately follow it with the slide-step change. Remember, hitters hit what they see, so the slide-step change must be thrown with the same arm slot as well as the same arm speed as the fastball for good results.

Forkball and Split-Finger Change-Up

More and more pitchers try to use the forkball and split-finger fastball as change-ups. These pitches as change-ups have both good points and bad points. If a pitcher can get good topspin on the baseball while still throwing the pitch 12 miles per hour slower than the fastball, then these pitches make good change-ups. However, if the pitcher is getting a knuckleball spin on the baseball, then regardless of how much it breaks, its value as a change-up is weak.

The change-up is supposed to resemble the fastball so that the hitter will be tempted to swing when the pitcher is behind in the count. If the pitch is not spinning, the good hitter will not swing on 2-0 count because he knows the pitch is not a fastball. This is why the forkball is better used as a strikeout pitch. With two strikes, the batter has to swing no matter what type of spin the pitch has. The forkball and split-finger fastball are very similar and appear to be the same pitch. The difference between the two pitches is the amount of ball between the fingers.

With the split-finger fastball, the fingers are spread along the outside of the seams, starting at the narrowest area between the seams and spreading out toward the wide part of the horseshoe (figure 2.16). The split-finger is thrown the same way as a regular fastball. Each pitcher should start with this grip and make small adjustments until he can find a good down break. Many pitchers never find the groove with this pitch; it takes a lot of practice, and long fingers help. The split-finger fastball, if thrown correctly, looks like a fastball until the last six feet and then breaks down, creating an excellent strikeout pitch.

The forkball grip is somewhat different because the ball is divided down the middle by the fingers. Long fingers are a must with

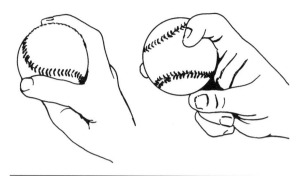

Figure 2.16 The split-finger fastball grip.

this pitch. Topspin is created because the fingers act as an axis on which the ball can spin. The longer the fingers, the more room the ball has to spin, creating topspin and a good down break. Pitchers with fingers that are not quite long enough will get a knuckleball spin on the forkball; pitchers with long fingers get more topspin on the ball.

Pitch Adjustments

When a particular pitch is not working quite as it should or the pitcher is wild, there is a reason. The following is a list of physical adjustments that a pitcher can make when things aren't going well. A coach can make only three trips to the mound to help out a pitcher; therefore, the pitcher needs to be able to make his own corrections and adjustments between pitches.

Missing Up

The pitcher's throwing hand must be up in the back when the stride foot lands. Something is causing the hand to be late, and the result is a high pitch. Following are some possible reasons for missing up.

• *Rushing.* The pitcher may be running out from under his arm. The body goes to the plate before it is supposed to, leaving the throwing hand before it is set up in the back. The pitcher can try two things to give the arm time to set up. First, the pitcher should just try to stay back with his weight on the inside of his back leg while his arm is being set up for delivery. Second, the pitcher can either

slow down his leg lift or lift his leg a little higher to give the arm time to get set up in the back. The higher or steeper the mound, the more the pitcher has to try to stay back.

• *Shoulder tilt.* When the pitcher's front-side shoulder and elbow aim up over the target as he strides toward the plate, the throwing arm will not get set up high in the back. The pitcher appears to be throwing uphill. The overhand pitcher may have a little shoulder tilt and be effective; however, the three-quarter or side-arm pitcher should keep the shoulders lined up to the plate.

• *Overstriding.* The pitcher who jumps at the target and lands on his heel is overstriding and will miss up in the zone. The pitcher should only stride as far as he can land on the inside of the ball of his stride foot.

• *Collapsing the back side.* A pitcher who collapses the back leg will have problems keeping the ball down in the zone. The pitcher should stay tall and throw downhill. A slight bend in the back leg is necessary for balance; but when a pitcher's first move is to sit on his back leg, he is collapsing and appears to be throwing uphill.

Missing Down

When the pitcher's throwing hand gets set up too early in the delivery, the result is that he misses down. Following are some possible reasons as to why a pitcher misses down.

• *Understriding.* The most obvious solution to missing down is to encourage the pitcher to stride a little farther. The pitcher may need to push a little more with the back leg to increase his stride. Perhaps the leg lift is too slow and the pitcher's timing is off. Speeding up the leg lift will help to get the throwing arm in the proper position in the back.

• *Squeezing the baseball.* Many times a pitcher who is missing down is simply squeezing the ball, which will affect the release point. For best results, the pitcher should have a loose grip on the baseball. Squeezing the ball too tightly usually comes to play more with breaking balls caused by the pitcher's intent to really break one off and throw a strikeout pitch.

It is common to see pitchers throw a great breaking ball early in the count and then, with two strikes, squeeze the ball and bounce it three feet in front of the plate.

Hanging Curveballs

The hanging curveball is that curve that starts high and finishes up in the zone with little break. This curveball is usually hit very hard.

The curveball must be thrown out in front. The proper sequence is reach, turn, and pull. Pitchers will sometimes turn the ball for the curveball before they get to the release point. When a pitcher turns the ball back by his head, the arm slows down and the wrist gets locked into curveball position. The result is a slow, flat, hanging curveball. The pitcher should throw a fastball and turn the ball during release for a quick, sharp break on the curveball.

The pitcher may turn the ball during release and still have a flat curveball if he does not pull his throwing hand into his body by bending the elbow after release. Pulling the hand around the ball and back toward the waist creates better spin, and it helps to keep the arm healthy by eliminating hyperextension of the elbow.

Hanging Change

As with the hanging curveball, a change that is flat and up in the zone becomes a very hittable pitch. A pitcher should miss low with the change if he is going to miss. A batter will often chase a low change; should the batter hit a low change, there is usually very little damage.

When a pitcher is pushing his change, he simply has his elbow down during delivery, causing the ball to be pushed up in the zone. The change should be thrown with fastball mechanics, including a high elbow. The change grip will take care of the change of speeds.

As with the fastball, the breaking ball, and the curveball, the change must be thrown out in front to be effective. Encouraging the pitcher to bend at the waist and reach to the plate with the pitch will help him to get the change low in the zone.

Pitching Only to One Side of the Plate

Many pitchers have the ability to throw the fastball only to the arm side of the plate. To be effective in the long run, a pitcher must be able to pitch to both sides of the plate. In many cases a small adjustment will help the pitcher to pitch to either side of the plate. Some common errors and corrections follow.

- *Throwing across the body*. A pitcher who does not stride in a direct line to the target will have problems with pitching from side to side. Many pitchers who throw across the body are blocking out their ability to throw to the opposite arm side. When a pitcher lands to the outside of a straight line to the target, it is almost physically impossible to locate the ball low and away.

- *Spinning the pivot foot*. A pitcher who appears to stride straight to the target in drills and even the slide step, yet has problems in the full windup, may be spinning on his pivot foot.

When the pitcher lifts his leg up and back into the gathered position, sometimes his pivot-foot heel will travel away from the rubber so that the pivot foot is not square to the target. The pitcher is now physically lined up to the arm side of the plate and will throw across his body. Three-quarter and side-arm pitchers are prone to pivot-foot spin because of the amount of coil in the gathered position.

- *Overrotating the upper body*. In some cases a pitcher may be overrotating the shoulders in the gathered position. The lower body may coil a small amount behind the rubber, but the shoulders should hold the line between home plate and second base. With too much shoulder rotation, the throwing arm may not catch up and the result is the inability to throw down and away.

• *Positioning the head away from the target*. The body goes where the head goes. When the pitcher's head does not go directly to the target, the body and the throwing arm will not go to the target.

Many pitchers will tilt the head back and away from the center of gravity, causing the upper body to spin out. When the head goes, the front shoulder goes; the throwing elbow will drop, causing an early release point. The result is an inside (and usually upward) pitch.

To pitch down and away, the pitcher must keep his head over his center of gravity and on line to the target. When the head is aligned, the eyes will remain parallel to the ground. When the eyes are tilted with the arm-side eye higher than the glove-side eye, the head is tilting and going off line.

chapter 3

Instructing How to Hold Runners and Field the Position

The pitcher's defensive responsibilities include fielding groundballs and bunts, backing up bases, and holding runners. If the pitcher is able to field his position, he will allow fewer base runners and runs. Holding runners is also important for keeping them out of scoring position. The bottom line is that the pitcher who can field and hold runners allows fewer runs and therefore is successful.

Fielding the Position

The pitcher's fielding role is often overlooked or ignored, yet it is often important to the outcome of the game. Some type of pitchers' fielding practice should be held daily to ensure proper fielding and throwing techniques, and pitchers should learn their defensive responsibilities for different situations.

Position players spend hours practicing fielding and throwing, yet pitchers are generally ignored in this phase of the game. The pitcher is involved in 10 to 15 percent of fielding situations. These figures may even be higher if the pitcher throws a lot of groundballs. (These figures were attained by dividing the total number of times a pitcher handled the ball after it was hit by the total number of times the ball was handled by the team.)

The pitcher handles the baseball in many situations, including bunts, comebackers, rundowns, and backing up the bases. The percentages alone show the importance of daily fielding practice for pitchers.

Guidelines for Fielding Groundballs

The pitcher should follow some basic guidelines when attempting to field any type of groundball:

- The slower the ball is hit, the faster the pitcher must move to the ball.
- The slower the ball is hit, the more important it is to get the feet and body set to throw before the pitcher catches the ball.
- The pitcher should use two hands to field the ball when the ball is moving and only the bare hand if the ball is completely stopped.
- The pitcher should attempt to turn his body toward the glove side when setting up to make a throw. Turning away from

the glove side takes more time and is less efficient.

- The pitcher should always catch the ball before throwing it. Throws are often errant because pitchers are too hurried.

Bare-Handed Play

The only time the pitcher should bare-hand the ball is when it is completely stopped. Any time the ball is rolling, the pitcher should use two hands. The correct procedure for bare-handing a baseball is as follows: The pitcher should approach the ball in such a way that he can set his feet in line with the target before he picks up the baseball. Setting the feet before pickup saves time, which is always important on the bare-handed play or on any slow-rolling groundball (figure 3.1). When the pitcher approaches the ball, he should attempt to field the ball by his back foot. This saves time when he throws to the target (figure 3.2).

When the pitcher bends to pick up the baseball, he should push the ball into the ground with his bare hand, thus ensuring a

Figure 3.1 Set the feet before picking up the ball.

Figure 3.2 Field the ball by the back foot.

good grip. Most pitchers who misplay the bare-hand play start to straighten the body to make the throw without having a good grip on the baseball. Another common mistake is to look up to see the base runner before getting a good grip on the ball. Pushing the ball into the ground enables the pitcher to always get a good grip (figure 3.3).

Figure 3.3 Push the ball into the ground.

Time is of the essence during the bare-handed play, so the pitcher should throw the baseball without first putting it in the glove. If he takes the ball to the glove before making the throw, he gives the base runner one more step to the base (figure 3.4).

Making Throws From the Field

To ensure accuracy, a pitcher should follow some basic guidelines when making a throw after fielding a ball.

- The feet must be lined up in the direction of the target. The front foot should step toward the target during the throw to ensure accuracy. The direction of the front foot dictates the direction of the throw (figure 3.5). Improper front-foot alignment is the number one cause of inaccurate throws among fielders.

- The shoulders must be parallel to the ground. When the front shoulder is aimed over the target, the throw will be

Figure 3.4 Throw the baseball without first putting it in the glove.

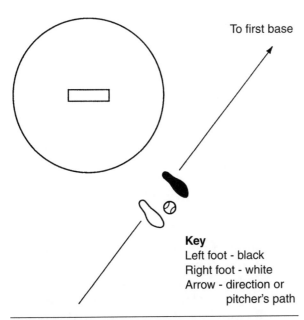

Figure 3.5 The direction of the front foot dictates the direction of the throw.

To first base

Key
Left foot - black
Right foot - white
Arrow - direction or
pitcher's path

Figure 3.6 The shoulders must be parallel to the ground: *(a)* correct, *(b)* incorrect.

over the target. When the front shoulder is aimed below the target, the throw will be short of the target (figure 3.6).

- All throws should be overhand, except for the throw that must be made off balance (do-or-die play). Overhand throws do not tail as much as a side-arm throw, making them easier to handle.
- A four-seam grip should be used. A two-seam grip creates more movement, making the throw tougher to handle.
- When the ball has been caught with two hands, the hands should not break until the throw is made. While the pitcher is waiting for the fielder to cover the base, his hands should remain together until he makes the throw.
- The farther the throw, the harder the throw should be. The shorter the throw, the softer it should be.

Pitcher to First Base (1-3 Play)

The basic guidelines for fielding and throwing previously mentioned in this chapter should be followed in the 1-3 play attempt. The pitcher should make a firm throw and keep

Position by Number			
Pitcher	1	Shortstop	6
Catcher	2	Left fielder	7
First baseman	3	Center fielder	8
Second baseman	4	Right fielder	9
Third baseman	5		

the ball in the glove until the first baseman is on or close to the base. The throw should be chest high and to the inside of the base.

Pitcher to Second Base (1-6-3 or 1-4-3 Play)

The basic guidelines for fielding and throwing should be followed in the 1-6-3 or the 1-4-3 play attempt.

The shortstop covers second base in 95 percent of all plays to second base. With this in mind, the pitcher should communicate with the shortstop before the pitch about the possibility of a play at second base.

The only times the second baseman covers the base are when (a) the ball is hit to the pitcher's right and the shortstop has to charge the groundball if it gets by the pitcher, (b) the shortstop is playing way over toward third base because a pull hitter is up, and (c) the shortstop is covering third base in a predetermined bunt defense.

On the play to second base, the throw should be firm and chest high over the base. In the case of a hard-hit groundball, the pitcher should keep the ball in the glove until the shortstop is close to the base.

Pitcher Back to the Plate (1-2 or 1-2-3 Play)

The basic guidelines for fielding and throwing previously mentioned in this chapter should be followed in the 1-2 or 1-2-3 play attempt. The throw to the catcher should be firm but not too hard because the pitcher is very close to the catcher. The throw should be chest high and over the base.

The situation for throwing to the plate is when bases are loaded with no outs. The only other time is when there is one out and the tying run is on third. The pitcher should communicate with the catcher before the pitch about the possibility of a 1-2 or 1-2-3 play.

In the case of a hard-hit groundball, the pitcher should keep the ball in the glove until the catcher is on or close to the plate. In the case of a routine groundball, the pitcher should try to get his feet lined up before making the catch, for a quicker throw to the plate.

It is better for the pitcher to be a little slow in the throw to the plate, and get only the force-out at the plate, than to try to hurry the throw for the 1-2-3 double play and make a bad throw. The force-out at the plate is the first priority.

Covering First Base (3-1 Play)

A pitcher's first reaction when the ball is hit to his left must be to go toward first base in case he is needed to cover the base. This must be an immediate reaction because the base runner will probably be safe if the pitcher has to think about it before covering first. The only way to make this a natural reaction is through repetition. Countless executions of this play in practice will ensure that the pitcher reacts, rather than remembers, to cover first.

The following are guidelines for covering first base on a 3-1 play.

- When the ball is hit on the ground to his left, the pitcher should immediately (reactively) break toward first base. The path to first base is the same regardless of the speed of the groundball. The pitcher should sprint to a point 10 feet in front of first base, toward home plate, on the foul line. When he gets to this point, he turns up the foul line toward first base. In the remaining 10 feet the pitcher should slow down and get himself under control, giving the first baseman a target with his glove. The target should be chest high and to the inside of the base (figure 3.7).

- During his approach, the pitcher should prepare to touch the inside of the base with his right foot. (Regardless of which

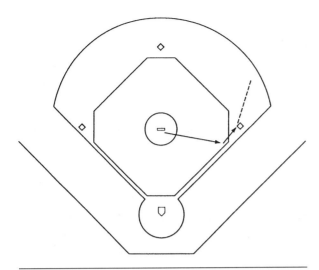

Figure 3.7 The target should be chest high and to the inside of the base.

hand the pitcher throws with, the right foot is always used in this play.) Using the right foot and touching the inside of the base will keep the pitcher's body from crossing the foul line and going into the runner's path.

- The first baseman should throw the ball before the pitcher gets to the base, enabling the pitcher the opportunity to look at the base and make the play. Upon receiving the throw and touching first base, the pitcher should take one more step to the inside with the left foot and immediately turn to look at the plate; if second base is occupied, the runner may try to score on a 3-1 play. It is a good habit to turn and look at the plate whether or not a runner is on second base.

- If the first baseman bobbles the ball, the pitcher should get to the base and set up as a first baseman does to receive the throw. The pitcher can stretch to the ball, if needed, from this position.

A 3-1 play on a slow groundball is simple to execute, yet it is often misplayed. Following these basic guidelines will eliminate any communication problems between the first baseman and the pitcher.

The pitcher follows the same path to first base regardless of the type of groundball that is hit to his left. When the ball is hit slowly, the pitcher starts toward first base in the usual

manner. If the batted ball goes between the pitcher's path to first base and the plate, the pitcher goes to get it and throws it to the first baseman. The type of throw depends on how far the pitcher is from first base. (See the throwing guidelines on pages 40-41.) When the batted ball is close to or on the designated path to first base, the pitcher catches the ball and either flips it to the first baseman or takes it to first base himself.

If the batted ball goes to the left of the pitcher's designated path to first base, the pitcher should continue to first base. The first baseman will catch this ball and flip it to the pitcher covering the base. The pitcher should turn inside to face the first baseman upon arrival at first base.

Communication between the first baseman and the pitcher is crucial. When the ball is hit to the right of or on the pitcher's designated path to first base, the pitcher yells "I've got it" and proceeds with the play. Should the ball go to the left of the designated path, the pitcher says nothing and continues to first base. The first baseman goes after all groundballs hit in his direction until he hears the pitcher say that he has it, at which time he goes to first base to receive the throw. The only player who ever says anything is the pitcher, and then only if he is going to field the ball.

3-6-1 Double Play

The 3-6-1 double play is a play that seldom happens, but it is still important for the pitcher to be able to complete it. Base runners must be on first and second base, or bases may be loaded. The first baseman must be playing back behind the runner at first base.

In making a 3-6-1 double play, a pitcher must follow these guidelines.

- When the ball is hit to the pitcher's left, he must follow the designated path to first base.

- As the first baseman throws to second base, the pitcher should set up at first base as a first baseman does.

- Should the first baseman bobble the baseball, the throw should go directly to first base.

Bunt and
Slow-Roller Defense

The basic guidelines for fielding and throwing should be followed in fielding bunts and slow rollers. The pitcher's plan of action in bunt defense will vary from team to team, but the basic fielding and throwing guidelines should remain the same.

When fielding bunts, pitchers should follow these guidelines.

- The pitcher should be aware of all bunt situations, whether sacrifice or for a base hit, and pitch accordingly. In a definite sacrifice-bunt situation, the pitcher should throw high four-seam fastballs for strikes. High fastballs are not easy to bunt and may be popped up. A hard-breaking ball is also a very hard pitch to bunt. The key is to throw strikes, forcing the batter to bunt. *Take the out.*

- The pitcher becomes a more efficient fielder when he takes the appropriate angle on bunts and slow rollers. He must know his particular lane in the predetermined bunt defense and get there under control.

- Having taken the appropriate angle to the ball, the pitcher can now set his feet to make the throw before he fields the ball.

- The pitcher should always use two hands to field the ball if it is moving. When the ball is stopped, a bare-handed play is advised.

Here are several specific bunt plays and the pitcher's respective defensive responsibilities.

Runner on first base, bunt fielded by the pitcher. In this situation the pitcher should anticipate the throw to second base and preset his feet accordingly. The theory behind this is that the pitcher can always shift his feet and go to first base, but setting his feet to first base makes it impossible to get the lead runner going into second base.

Bunt down the first baseline to be thrown to first base. When the ball is bunted well to the inside of the baseline, the pitcher presets his feet and throws the ball to the first baseman, who should be set up on the inside of the base. Staying on the inside of the baseline is necessary for avoiding the running batter.

When the ball is bunted close to or on the baseline, the pitcher should field the ball on the run and throw the ball underhanded to the first baseman on the outside of the base. This is a tough play, and players must practice it to perfect it. The first baseman will know to go to the outside when he sees the pitcher's momentum carry him to the outside of the baseline.

The left-handed pitcher must take a different angle than the right-handed pitcher takes when fielding the bunt down the first baseline. The left-handed pitcher must go around the bunt, cutting it off on the first-base side.

The pitcher should step over and in front of the bunt with his left foot. Before his left foot hits the ground, the pitcher starts to spin so that he is fielding the bunt facing the pitcher's mound. As the pitcher spins, his right foot swings around to set up in a straight line to first base. The phrase "hopping the fence" is often used for this particular type of play because, when properly executed at full speed, it does indeed look as if the pitcher is hopping a small fence (figure 3.8).

Bunted ball on the third baseline to be thrown to third base. In this instance it is the right-handed pitcher who must hop the fence. He should first cut the ball off and step over and in front of it with his right foot. Before that foot hits the ground, the pitcher starts to spin so that he is fielding the bunt facing the pitcher's mound. As the pitcher spins, his left foot swings around to set up in a straight line to third base. For effectiveness, this move (as with the left-handed pitcher's fielding of a bunt to first) must be performed as a continuous motion and not as a string of segments in which the pitcher steps, fields, spins, and throws (figure 3.9).

For the left-handed pitcher, if the ball is well inside the third baseline, the pitcher simply presets the feet to line up with third base and continues the play.

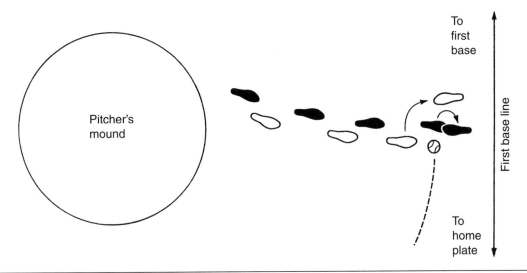

Figure 3.8 A left-handed pitcher "hopping the fence."

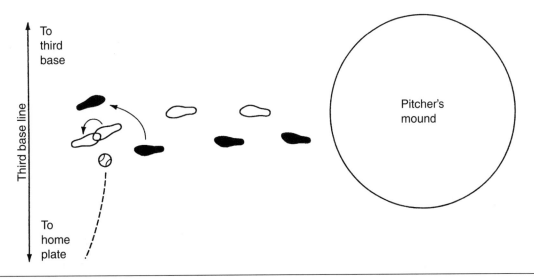

Figure 3.9 A right-handed pitcher "hopping the fence."

Should the ball be bunted close to or on the third baseline, the pitcher may have to field the bunt on the run. With no base runner between home plate and third base, the pitcher can throw directly to the third baseman instead of going outside or inside.

Squeeze bunt. A properly executed squeeze bunt is impossible to defend against. However, because of the delicate timing required and the pressure on the bunter, the squeeze play is often miscued.

In the perfect squeeze play, the bunter doesn't show bunt and the base runner doesn't show run until the pitcher's lead foot hits the ground. In such a case the pitcher has to take his chances because it is too late to change anything.

If the runner on third leaves early enough to tip off the squeeze play, the pitcher should pitch out, down, and away from a left-handed batter and 12 inches inside on a right-handed batter. By pitching out to the left-hander and in to the right-hander, the pitcher is trying to get the batter to miss the bunt. The catcher is on the appropriate side of the base for the tag.

When the squeeze bunt is bunted too hard back to the pitcher, it is possible to get the runner at the plate. The runner has a head start, so the pitcher must bare-hand this play. Many pitchers discard their gloves so that they can bare-hand the ball with either hand. Pitchers, catchers, and infielders must not forget the out at first base; if there is a runner at second base, they must realize that he may try to score also.

Pitchers and Rundowns

Many times a pitcher gets involved in a rundown either after a pickoff or after a comebacker in which a runner gets hung up. The following guidelines should be followed.

Rundown After a Pickoff

The pitcher should always go to the base with the fewest fielders and proceed with the rundown. For example, when picking off a runner at first base, the pitcher should go to back up first base. The shortstop and second baseman will be at second, leaving only the first baseman to cover first.

Rundown After a Comebacker

Runners often try to advance on a ball hit back up the middle. When the pitcher comes up with the ball, the runner either keeps going or stops and gets caught in a rundown. If the runner keeps going to the next base, the pitcher simply throws the ball to the appropriate base. If the runner stops or slows down, the pitcher should run to a spot in front of the runner, heading him off, and run him back in the direction of the previous base.

Once the rundown begins, the pitcher should follow the rundown procedure his team uses.

Pitcher and Catcher Fielding Communication

The catcher has the field in front of him; for this reason he is responsible for deciding which base the ball should be thrown to. Of particular concern to the pitcher are bunt plays, plays that include backing-up responsibilities, and balls that get by the catcher.

Catcher and Bunt Plays

In all bunt defenses, the catcher is responsible for choosing which base the ball should be thrown to. In handling bunt defenses, the catcher has the following responsibilities.

- He must make the call as early as possible. The pitcher is trying to preset his feet to properly field the bunt. The sooner the pitcher knows what base to throw to, the more easily he can set his feet.
- He should know the speed of the runners involved.
- He should be aware of any designed bunt defense that comes from the bench and the intent of that particular defense.
- He must be aware of the pitcher's qualities, including quickness and arm strength, and which arm the pitcher throws with.

Catcher's Involvement in Backing Up Bases

In most situations it is fairly routine which base the pitcher should back up. Any time there is a choice to be made between throwing the ball to third base and throwing it home, the pitcher should go to a spot halfway between third and home and respond to the catcher's call. The catcher must watch the play develop and call the play as early as possible to ensure that the pitcher is backing up.

Passed Ball–Wild Pitch

When a passed ball–wild pitch occurs and the catcher doesn't know where the ball is, the pitcher and catcher can use two forms of communication: a verbal signal and a physical signal.

Verbal Signal

The pitcher should yell out the number 1 if the ball is deflected behind the catcher toward the first baseline, the number 2 when the ball goes straight back, and the number 3 when the ball is deflected toward the third baseline. Even though the catcher will probably see the ball if it stays in front of him, the pitcher should still yell out, "In front." When the ball is straight down around the catcher's feet, the pitcher should simply yell, "Down."

Physical Signal

The pitcher should also give a physical signal. If there is a large crowd and the catcher can't hear, he can always look at the pitcher. In addition to yelling the direction of the passed ball–wild pitch, the pitcher should point in the direction the ball has gone. To avoid confusion, the pitcher should always give both sets of directions.

In covering the plate after a passed ball–wild pitch, the pitcher should do the following:

1. He should sprint to the clay in front of the plate and then slow down and get under control, facing the catcher and presenting a good target.

2. He should set his feet in such a way that he will never block the plate. His feet should be out of the baseline on the first-base side of home plate.

3. When making the tag, he should catch the ball, turn the glove so that the back of the glove is facing the runner, and make a swoop tag, putting the glove down for the tag and then getting out of the way.

Backing Up the Bases

Once the ball is hit, the pitcher becomes a fielder just like the other eight players on defense. And like the other players, when the pitcher is not involved with the original play he is responsible for backing up a base in case of an errant throw.

Pitchers should use the following tips when backing up bases:

- When crossing the baseline, the pitcher should be aware of base runners. Running into base runners constitutes interference, and the runner is awarded the next base.

- When backing up a base after a pickoff or in any rundown situation, the pitcher should back up the base that has the fewest fielders. For example, when picking off a man at first base, the pitcher should back up first base. The second baseman and shortstop will be at second, leaving only the first baseman to cover first.

- When backing up a throw from the outfield to a base, the pitcher should always get as far away from the base as possible and still be in a straight line with the outfielder and the base. When backing up third base and home plate, the pitcher should be back to the fence or backstop. This will keep the pitcher from being short-hopped or involved with a bad bounce.

- The pitcher should always back up the base that is two bases in front of the runner in situations other than a pickoff. Figure 3.10 shows the routes a pitcher should take to back up the bases in most situations.

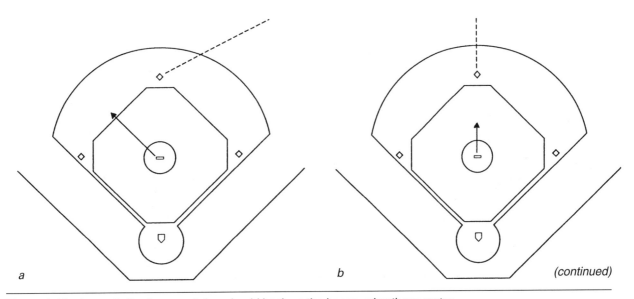

a   *b*   *(continued)*

Figure 3.10 In most situations, a pitcher should back up the bases using these routes.

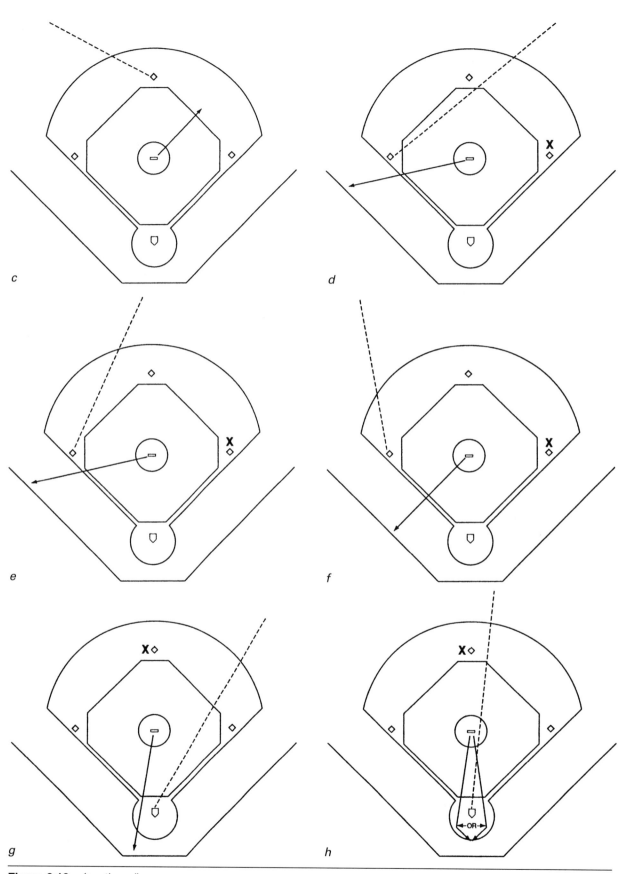

c

d

e

f

g

h

Figure 3.10 *(continued)*

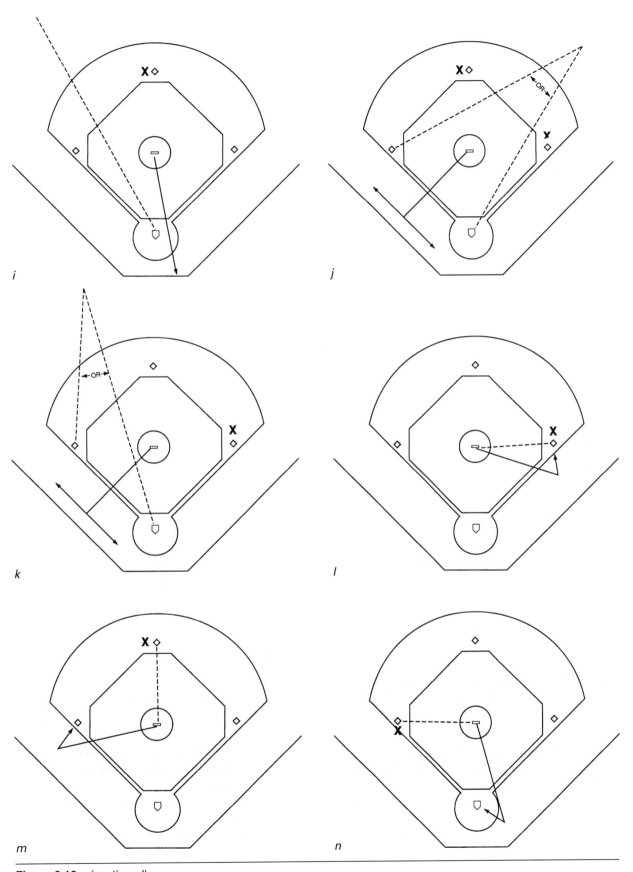

i

j

k

l

m

n

Figure 3.10 *(continued)*

Holding Runners

The skill of holding runners involves stretch mechanics, pickoffs at first base, and release times. The first thing a pitcher does differently when a batter reaches first base is to use the stretch position instead of the full windup. For this reason, stretch mechanics are discussed in this chapter rather than in chapter 1, "Developing Proper Mechanics." Pickoff moves, release times, and other criteria for holding runners are also discussed in this chapter.

Stretch Mechanics

Stretch mechanics are perhaps more important than full-windup mechanics because they are used when a runner is on base. A pitcher who can pitch effectively with men on base is truly a great pitcher.

Perfect stretch mechanics are very similar to full-windup mechanics. They differ only until the gather; then the stretch looks identical to the full windup. The same mechanics should be used for two reasons. First, it is difficult enough to master one set of mechanics—let alone two—and throw the ball with control. When a pitcher uses an entirely different set of mechanics from the stretch, he has to learn two deliveries. This can also affect his full windup. Second, when a pitcher uses two completely different deliveries, he is at higher risk of injuring his arm. When a pitcher tries to match the two deliveries, he sometimes must change his full windup to match his stretch because he must follow certain guidelines out of the stretch.

The mechanics of the stretch are very similar for the right-handed pitcher and the left-handed pitcher, except that the left-hander usually has a slower delivery because he has the advantage of facing the runner at first base. The right-handed pitcher needs to have good, sound mechanics yet be quick enough to the plate to deter the runner from stealing a base. The left-handed pitcher can use good, sound mechanics without worrying about how fast he delivers the pitch, because he doesn't have to commit to the plate until he decides to.

A pitcher needs to practice pitching in the stretch position at least twice as much as in the full windup. Most pitchers think they should do just the opposite, so coaches should force pitchers to spend time in the stretch.

Taking the Signal

When beginning the stretch, the pitcher should first straddle the rubber, with his arms dangling by his sides (figure 3.11).

When he sees that all of the fielders are in position and the umpires are ready to go, the pitcher assumes position on the rubber. The pivot foot is located next to the rubber at the appropriate end. The stride foot is located 12 to 18 inches closer to the plate, on a line to the plate with the pivot foot (figure 3.12).

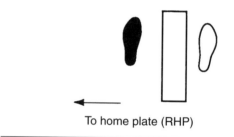

To home plate (RHP)

Figure 3.11 Beginning the stretch.

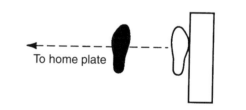

To home plate

Figure 3.12 Assuming position on the rubber.

The pitcher can hold the glove in front of his body or dangling at his side. However, he must hold the throwing hand at the side or behind. (This rule was adopted to eliminate the quick pitch.) The pitcher should stand up straight, letting the arms hang in a relaxed fashion. Many pitchers prefer to bend at the waist with the glove hand resting on the front knee. There is nothing wrong with this, but the body must straighten again to get into the set position. This bending and straightening, multiplied by several pitches, could cause lower back fatigue and stiffness.

Coming to the Set Position

Once again, simplicity is best, so the pitcher should avoid all unnecessary movement when coming to the set position. Instead of taking a step back to where the foot will be planted, he should put it there when taking the signal. If the pitcher can eliminate this step and not bend over, the only thing he needs to do is bring the glove and the ball together in front of the body and slightly flex the legs. (The pitcher should avoid bringing both the glove and the ball over the head and down to the set position because this is also a big waste of movement.)

The pitcher moves into the set position after he receives the sign and finishes his preliminary movements. The pitcher can remain in the set position for as long as he wants. When in the set, he can move his head to look at the base runners, but he cannot move any other part of his body unless he is going toward the plate in the delivery. If he moves his shoulders or anything else, it's a balk.

Should the pitcher want to stop and start over for whatever reason, he must step behind the rubber with the pivot foot. He is then free to move the rest of his body, because after he clears the rubber he becomes a regular fielder and no longer must adhere to pitching rules.

The pitcher brings his hands together in front of his chest or belly when he comes to the set position. Here are some guidelines he should follow:

- The hands must change direction before the pitcher can go to the plate.
- The change of direction must take place in front of the body and lower than the chin.
- It is up to the pitcher when to throw the ball after he becomes set. He may set and go, or he may pause before the pitch.
- The pitcher should hold his hands next to his body. This ensures that the ball hand is free to take the correct path when he starts to the plate. The hands

break in exactly the same way in the stretch as in the full windup.

When the pitcher comes to the set position, his legs should be slightly flexed. Whether he goes to the plate or throws to a base, his first movement is to flex his legs slightly. By having the legs already flexed in the set position, he eliminates some movement and can be quicker to the plate.

The pitcher's stride foot must be located on a line from the appropriate side of the rubber to the plate. The feet should not open up; any advantage gained by being able to see the runner at first or having a quicker move will be nullified by slowness to the plate. It is also very easy to run on a pitcher who has opened up, because before he can go to the plate he must close his hips and shoulders. This gives the runner a good jump (figure 3.13).

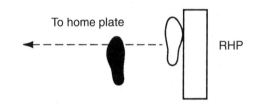

Figure 3.13 The open set position is not necessarily the best position in the set.

Right-Handed Pitcher

Following are considerations for right-handed pitchers when working on stretch mechanics.

Right-Handed Pitcher to the Plate

Right-handed pitchers should concentrate on being quick to the plate, within the boundaries of proper stretch mechanics. A base runner can decide when to steal much earlier with a right-handed pitcher than with a left-handed pitcher, so a right-hander must be quick to the plate. The right-handed pitcher should not alter his mechanics but only speed them up. It takes a lot of practice for a pitcher to do this without losing his rhythm and velocity.

Stride leg. The right-handed pitcher's stride leg is the key to a quick delivery. The higher the leg kick, the slower the time to the plate. Instead of using a high leg kick, the pitcher should bring the knee back and up at the same time. This enables him to get into a closed gathered position more quickly than if he lifted his leg up first and then back. The result should be the same gathered position as in the full windup. From the gathered position, the pitcher's delivery should be identical to his full-windup delivery.

Release times. When calculating a pitcher's quickness to the plate, a coach can use a stopwatch to measure the release time. The watch should be started at the first sign of movement from the pitcher and stopped when the ball hits the catcher's mitt.

A good release time is 1.4 seconds or less. Anything more than 1.4 seconds makes it difficult for the catcher to throw out the base runner. To practice release times, the coach should put the watch on his pitchers in the bullpen every time a pitcher throws from the stretch. Constant reminders to be quick will help the pitcher reduce his release time. Don't expect a low release time if the only time it is mentioned is during a game. In a game, you want the pitcher concentrating on getting the opposition out and winning the game.

Common Stretch Problems for Right-Handed Pitchers

Some problems often arise with the right-handed pitcher's stretch mechanics. Rushing, loss of rhythm, and the development of bad habits are common and should be attended to immediately.

Rushing from the set position. When pitchers try to speed up the stretch, one of the most common problems is rushing. The pitcher tends to go too hard to the plate with the legs and leave the arm behind. The key to speeding up the stretch delivery is to quicken all aspects of the delivery, not just the legs.

Loss of rhythm from the stretch. When the pitcher tries to speed up, his rhythm suffers. Rhythm is a major factor affecting velocity. To keep a rhythm, the pitcher should try bouncing the hands before going to the plate. When the knee goes up, the hands go up. When the stride leg starts forward, the hands break. It is a very small bounce designed to help keep rhythm, not a big bounce that will slow down the stretch delivery. (The bounce can also be done in the full windup if there is a loss of rhythm there.)

Right-Handed Pitcher's Move to First Base

The key to the right-handed pitcher's move to first base is quickness. A pitcher with fast, dartlike throws to first base not only holds runners close but also occasionally picks off a base runner.

Pickoff move. The move of a right-handed pitcher can best be described as a jump-spin. The pitcher's feet start with the standard set position and jump-spin into the position shown in figure 3.14.

The emphasis should be on spin quickness and not on the height of the jump. The pivot foot must clear the rubber, and the stride foot must go toward first base to avoid a balk. The faster the legs get set to throw to first base, the faster the entire move will be. Throwing without the legs set results in inaccurate throws.

Quick feet help the pitcher's move only if arm speed is equally as quick. A common mistake that right-handed pitchers make is to work hard on their footwork only to have a slow arm movement. The proper arm mechanics for the move to first base are *dartlike*. Simultaneous with the initial jump, the throwing arm should go up by the pitcher's ear.

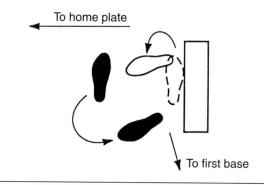

Figure 3.14 Proper foot position for a right-handed pitcher's pickoff move.

From here the pitcher can throw to first in a dartlike manner. The pitcher should throw as forcefully as possible while maintaining accuracy.

The pitcher should not drop the hand below the belt as in regular throwing mechanics (figure 3.15). The coach can use a stopwatch to time moves to first base.

Quick arm and quick feet go a long way toward holding runners. Of course, knowing when to throw over is just as important.

Figure 3.15 The arm should go up (a), not down (b), in the pickoff move.

Pickoff variations. The pitcher can use variations to help hold runners closer to first base. The more looks a pitcher can show a baserunner the better. When a pitcher uses variations in his pickoff move, the runner will not get comfortable and will lose confidence.

• *Decoy move.* Lobbing a throw over to first base doesn't fool anybody and is a waste of time and effort. To decoy a runner, the pitcher should throw a couple of attempts over to first base using the jump move, only with a long-arm throw.

If the pitcher feels that the runner is getting too big a lead, he should shorten the arm and attempt the pickoff. The key is to make the first couple of throws look as if they are the best pickoff moves the pitcher is capable of. Doing everything quickly, with the exception of the long arm, will accomplish this. The difference between the long and short arm is enough to throw off the runner's timing and perhaps catch him leaning toward second base.

• *Balk move.* Base runners often look at the pitcher's stride-foot heel to determine whether the pitcher is going to the plate or coming to first base. If the heel comes up, more often than not he is starting to the plate. To get an advantage, the pitcher can lift his heel and then throw to first base. This is a balk by the rules, but it is so difficult to see that it is rarely called. The heel lift must be very slight, or it will be detectable by the umpire.

• *Moves from different phases of the stretch.* A pitcher can and should throw to first base at any time during the stretch delivery. A pitcher can throw over before getting the sign, while getting the sign, or while getting into the set position. Each different look gives the opposing team more to think about.

• *Quick pitching.* When a pitcher has a good base stealer on first base, and his best move is not working to keep the base runner close, an occasional quick pitch can help. When a pitcher steps back off the rubber, the base runner's first reaction is to retreat to the base. If the base runner does retreat to the base, the pitcher can step back in front of the rubber and pitch to the hitter. In quick pitching, the hands must break when the pitcher steps back off the rubber. When getting back in front of the rubber, the pitcher must follow the rules governing the regular set position. The hands must come together, and he must pause or change direction. Of course, the best way to foil the quick pitch is for the batter to step out of the batter's box when he sees the pitcher step back.

Left-Handed Pitcher

The left-handed pitcher has a huge advantage with a runner on first base, as he is facing the runner in the stretch position. The advantage goes back to the right-handed pitcher with a runner on second or third base, so left-handed pitchers should pay close attention in these situations.

Left-Handed Pitcher to the Plate

Taking the signal, becoming set, and the basic set position are the same as for the right-handed pitcher. The differences between left- and right-handers begin when the left-handed pitcher goes to the plate. The right-handed pitcher relies on quickness to the plate, whereas the left-handed pitcher relies on deception. The left-hander can lift the stride leg up to the gather point and decide at this point whether to go to first base or go to the plate, depending of course on what the base runner is doing (figure 3.16). If the runner appears to be stealing, the pitcher throws to first base. If the runner stays close to first base, the pitcher goes to the plate. Because the left-handed pitcher relies on deception, he can use the same tempo as in his full windup.

Figure 3.16 The left-handed pitcher relies on deception.

Left-Handed Pitcher's Move to First Base

The key to a left-handed pitcher's move to first base is to *appear* as if he is going to home, then throw to first base while staying within the legal boundaries. (It sounds very simple, but very few left-handers have good moves to first base.)

An imaginary plane runs from the pitcher's rubber to first base. If the pitcher's stride foot goes to the second-base side of this plane, the pitcher is required to go home with the pitch. If the pitcher breaks the plane and throws to first base, a balk should be called. (When two umpires are officiating the game, it is very hard to make this call because one umpire is behind the plate and the other is between the pitcher and second base. A disadvantage of using this balk move is that four umpires are often used in championship games.)

An imaginary line also runs from the pitcher's rubber to a spot on the first baseline halfway between home plate and first base. The stride foot must hit on the first-base side of this imaginary line if the pitcher is throwing over to first base, or a balk should be called (figure 3.17). (Once again, this is a difficult call to make with two umpires.)

Unlike the right-hander's move, where there is one best way to attempt a pickoff, the left-handed pitcher's move is clearly individualized. There are as many different left-handed moves to first base as there are left-handed pitchers. The key is to stay within the rules and still make the pickoff look identical to the delivery to the plate.

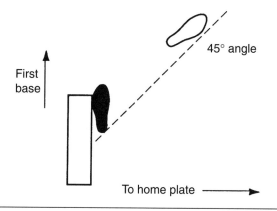

Figure 3.17 An imaginary plane runs from the pitcher's rubber to first base.

Throwing arm. The arm should make the same movements as it does when going to the plate. If a pitcher has good arm action, the arm will go down and back in both the delivery and the pickoff.

Many young left-handers want to shorten their arm motion for a quicker move to first base. That may be quicker, but it is obvious to the runner that the pitcher has changed his delivery and is coming to first.

The pitcher who goes down and back with his arm should throw to first from an area that is down and back. The short-arm pitcher's arm movement will be back and up when going to the plate and should also go back and up when going to first base.

A pitcher should find the arm groove he uses in the delivery to the plate and use the same groove when throwing to first base (figure 3.18).

Lead arm. The lead arm must appear to be heading toward the plate as if the pitcher were throwing a pitch. Many pitchers want to throw the lead arm toward first base, which only tips off the runner.

Shoulders. The shoulders should stay on the same line as when going to the plate. Many left-handers dip the back shoulder when throwing to first base; they must work to make the shoulder rotation the same in both movements.

Hip rotation. The amount of hip rotation in the gathered position should be the same in both movements. Many pitchers will not rotate the hips as much as when going to first base. To ensure a good move, left-handed pitchers must make certain that they do not break the plane of the rubber in the full windup and in the stretch.

Legs. Leg work should be the same in both movements. It is illegal to break the plane with the stride foot. This should not be a problem if the pitcher brings the stride foot to the edge of the plane in both deliveries. If the pitcher breaks the plane when going to the plate and doesn't break it when he is throwing over, base runners will quickly figure this out. Sometimes a pitcher will point his toe down when going to the plate and point his toe up when going to first base. (To prevent detection, the pitcher should always point the toe down.)

A good left-handed pitcher's move to first base requires the stride foot to hit as close as possible to the 45-degree line. To disguise this effort and avoid an umpire's calling a balk, the pitcher should step with the stride foot and continue to walk toward first base with the left foot. Many left-handers can get away with stepping on or over the 45-degree line because the walk-off makes the move appear legal.

Figure 3.18 *(a)* Correct throw and *(b)* follow-through; *(c)* incorrect throw.

Head. A left-handed pitcher can use three ways to look at the base runner at first base, and all three looks will work. Each pitcher usually has a preferred look; as long as each pitcher has a good move, there's no reason to change it.

The pitcher picks a spot halfway between first base and home plate. When he comes to the set position, he looks at this spot. He should be able to see whether the runner is getting a big lead, and he should be able to pick up the target if he decides to throw to the plate. The pitcher stares at the runner. Many left-handed pitchers will say that they like to look into the base runner's eyes and hopefully freeze them.

The pitcher looks back and forth from the runner to the plate and throws to first base or home plate while looking at one or the other. The pitcher should not become predictable by looking to home and throwing to first base or vice versa.

Alternatives to the Conventional Move

A left-handed pitcher can do several things if he has trouble with the conventional move or if he wants a variation.

Quick move. The left-handed pitcher can use a quick move when throwing to first base. This move is ideal for the left-hander who cannot master a good conventional move and needs something to hold runners.

From the set position, the pitcher steps off the back of the rubber with the pivot foot and simultaneously starts to throw to first base. Quickness rather than deception is the key. The left-handed pitcher's quick move is a great move when the base runner jumps to a lead and has his right foot in the air or when the base runner takes his eyes off the pitcher.

Right-handed left-hander. Often a left-handed pitcher with a quick full-windup delivery has trouble holding runners in the stretch. For this type of pitcher, the standard slow deception move to first base is not the ideal move. Left-handed pitchers with quick deliveries should think as a right-handed pitcher in the stretch position. Instead of relying solely on deception, the left-handed pitcher must also add quickness to the stretch. He still has an advantage because he can see the base runner. The mechanics of the left-hander's move to first base remain the same, differing only in the *quickness* of the stretch delivery and the move. Left-handers who use this type of stretch should have release times similar to those of right-handers. The left-handed pitcher using the quick stretch should also vary rhythm and looks.

Holding Runners at First Base

The game of baseball has changed recently. There are far more players now with speed, and stolen bases are up in all levels of play. With this greater emphasis on the running game, pitchers have to work harder than ever at holding base runners close to the base.

Pitchers have several ways to slow down the running game, such as using pickoff moves, pitchouts, and variations in tempo, and of course, having all the knowledge necessary to predict base-stealing situations. The bottom line is that base stealing is here to stay, and today's pitcher has to effectively hold runners to be successful.

Variation of Looks and Tempo

The pitcher decides how long to stay in the set position before throwing to the plate or throwing to first base. One of the easiest and most effective ways to hold base runners is to vary the time spent in the set position (that is, with the glove and throwing hand in front of the body, before the hands break).

Good base runners time a pitcher's delivery. If a pitcher repeatedly comes set, looks to first base, looks to home, and then pitches, the opposing team will quickly pick up his habit and steal when he looks back to home plate. A pitcher should not become predictable. He should change the amount of time between the set and delivery and mix up the number of looks to the base. That way, a base runner who wants a good jump will have to guess. The more different looks from the pitcher, the harder it is to guess. And if the pitcher believes the runner is stealing, a long pause is just what is needed. When a runner is ready to steal, his legs will be slightly flexed; if the runner has to wait for a long time, the flexed legs will get tired, resulting in a bad jump.

The pitcher should also vary the number of looks he gives the base runner. This is particularly important with a base runner at second base. Often pitchers get in a pattern of looking at the runner. When a runner knows that the pitcher will only look one time, it is easy to steal a base.

Ideal Base-Stealing Situations

There are obvious times in a ball game when it's likely that runners will try to steal bases. When a pitcher knows these situations, he can better guard against the stolen base.

Known base stealer on base. Of course, any time a known base stealer is on base there is a good chance that he will try to steal, depending on the score. Most teams have at least one player who fits this category, and the pitcher knows to concentrate on holding those runners.

Breaking-ball count. Many coaches give the steal sign when it appears that the pitcher will throw a breaking ball. A breaking ball takes longer to get to the plate and is often thrown low and away, which makes it harder for the catcher to throw to second base. A pitcher can combat this by trying pickoff moves or tempo variations when he throws a breaking ball. Of course, if a pitcher throws over before every breaking ball, opposing batters will soon pick this up; so he should use good judgment and not be predictable.

Opposing team is ahead. Teams prefer to run when the score is tied or they are ahead. Stealing bases involves some risk, and teams are not so willing to gamble when behind in the score.

Stay out of the double play. Coaches often start a runner at first base when they think that the batter may hit into a double play. That way, even if the batter hits a double-play groundball, the defense can only get the runner at first base.

Full count, one out, man on first base. Coaches like to start the runner in this situation. First, it can keep them out of the double play as just explained. Second, if the pitcher throws a strike, the batter swings, creating a run-and-hit situation; if the pitcher holds the runner close in this situation, it may be a strikeout, caught-stealing double play.

First and third double-steal situation. Many teams try to steal a run by having the runner at first base attempt to steal second so that the runner at third base can try to steal home on the throw to second base. Holding the runners in this situation helps to defend the double steal.

When to Throw Over to First Base

The pitcher should throw over to first base in the following situations:

- The count dictates the runner is going (for example, full count, two outs, runner on first base).

- It is a steal situation.

- The runner on first base likes to run. (A glance at the opposing team's stats before the game can reveal this.)

- The runner on first base jumps into his lead. (Any time a pitcher can catch a runner with his right foot in the air, either by jumping off the base or shuffling, the pitcher should throw over.)

- The base runner at first base has a big lead. (The pitcher should make a mark in the grass to inform himself of the length of a base runner's lead. By making a mark, the pitcher can concentrate on the mark and not the runner. If the runner is beyond the mark, it is time to throw over. Some pitchers use the cut of the grass as a marker; others use a fence post in foul territory.)

- The runner takes his eyes off of the pitcher. (Some base runners, particularly inexperienced ones, will look back to the base or over to the coach at third. The pitcher should throw over immediately when this happens.)

Slide Step

In an effort to keep the base runner from stealing a base or preventing a good jump on a hit and run, the pitcher should develop a slide-step pitch. The slide step does not need to be used all the time from the stretch, but it should be used for running situations or at least often enough that the opposing coach and base runners know that it is in the pitcher's bag of tricks. Just knowing this information will slow down the offense. The slide step should be practiced daily in flat-ground work and should at least be thrown a proportionate number of times in the bullpen.

Working backward from the T-position where the stride foot has landed and the pitcher's arm is loaded high in the back with the fingers on top of the ball, the pitcher has to begin to shorten the height of the leg lift and the circle of the throwing arm. Timing is everything in the slide step, so the pitcher should remember *quick feet—quick hands*. Many pitchers make the mistake of speeding up their legs and using the same arm swing. The result is that the stride foot lands before the hand is set up in the back, causing the release point to happen too soon (not out front) and the pitch to be up in the zone.

Shortening the leg lift and the arm swing simultaneously will give the pitcher a quality pitch low in the zone with a quicker release time to deter the base runners and give the catcher the opportunity to throw out a base runner. The catcher should have the option of calling a slide step whenever he thinks that perhaps it is a base-stealing situation.

Holding Runners at Second Base

The mechanics of pickoff moves to second base, as well as the theories involved with holding runners close at second base, are the same for both right- and left-handed pitchers. Right-handers may have a slight advantage because of their line of sight when they look at a base runner taking a lead off second base and because their stretch delivery is usually quicker, given their practice at holding the runner at first base. The left-hander has the advantage when the base runner is on first base, but the right-hander has the advantage when the base runner is on second or third.

Release Times With a Man on Second Base

There has been less emphasis on release times with a man on second base than on release times with a man on first. The runner on second is in scoring position and the runner at first base is not, so the emphasis on release times does not have much merit. Consider these points:

- The base runner at second base can get a bigger lead, cutting down the distance between bases.
- It is more difficult for the pitcher to make a pickoff at second base.
- Base runners are taught to get walking leads at second base for momentum, which lets them get to third base in a shorter time.
- Base runners can get longer secondary leads at second base because the catcher has to make a longer throw.
- The catcher has a shorter throw to third base than to second base. However, if a right-handed hitter is at bat, the catcher's vision may be hindered. And the catcher is required to step behind or in front of the hitter to make the throw to third base.

Both left- and right-handed pitchers should work on their release times to keep them under 1.5 seconds (preferably 1.3 seconds).

Pickoff Moves to Second Base

Two basic moves to second base are the spin move and the inside move. The spin move is designed to pick off a runner. The inside move is designed to keep the runner close. A third and fourth type of move to second base can be used in unique situations, as will be discussed.

Spin Move

Quick feet are the key to the spin move. The quicker the feet get set, the quicker the throw can be made. Starting in the set position, the pitcher attempts to jump and spin so that when he lands, his feet are switched (figure 3.19).

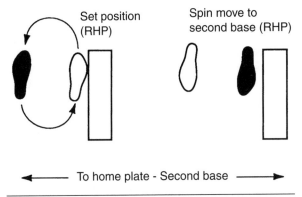

Set position (RHP) Spin move to second base (RHP)

◄——— To home plate - Second base ———►

Figure 3.19 Quick feet are the key to the spin move.

The pitcher spins (right-hander toward first base; left-hander toward third base), setting up the body for the throw. A common mistake pitchers make when throwing to second is dropping the arm straight down. This movement takes too long.

After the spin, the arm is set up and the stride foot points toward second base. A firm throw should be made to a spot one foot over the base. *Remember that the pitcher does not have to throw the ball to second base.*

Some pitchers prefer to spin the other way (right-hander toward third base; left-hander toward first base). This movement is less efficient. All baseball players are taught to turn toward their glove side. Turning toward the glove side is generally quicker and places less strain on the arm.

The pitcher should throw to second base when the following conditions are present:

- The runner has too big a lead.
- The runner does not stop after the pitcher becomes set.
- The pitcher can see the shortstop between the runner and the base. (This generally requires some kind of signal from the shortstop.)

- The runner takes his eyes off the pitcher. (Runners at second base tend to do this more than runners at first base. The runner may look at the coach, the base, or one of the middle infielders.)
- The runner jumps or runs into his lead.
- The runner at second base is a known base stealer.

Inside Move

Deception is the key to the inside move. The pitcher starts his stretch delivery and, at the top (gathered position), turns and throws to second base. This move is legal only if the stride leg does not start forward. Once the stride leg starts forward, the pitcher must throw to the plate, or a balk should be called.

The key to a good inside-move deception is the tempo of the movement. The stride leg should come up to the top at the same speed as when going to the plate. Many pitchers slow down this movement significantly, tipping off the base runner. The pitcher should use the inside move in the following situations:

- The base runner is taking a fast secondary lead.
- The base runner is taking a walking lead.
- The runner is going on a full count (runners on first and second, two out, and a full count).
- There is a base runner on second base, with zero outs (bunting situation). (The inside move will help to keep the runner closer for a possible play at third base.)
- The winning or tying run is on second base in late innings. (The inside move is not designed to pick runners off, but it does a good job of holding runners close.)

Full-Windup Pickoff to Second Base

With runners on second and third, or bases loaded and two outs, a pitcher can attempt a pickoff at second base out of the full windup. Upon receiving a signal from the catcher, the pitcher pushes off the rubber with his pivot foot, steps toward second base with the stride foot, and throws to second base.

- The pitcher takes the signal with the pivot foot on the rubber and the stride foot behind.
- The catcher gives the pitcher the sign to turn and throw to second base. (The catcher waits for the middle infielder to break behind the runner.)
- Upon receiving the sign from the catcher, the pitcher turns and throws to the middle infielder covering the base.

The full-windup pickoff is an excellent play to try when the runner on second base is getting an extra-big lead on the full windup.

Relay Pickoff at Second Base

When the runner on second base is walking back to the base with his head down after each pitch, the relay pickoff should be put on.

- The pickoff is put on.
- The pitcher pitches to the batter. After the pitch, the pitcher sets up so that he is facing first base (right-handed pitcher).
- The catcher throws the ball back to the pitcher from his knees.
- The pitcher catches the ball much as a relay man would and throws to the middle infielder covering second base.

This pickoff works only for the runner who is not watching the action on his way back to second base.

Holding Runners at Third Base

Holding runners at third base is important because the pitcher wants to keep the base runner as close to third as possible to have a better chance for a play at the plate. However, the pitcher should not try too many pickoffs at third. Holding the runner close at third is not of paramount importance, and a foul-up in a pickoff play at that base could let a run score.

Pickoffs at Third Base (Stretch Position)

Again, pickoff attempts at third base can be very hazardous because a bad throw or a fielding error can let a run score. Therefore, the pitcher should practice pickoff attempts at third many times before trying them in a game. The mechanics of the pickoff move to third are the same as for the move to first base, only in reverse. Now the left-handed pitcher uses the jump-spin, and the right-handed pitcher uses the deception move.

The following guidelines apply to pickoff attempts at third base.

- Communication with the third baseman is a must because he is not standing on the base.
- The pitcher does not have to throw the ball. If the pitcher has not practiced a pickoff move to third base, a fake may be the better play.
- A right-hander using the deception move to third base must be sure to stay to the right of the imaginary 45-degree-angle line. A balk in this situation means a run.
- The pitcher should not attempt a pickoff at third base unless the runner is way off the base or taking a running lead. He cannot go anywhere unless he steals home, and this is very unlikely.
- The runner must come to a complete stop when he is taking his lead.

Checking the Runner at Third Base (Full Windup)

When there are two outs with a man on third, men on second and third, or bases loaded, the pitcher can throw from the full windup. (The exception is when bases are loaded with two outs and a full count. At this time the pitcher should throw from the stretch to hold the runner closer at second base. See the section on the inside move, page 59.)

The pitcher should use the following guidelines for a full windup:

- The pitcher should place the pivot foot on the rubber and keep the stride foot off of the rubber, in back. He should get the sign from this position.

- After receiving the sign, the pitcher should look at the runner on third base. If the runner doesn't stop or has too large a lead, the pitcher should simply step off the rubber with the pivot foot. (When the pitcher places both feet on the rubber to take the sign, he is apt to step off with the stride foot. This is a balk, and the runner will score. If the stride foot is already off the rubber, then there is no chance of stepping off with the wrong foot.) After stepping back, the pitcher is considered an infielder and can react in whatever way the situation requires.

- If the runner stops his lead, the pitcher continues his usual full-windup delivery.

- The pitcher should check the runner at third base before every pitch to prevent the runner from stealing home.

If the runner at third base attempts to steal home, the pitcher should throw the ball on the third-base side of the plate for a strike. If the pitcher has checked the runner before the pitch, and if he makes a good pitch, the runner will be out. The hitter will not swing if the runner at third base is trying to steal, so the pitcher should not be concerned about that.

The pitcher should not alter the regular delivery because that would be a balk. (The pitcher shouldn't have to hurry, provided he checked the runner before the pitch.)

chapter 4

Practicing, Drilling, and Using Training Aids

Drills executed with precision lead to mastery both on the mound and in defensive positions once the ball is pitched. This chapter is divided into four areas of emphasis. Delivery drills break down the pitching mechanics and can either isolate a certain skill of the delivery or work on a whole phase of the delivery. Defensive drills concentrate on playing defense after the ball has been pitched, and bullpen work will help the pitcher perform on the field when he crosses that white line from bullpen to game mound. Training aids are pieces of equipment that help pitchers improve their technique. Practice techniques are discussed at the end of the chapter.

Delivery Drills

Delivery drills are designed to help a pitcher with a certain aspect of a delivery. All pitchers should not do all drills all the time. Instead, a pitcher should focus on areas of his delivery that need attention. Many coaches will try to get pitchers to have identical deliveries, but this is not good practice. A doctor would not prescribe the same medication for all ailments;

only after some serious study and testing would he prescribe a specific medicine for each illness.

A large part of a drill's effectiveness is how well the coach sells the drill to a pitcher. A pitcher has to believe that doing countless repetitions of a drill will help him improve his pitching performance. Many of the drills isolate a certain area of the pitching delivery and therefore can become tedious when performed daily. Old habits are always hard to break, and they are even harder to break when the pitcher doesn't want to work to break them. Coaches must also be sure that each drill is executed correctly, or else new bad habits will be created.

Many of the drills work for more than one aspect of pitching. Most can be done daily because they involve only light throwing. Many of the lower-body drills don't even use a ball, so the pitcher is working strictly on his form. The pitcher can either use a partner or throw into a net. Both ways are effective, but for some drills it may be more effective to use a net because this eliminates competition and worries about hitting a target. The pitcher should focus on whatever area he is working on and not on throwing a strike or hitting targets.

The drills presented here are broken down in the following ways: purpose of the drill (the area of delivery the drill will isolate), equipment for the drill, procedure (execution of the drill), and the number of repetitions necessary to improve performance.

Lower-Body Drills

Lower-body drills involve the feet, legs, and hips, although many still involve throwing a ball. Most of the drills work more than one area.

CHAIR DRILL

Purpose

The chair drill works several different areas of the delivery simultaneously. The pitcher can practice the turning sequence of hips, torso, and shoulders as well as work on throwing-arm extension and follow-through. Balance throughout the delivery as a result of having the back foot on the chair is an added bonus.

Equipment

A bucket of balls, a folding chair or bench, and a target. (If players work in pairs, a single ball will work with the partner in a catching position for the target.)

Procedure

Place the pivot foot on the chair, instep down. The stride leg should be out in front with the foot in line with the target. The stride foot should be slightly closed and the weight should be on the inside ball of the foot. The hands start together in the gathered position, and the shoulders should be in line with the target (figure 4.1a). From this position, the pitcher will rock back for some momentum and then pitch to the target. The pitcher should end up in a balanced position, with the throwing arm extended well and the head out in front of the stride leg (figure 4.1b). The back foot remains on the chair with the top of the foot aiming down as the pitcher completes the delivery. (If the pitcher is having serious

balance problems, his stride foot is probably too close and he needs to stride it out until he can attain some balance.)

Repetitions

The pitcher should not throw hard during this drill; therefore, he can do several repetitions.

Figure 4.1 Chair drill.

BAT DRILL

Purpose

The bat drill is designed to isolate the hips to practice staying closed until the last second and also work on the turning sequence of the hips, torso, and shoulders. This drill can also be used to practice proper stride mechanics, balance, and throwing over the stride leg.

Equipment

A bat or broomstick.

Procedure

Place the bat behind the back, holding it in place with the elbows (figure 4.2a). This prevents the player from thinking about the upper body and fully demonstrates when the hips open up. Starting in the gathered position, the pitcher takes a stride to the plate as if pitching (figure 4.2b). The idea is for the end of the bat to point to the plate for as long as possible before throwing. When the bat turns, the hips have opened (figure 4.2c). The hips should open as close to the plate as possible for ultimate power.

Figure 4.2   Bat drill.

LEG SWING DRILL

Purpose

This drill promotes proper stride-leg action for getting into the gathered position. Some pitchers like to swing the leg up and behind them instead of just lifting the leg and slightly rotating the hips.

Equipment

None.

Procedure

Start in the stretch position, but place the stride foot on the second-base side of the pivot foot (figure 4.3). With the stride foot on top of the rubber, lift the leg straight up to the gathered position, pause, and proceed to pitch. The adjustment with the foot makes leg swinging impossible. The pitcher should practice the up, down, skim-the-ground leg action when doing this drill.

Keys

A serious leg swinger should do this drill every time he throws in the bullpen until it becomes habit. Leg swinging causes rushing in the lower body.

Figure 4.3   Leg swing drill.

FOOT-UNDER-KNEE DRILL

Purpose

This drill promotes the proper action of keeping the foot under the knee in the delivery. Many pitchers like to have their foot out away from the body, which causes the pitcher to lean back to compensate.

Equipment

A chair or something similar to block the player's foot.

Procedure

Place the back of the chair in the path of the straying foot. Pitch the ball without kicking the chair. When the pitcher can throw without hitting the chair, his foot should be under the knee (figure 4.4).

Keys

This is a hard habit to break. Many repetitions of this drill may be necessary.

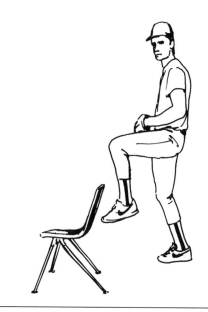

Figure 4.4 Foot-under-knee drill.

Upper-Body Drills

Upper-body drills are best performed with the pitcher kneeling on the pivot-leg knee. This prevents the pitcher from thinking about the lower body, so he can concentrate on his upper-body. To break bad habits, a pitcher should do upper-body drills whenever possible; therefore, he should not throw hard during these drills. Ideally, the pitcher should throw into a net when doing these drills to eliminate thinking about a target. The pitcher can then watch himself during the drill to make sure he is doing it correctly.

BREAKING THE HANDS

Purpose

This drill promotes the thumbs-down approach to breaking the hands.

Equipment

Baseballs.

Procedure

Kneeling on the pivot-leg knee with the stride foot in line with the target and the foot slightly closed, the pitcher will start with the hands close to the navel (figure 4.5a). He then will bounce his hands up for rhythm and bring them down to break (figure 4.5b). The front elbow will lead to the target, and the backside arm will get into the load position with the fingers on top high in the back (figure 4.5c).

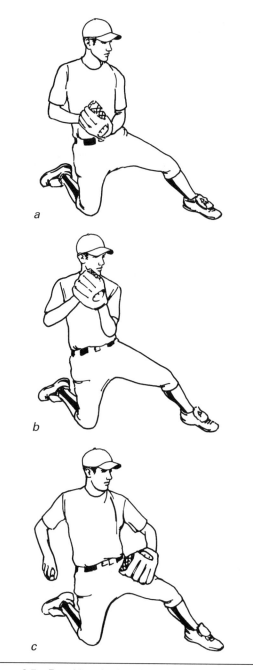

a

b

c

Figure 4.5 Breaking the hands drill.

STAND-UP DRILL

Purpose

This drill is a follow-up to the breaking the hands drill. The drill promotes good direction to the plate and good balance on the front leg; it also encourages throwing out over the front side and emphasizes the follow-through.

Equipment

Can be done with or without baseballs.

Procedure

From the kneeling position, the pitcher will bounce his hands up and break his hands on the way back down. As he drives his upper body and head toward the target, during the throw he will stand on his stride leg as he completes the pitch. After release the pitcher should be in a good balanced position with his head out in front (figure 4.6).

WALL DRILL

Purpose

The wall drill may help the pitcher who throws over the top or high three-quarter pitcher who takes his throwing hand too far back behind his body.

Equipment

A baseball and a fence or wall.

Procedure

The pitcher stands with his back to the wall or fence and goes through his stretch delivery. The lower the arm slot, the farther away the pitcher should stand from the wall or fence to allow for more horizontal rotation. The pitcher should start slow so that he won't bang the knuckles into the wall or fence. An actual throw is not needed in this drill (figure 4.7).

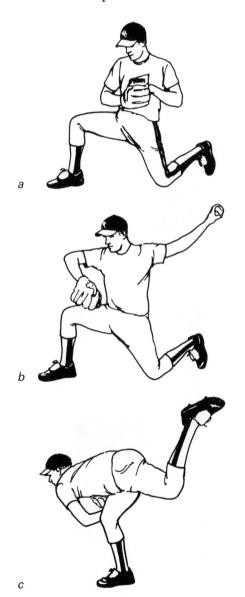

Figure 4.6 Stand-up drill.

Figure 4.7 Wall drill.

BACK SIDE OF THE MOUND

Purpose

The back side of the mound drill is to help pitchers learn to throw out front (develop extension). It also helps a pitcher to move more on the downhill plane.

Equipment

The pitcher's mound or the bullpen mound, a baseball, and a catcher. (If the mound does not have much slope on the back side, the pitcher can throw uphill toward second base.)

Procedure

The catcher gets in the down position about five or six feet in front of home plate. The pitcher sets up behind the mound and throws uphill from the stretch, trying to throw low strikes. After several attempts, the catcher and pitcher assume their normal positions and pitch. The pitcher will probably bounce the first couple but he will begin to feel extension and movement on the downhill plane (figure 4.8).

HAT DRILL

Purpose

The hat drill teaches extension out in front, proper front-side mechanics, and direction of the stride.

Equipment

Hat or small towel and a partner.

Procedure

The partner will take one knee and hold his glove out in front of his other knee. The pitcher places his hat in his hand, with the bill

Figure 4.8 Back side of the mound drill.

Figure 4.9 Hat drill.

between his fingers and his thumb. Simulating the stretch position, the pitcher strides toward his partner and tries to slap his partner's glove with his hat. If it's easy to do, the pitcher should adjust his starting point by backing up until he is just out of range. From this point the pitcher continues to try to slap the glove with the hat (figure 4.9).

Adjustments to Lengthen Extension

- The body goes where the head goes. Is the pitcher's head going right at the target or is it going off line?
- The pitcher must step toward the target. When a pitcher throws across his body it's impossible to get extension out front.
- When the pitcher's glove goes behind his body it alters forward motion and cuts down extension. The glove should never go behind the body.

- When a pitcher's stride leg locks up too early, it cuts down on extension. The stride leg should be slightly bent but firm so that the upper body can get through the pitch.

STAYING BEHIND THE BALL

Purpose

This drill encourages players to stay behind the baseball and not cut the ball during release. Many pitchers cheat themselves out of velocity because they cut the ball (throw the ball slightly off center).

Equipment

A baseball that is half white and half black.

Procedure

Pitchers can do this drill while standing or kneeling on the ground or sitting on a chair. Grip the ball so that one finger is in the white, one is in the black, and the thumb is on the border (figure 4.10). When playing catch, you should see two distinct halves of the ball if you are staying behind the pitch. If not, you will see a flutter of black and white.

Keys

If a pitcher is having trouble staying behind the ball, this drill can be incorporated into his daily program.

Figure 4.10 Grip for the staying behind the ball drill.

Developing Feel

Major league pitchers know the importance of being able to "feel" their delivery. This skill is developed over many years of working to understand the signals that the body sends out to them as they make a pitch. The scientists call this kinesthetic awareness—being aware of what the body is doing in space and time.

Pitching in the dark is a great way to learn what the pitcher's body is saying as he delivers the baseball. Eliminating the sense of sight forces the pitcher to feel his mechanics and develop awareness of timing in his delivery.

DRILLING WITH EYES CLOSED

On occasion, when a pitcher is working on delivery drills, he should close his eyes to really feel what his body is doing as he delivers the baseball. In the beginning stages, the pitcher should perform this drill without a baseball until he develps a feel for this drill. In time the pitcher can throw a baseball to a tire or net and eventually to a partner.

Throwing a baseball with the eyes closed can also help a pitcher learn to visualize (use his mind's eye) the pitch before it is delivered, which will help him in his pre-pitch visualization skills.

PITCHING IN THE DARK

Purpose

Along with helping the pitcher develop feel in the delivery, this drill emphasizes the ability to focus on a target. If a pitcher has learned to block out everything (hitter, umpire, and fans) except the target, he will be more effective. Pitching in the dark emphasizes the mechanical motion as well as the visual focus toward the target, in this case a light. A pitcher simply gets into the gathered position and goes toward the light.

Equipment

A target (tire) and a penlight.

Procedure

Pitching in the dark is exactly how it sounds. Set up a target behind home plate and place a penlight immediately behind the target for illumination. Using darkness, the pitcher can keep his eyes open to see the target, but he still has to feel his mechanics. After a few warm-up deliveries with no throw to get acclimated to the darkness, the pitcher will then throw to the light. The sound of the ball hitting the tire is unmistakable, so a pitcher can gain feedback as he throws.

Defensive Drills

A team may have 3 to 12 pitchers who need weekly work on various defensive parts of the game. The following drills will work several pitchers at one time and require very little space and management.

THREE-LINE BUNT DRILL

Purpose

This drill emphasizes repetitions of basic pitcher defensive plays in a short amount of time. The drill can be performed with pitchers only or with infielders and pitchers.

Procedure

Arrange pitchers so that three pitchers are on the mound; three pitchers are at home plate;

and one pitcher each is at third base, second base, and first base. The three pitchers on the mound will simultaneously make three different bunt plays. The pitcher at home plate on the first-base side will roll a bunt down the first baseline and yell, "One, one, one." The pitcher on the first baseline will set his feet properly and make the play to first base.

The middle pitcher at home plate rolls the ball (this should be a hard bunt) to the middle pitcher, who sets his feet and throws to second base. The pitcher at home plate on the third baseline rolls the ball down the third baseline and yells, "Three, three, three." The pitcher sets his feet and makes the throw to third base (figure 4.11).

Pitchers will rotate positions and begin again.

base side will hit a groundball to the first baseman, who will throw to the pitcher covering first base.

The pitcher at home plate in the middle will either hit or throw a groundball to the middle pitcher, who will start the double play at second base. The pitcher at home plate on the third baseline will roll a bunt between the pitcher and third baseman to practice communication on a bunt play (figure 4.12). Pitchers will rotate positions and begin again.

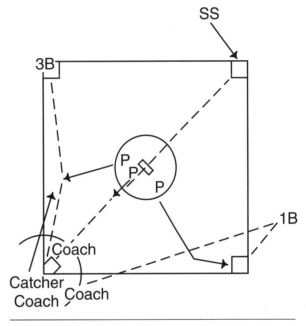

Figure 4.12 Three-line fielding drill.

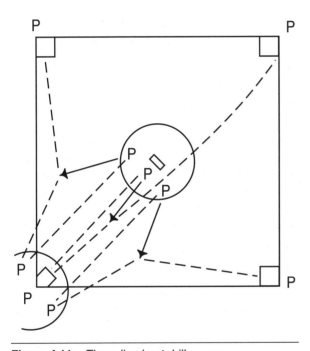

Figure 4.11 Three-line bunt drill.

THREE-LINE FIELDING DRILL

Purpose

This drill emphasizes repetitions of basic pitcher defensive plays in a short amount of time.

Procedure

Use the same setup as the three-line bunt drill. The pitcher at home plate on the first-

FOUR-CORNER BUNT DRILL

Purpose

This drill emphasizes bunt defense and the ability to think ahead and set the feet.

Procedure

Four pitchers assume a position on one of the four bases. A pitcher will be in the middle of the field. (If the main field is in use, throwing down bases in the outfield will work.)

The pitcher will start the drill by pitching to a base. Whichever base he throws to becomes home plate, and of course, the base on his left is first base, the base behind him is second base, and the base on his right is third base. The person catching the ball will wait until the pitcher is back in the middle, roll a bunt, and call out a base for the pitcher to throw to. (If the pitcher who caught the throw calls out, "Three, three, three," then the pitcher in the middle will field the bunt and throw to the base on his right. At this time the person who catches the throw is now rolling the bunt and giving directions (figure 4.13).

This drill should run fast enough for the pitcher to get some conditioning but not so fast that he doesn't get back to the middle of the field before another bunt is rolled out. Pitchers will rotate into the middle.

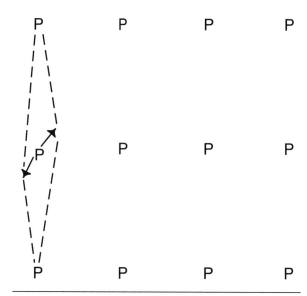

Figure 4.14 Three-man double-play drill.

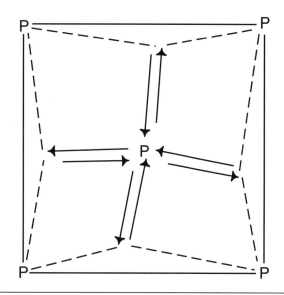

Figure 4.13 Four-corner bunt drill.

THREE-MAN DOUBLE-PLAY DRILL

Purpose

The pitcher gets lots of repetitions on the 1-6-3 double play. This drill is excellent for working on footwork.

Procedure

Three pitchers get in a straight line 80 to 90 feet apart. The pitcher in the middle will go through his stretch delivery and fake a pitch to the end man (catcher). At the appropriate time the catcher will throw a groundball to the middle man (pitcher), who will turn and throw the ball to the other end pitcher (shortstop). The drill is then repeated the other way. After several repetitions, the pitchers will rotate into the middle (figure 4.14).

THREE-MAN COMMUNICATION DRILL

Purpose

Players will practice communication among the pitcher, catcher, and shortstop. Before the pitch, the pitcher will look to his shortstop for any signals concerning a pickoff to second base or perhaps the number of looks to give the runner. The pitcher will then get the signal from the catcher about what pitch to throw. This drill will provide much-needed repetition in communication so that it becomes a habit in game time.

Procedure

The pitcher in the middle starts with the ball and will first look to the pitcher at second base. The pitcher at second base will give a sign for a pickoff or a certain number of looks at second base. After receiving these signals, the pitcher will then get the signal from the catcher about what pitch to throw.

The pitcher will then react to the signals. If it's a pick at second, he will do that. If it's a certain number of looks before throwing, he will perform his looks and then throw the appropriate pitch to the catcher (figure 4.15).

Keys

Using pitchers at all three positions is a great way to make sure that the pitchers know all

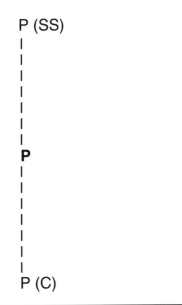

Figure 4.15   Three-man communication drill.

the signs. This is a great preseason drill and can be executed indoors or outdoors.

BACKUP DRILL

Purpose

In the majority of plays at a base, the ball is caught so that a pitcher doesn't get a lot of repetitions at backing up bases. This drill will help them to get where they need to be and give them practice watching the flight of the ball and reacting accordingly.

Procedure

The coach will take a bucket of balls and a fungo bat into the outfield and will hit balls to the bases. The coach will give the situation and hit to the base where the pitcher should be backing up. For example, a runner is on first base, and there is a base hit to centerfield. The pitcher will start on the mound and go to the backup position behind third base. The coach should simulate a game situation and give the pitcher a good start to the backup position before hitting the ball. (See figure 4.16.)

Keys

This drill is especially good when a runner is on first base and a double is hit. Not knowing whether there will be a throw to third base or home plate, the pitcher will go halfway and read the throw.

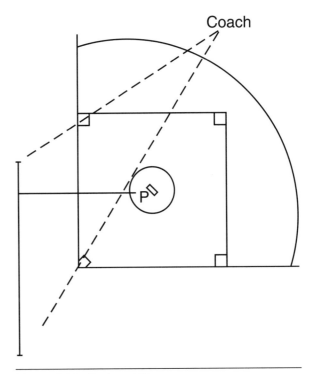

Figure 4.16   Backup drill.

Footwork-Only Drill

In that instance when the pitchers have tired arms yet still need to work on fielding their position, the coach can do the footwork-only drill. The coach will need a bucket of balls and an empty bucket to put the caught balls in after a pitcher has made a play. The coach will determine the situation and either hit or roll a ball to the pitcher. The pitcher will use the proper footwork to get to the ball. He'll use proper fielding fundamentals and, after catching the ball, will use the proper footwork for the throw to the appropriate base. The pitcher should break his hands and get the ball up in the throwing position using proper throwing fundamentals. When the pitcher gets to this position, he stops, goes back to the mound, and places the ball in the empty bucket by the mound.

Players can practice the following situations with no throws:

- Sacrifice bunt to first base from anywhere in front of the mound
- Sacrifice bunt to second base from anywhere in front of the mound

- Sacrifice bunt to third base from anywhere in front of the mound
- 1-3 play
- 1-3 play checking runner at second base
- 1-3 play checking runner at third base
- 1-6-3 play
- 1-2-3 play
- 3-1 play (coach takes a bucket of balls to first-base area and flips to pitchers covering first base)

Training Aids

A training aid can be just about anything that assists the training of an athlete to perform a specific skill or movement. Training aids can cost hundreds of dollars or can be very inexpensive. The bottom line is that training aids will help an athlete to perform at a higher level, but only if that athlete puts forth the effort to train.

Tire Drills

Tire drills are a form of target practice so that a pitcher can work on the location of his pitches. Although several products on the market will encourage hitting spots, tire drills are easy to set up, can be changed at any time for different pitchers and different pitches, and can be performed indoors or outdoors; also, the setup cost is minimal. Equipment includes fielding screens, lawnmower tires, bungee cords, and a bucket of balls.

From a coaching aspect, tire drills provide an opportunity for pitchers to practice without a catcher. Just as a basketball player can practice his shot by himself, a pitcher can get quality practice reps whenever and wherever he desires. Instant feedback is a wonderful teaching tool in any sport. The basketball player either makes his shot or he doesn't. If he misses, he makes the adjustment and shoots again. The pitcher either hits his spot (tire) or he doesn't. If the pitcher misses, he can instantly make a correction with his delivery or his release point.

The coach can use the tire drill setup to encourage a particular pattern of pitching (see figure 4.17). For example, a pitcher who has good sink on his ball will want to work the bottom of the zone, so the coach can place two or three tires along the bottom of the strike zone. With the instant feedback, the coach has a valuable grading tool to keep track of a pitcher's success rate, which will also encourage and motivate pitchers to improve their techniques and improve their location.

Finally, by adding a point value to hits and misses, a pitcher will also have fun and maybe will want to work on his own. An example of this is to assign 0 points if the pitcher hits the center of a tire, 3 points if he hits the tire, and 5 points if he misses the tire completely. By tallying the points and dividing by the number of pitches, the pitcher will have a score for the practice. (This type of scoring is used because lower is better, similar to an earned run average.)

The tire drill station is a valuable tool during the winter as pitchers work on their skills. It's easy and fun, and working on throwing to spots is never a bad thing. The major league hall of fame is full of pitchers who learned their trade by throwing rocks at bottles and baseballs at everything—tires, barn doors, and old mattresses. Coaches should encourage pitchers to practice on their own with the makeshift equipment they have available. If a concert pianist only practices when he is with the piano teacher, he will never get to Carnegie Hall.

The tire drill can also be used as a batting-practice catcher to help both the pitcher and the hitter. The pitcher sees the value of hitting his spots by the hitter's swings, and the hitter learns the strike zone and gets a feel for his strengths and weaknesses.

Strike Zone Strings

The use of strings to determine the strike zone has been around for many years and continues to be a good training aid for pitchers. A string strike zone gives the pitcher and catcher a good visual reference of pitch location. The string strike zone is like the tire drill in that it offers instant feedback, which supplies pitchers with information to make

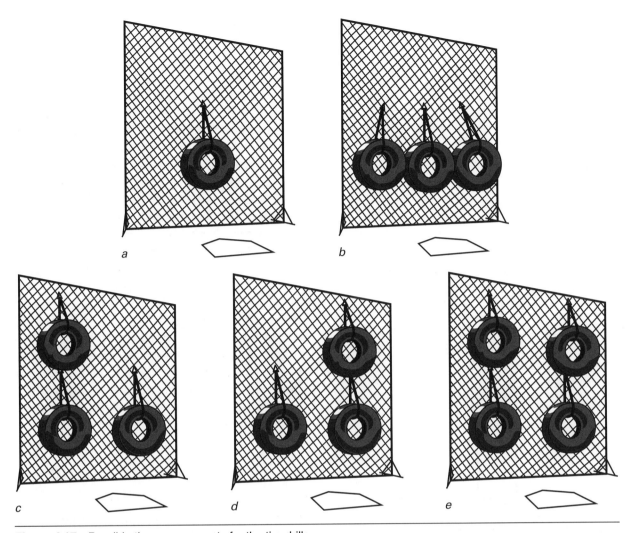

Figure 4.17 Possible tire arrangements for the tire drills.

adjustments pitch by pitch, just as they must do in a game.

The strike zone strings can be used in a variety of ways depending on a pitcher's practice needs (figure 4.18). Lengths of bungee cord are used for these drills.

Strings and Tires Together

By combining strike zone strings with a tire drill, pitchers can understand the value of deception. For example, a pitcher will throw two types of breaking balls. One breaking ball will appear to be a ball and end up a strike, whereas the other appears to be a strike and ends up out of the zone.

By setting up the strings out in front of the plate, a pitcher can get great feedback on his breaking ball (figure 4.19). When the pitch goes through the strike zone strings yet hits a tire outside of the zone, a pitcher can truly see and understand the concept of throwing a breaking ball that appears to be a strike (that is, through the strings yet it ends up a ball). When the pitch goes around the zone yet hits a tire in the zone, it appears to be a ball yet it ends up a strike. Players will need to make many pitches to understand this concept and be able to perform this skill.

Wiffle Balls

Anyone who has ever pitched a Wiffle ball knows the tremendous amount of break he can get on his pitch. Because of the weight of the ball and the resistance of the air, the Wiffle ball can do many things. Throwing into the wind, for greater feedback, a pitcher can work

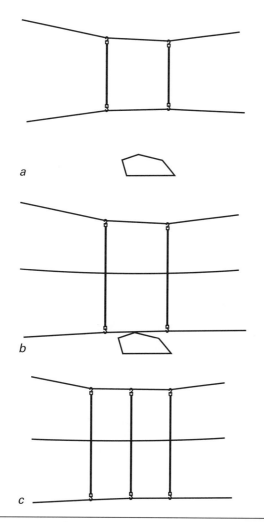

Figure 4.18 Strings can be set up in different ways for the strike zone.

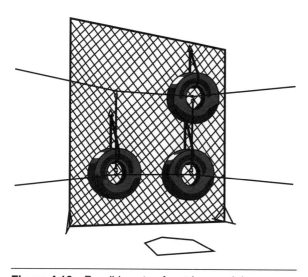

Figure 4.19 Possible setup for strings and tires.

on his grips to acquire movement. *Throwing Wiffle balls with full arm speed is not recommended because this is not good for the arm and may cause injury.* Easy throws with emphasis on the release point will enable a pitcher to see and feel the differences in the pitches.

A pitcher can start by trying to stay behind the baseball and develop backspin. Instantly he will see his ball rise and will understand the concept. Should a pitcher need work on his breaking ball or change, the break will be obvious and help him to feel and see the appropriate break for his arm slot.

A pitcher can go from fastball to cutter to slider to slurve and finally curveball and get a grasp of the amount of turn in the release point for all of these pitches. A pitcher who throws the circle change will immediately understand the importance of having his fingers on top as he sees the down-and-away break. Working with Wiffle balls is not to be done every day but only occasionally to demonstrate movement and help a pitcher to understand spin.

Practice Schedule

The following is a list of practice activities in the proper sequence to not only maintain a pitcher's health but also to maximize practice. The sequence of these drills is important to insure good health and to improve pitching skills. For optimal results the activities should be practiced in this order on a daily basis.

Warm Up to Throw

A pitcher should warm up to throw, not throw to warm up. The first activity a pitcher should do in practice is warm up the body. A warm-up may include any number of exercises to get the muscles warm, the heart pumping, and the blood moving.

Jogging a couple of laps around the field is the simplest form of warming up. Calisthenics such as jumping jacks or windmills are excellent warm-up drills as well as the use of a jump rope.

Flexibility Drills

Once the pitcher warms up, he should do some stretching drills to develop greater flexibility as well as reduce the risk of injury. A complete flexibility program can be found in chapter 5. The flexibility program should include the entire body and will take 10 to 12 minutes. This is also a good time for the pitcher to collect his thoughts for the day's practice.

Conditioning Drills

The best possible time to condition is immediately after the flexibility program. The body is warmed up and stretched, so conditioning at this time makes perfect sense. Conditioning before throwing also ensures that the body is loose and ready to throw, reducing the risk of injury to the arm. Conditioning before throwing also helps to eliminate stiffness in the joints from previous throwing. Conditioning drills can be found in chapter 5.

Surgical Tubing

The final preparation to begin throwing is a surgical-tubing workout for the shoulder. This can be very specific with exact exercises or a casual period to allow the pitcher to catch his breath from conditioning and use the tubing to go through his throwing motion with some resistance. Surgical tubing is fairly inexpensive. To make sure all the pitchers can get this work done in a quick, efficient way, they should attach several tubes to the fence so that many can work at one time. See figure 4.20.

Daily Throwing Program

After 30 minutes of warm-up, flexibility, conditioning, and shoulder work, the pitcher is ready to begin his throwing program. All pitchers should take part in the preliminary work on a daily basis regardless of how they feel or when they last pitched in a game or bullpen.

Only after the preliminary work has been completed should there be any decisions made about individual pitchers and the type or amount of throwing that should be done for that day. The pitcher who pitched the day before will obviously do less throwing than the pitcher who is fresh. It is suggested that all pitchers perform the preliminary work as a group, while the throwing programs should be individual for each of the pitchers on the team.

Long Toss

There are two distinct types of long toss, both of which are good for the pitcher at certain times depending on what season it is, when the pitcher last pitched, when the pitcher is pitching next, or depending on the health of the pitcher. All pitchers should lengthen their throws on a daily basis unless there is pain in the throwing arm (NOT to be confused with fatigue).

Long toss begins with the pitchers approximately 50 to 60 feet apart. The pitcher will use a step-behind crow hop during long toss to develop good habits with the feet. The distance is then increased as the pitcher and his partner get loose.

A *hard long toss* is one where the pitcher and his partner will really stretch it out and throw as far as possible. Hard long toss is the best single thing a pitcher can do to increase external rotation and create velocity. Hard long toss is excellent in the off-season for developing arm strength and on occasion during the season when it can be executed without affecting performance.

An *easy long toss* starts the same way as the hard long toss but only goes as far as is comfortable. The easy long toss is more of a maintenance long toss and should be done everyday, including the day after pitching. Comfortable is the key word as the pitcher determines how many reps and the distance depending on his arm.

When the pitcher has reached his peak distance, the amount of throwing at that distance will vary depending on the need of the pitcher. At some point the pitcher will start to shorten his throws, gradually working his way back to 50 feet.

Figure 4.20 Three possible exercises using surgical tubing.

a

b

c

d

e

f

Occasionally, the pitcher will want to throw long toss change-ups to keep the arm speed consistent with the fastball arm speed. A good distance for long toss change-ups would be 100 to 120 feet. The pitcher should not arch these throws but instead try to one hop his partner. This will help the pitcher to get on top of his change-up.

Daily Drills

After long toss the pitcher will begin his flat-ground daily drills with a partner. It is not necessary for every pitcher to do every drill. The coach should assign drills depending on the need of each pitcher.

Any flat-ground drill session should include the following guidelines. The two partners should be about 50 feet apart. The receiving pitcher should always get down like a catcher to help the pitcher get on top and throw downhill. A grading system should be used, either balls and strikes or the yes/no system (yes the pitcher hit spot, no the pitcher missed spot), to insure focus and concentration.

Bullpen Work

Those pitchers who are scheduled for a bullpen session will complete their session after they complete their flat-ground daily drills. (Those that do not have bullpen sessions should at this time change their undershirts and report to another part of practice.)

Bullpen work should be individualized for each pitcher but at least 50 percent of it should be done from the stretch position. The length of the bullpen session can be any number of pitches depending on the pitcher and when he pitched previously or will pitch again. For more information on bullpen sessions, see chapter 9.

Cool-Down

When a pitcher completes his bullpen session he should cool down by completing the surgical-tubing program again. He should then run some more before changing undershirts and joining regular practice. The amount of time spent on cool-down should be proportionate to the amount of pitching in the bullpen or game. For example, a 30- to 40-pitch bullpen might only require a 5- to 10-minute cool-down. A 75-pitch bullpen would require a longer cool-down of perhaps 10 to 15 minutes. (Many major league starting pitchers ride the stationary bike immediately after they are finished pitching in a game.)

chapter 5

Conditioning the Arm and Body

The physical development of pitchers involves flexibility, strength training, and cardiovascular training. All three are important for developing and maintaining high-level performance.

Flexibility and strength training go hand in hand. A pitcher should always surround a good strength workout with stretching sessions. Stretching the muscles both before and after strength training keeps the muscles lengthened and removes lactic acid buildup, which speed up the recovery period. Stronger legs and midsection produce more power during the delivery, which translates into more velocity on the fastball. Proper strength training of the arms and shoulders also reduces the chance of injury to the throwing arm. Cardiovascular training enables the pitcher to perform efficiently for longer periods without tiring. A tired pitcher loses control and velocity and becomes increasingly susceptible to injury.

This chapter presents a basic strength program for the entire body, as well as programs for in-season and out of season. Several ideas and suggestions for aerobic and anaerobic training for pitchers are also provided.

Stretching Program

Flexibility plays a big role in injury prevention and efficient pitching mechanics for players of all ages. To increase flexibility, an athlete must stretch the muscles, individually and in groups, to their fullest capacity; this also creates a fuller range of movement. Younger athletes require less stretching because their muscles are more elastic. Older and stronger athletes need to stretch more extensively to maintain flexibility.

There are three types of stretching. *Ballistic* stretching involves bouncing to reach a desired goal (for instance, touching the toes). With each bounce, the stretcher tries to stretch farther. Ballistic stretching is dangerous and should be avoided because the bouncing can tear muscles. In *static* stretching, the stretcher finds his ultimate stretch point and holds it, generally for 8 to 15 seconds. The third type of stretch involves isometric *contraction* after the peak stretch has been held for 5 to 10 seconds. After the isometric contraction, the stretcher increases the stretch and again holds. This process is repeated until the maximum range of motion is attained.

The static stretch is recommended as the primary form of stretching. The bounce becomes more dangerous as athletes age and their muscles lose elasticity. The stretch-isostretch method can be very effective for attaining flexibility, but it can also be very harmful if it is not closely monitored. Young athletes tend to be too aggressive and ignore the body's warning signals that they've reached their current maximum stretch, and some studies show that isometrics can be harmful to the heart.

At the start of the daily stretch regimen, first warm the joint areas to be stretched. This warm-up gets the blood flowing in the areas to be stretched and speeds up the stretching process. Warm-ups can include trunk rotations, arm swings, jumping jacks, or simply jogging a lap. Only after he stretches should an athlete begin his baseball activities or any type of conditioning (strength, balance, or cardiovascular training).

A young pitcher should add a stretching program to his daily routine at the age when he starts to notice some stiffness the day after pitching. Otherwise, he should start a stretching program when he starts to use strength training for development. The stretching programs outlined in this chapter involve all of the major muscles and muscle groups. The entire program takes approximately 15 minutes.

Individual Stretches

The following group of stretches should be performed without a partner. This group of stretches should be adequate for a pitcher who has no significant problem areas.

ANKLE ROTATIONS

Sit with one leg straight out and the other crossed over at the knee. Use the hands to work the ankle in all directions; this helps prevent sprains. Hold 8 to 15 seconds, then switch legs.

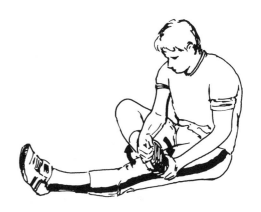

FOOT-UNDER-HAMSTRING STRETCH

Sit with one leg straight out. The other leg is crossed under at the knee. Reach with both hands to the ankles and pull back. Reverse the action. Hold for 8 to 15 seconds. This exercises not only the hamstrings but also the lower back.

STANDING HAMSTRING AND LOWER BACK STRETCH

Place left foot at a 45-degree angle, and lift the toes off the ground. The right foot should be

pointed straight ahead with the right leg slightly bent. Bend, grasp the left calf, and pull the upper body to the leg. Hold for 8 to 15 seconds, then switch legs. This exercise is also a good Achilles stretch.

CALF AND ACHILLES STRETCH

Place the left leg two to three feet behind the right leg. Shift weight toward back leg so that the heel is flat on the ground. Hold for 8 to 15 seconds, then switch legs.

QUADRICEPS STRETCH

Standing with feet together, lift left foot up in the back and grasp with left hand. Pull foot

toward body while balancing on right leg. Hold for 8 to 15 seconds, then switch legs. This exercise also stretches the hip flexors.

GROIN STRETCH

Sit on the ground and place feet with soles together as close as possible to the groin area. Place elbows inside of knees and push down. Hold for 5 seconds and resist with legs. Repeat three times, going farther each time.

LOWER BACK TWIST

Sit with one leg straight out and the other foot placed outside the knee. The elbow of the opposite arm is used for leverage to rotate the trunk to a position facing backward. Hold 8 to 15 seconds, then twist the opposite way. This exercise also stretches the abdominal muscles.

REACH BACK WITH BOTH ARMS

While sitting, place the back of the hands on the ground behind the body. Slide forward, stretching the shoulders and chest. Hold for 8 to 15 seconds. This stretch is excellent for the deltoid and pectoralis muscles.

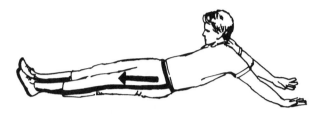

UPPER BACK AND SHOULDER STRETCH

Stand with feet together and legs bent. With the left hand, grasp the outside of the right shoe. Slowly straighten the legs, keeping hold of the shoe. Hold for 8 to 15 seconds, then switch arms. *This exercise is a must before a pitcher throws the ball.*

NECK STRETCH

Roll head from left shoulder to chin on chest to the right shoulder. Do not bend the head backward.

SHOULDER STRETCH

Lift the elbow of the left arm, and point it straight up. With the right hand, push the upper left arm back. Hold for 8 to 15 seconds, then switch arms.

ARM ACROSS THE BODY

Lift a straight left arm in front of and across the right shoulder. With the right hand, pull the left arm toward the body. Hold for 8 to 15 seconds, then switch arms.

ARM OVER TOP

Attempt to grasp hands together behind the back. Hold 8 to 15 seconds, then switch arms.

HANGING

Hang for 10 to 15 seconds. The top of the dugout or the fence surrounding the field work well as places to hang from.

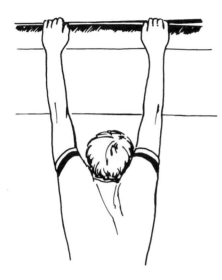

Partner Stretches

The following stretches require a partner for a more significant stretch. Partner stretching can be harmful if not done in moderation. An athlete should always pair up with the same partner and exercise caution on all partner stretches.

THROWING STRETCH

Athlete places arm at approximate throwing angle (elbow at shoulder height or higher). A partner places one hand on the elbow to stabilize it and one hand on the athlete's fingertips. The partner pulls down until the athlete says he has reached his limit. Hold for 8 to 15 seconds. (Athlete can apply force forward if he wishes, before repeating the procedure.) Be cautious when doing this exercise. Communication is vital. This stretch can also be done with a bat. The athlete can stretch himself by using a bat to do the work of the partner.

LOWER BACK STRETCH

The lower back is a significant area of stiffness for a pitcher. In this stretch, the athlete lies on his back with his head flat on the ground and places one knee on his chest, keeping the remaining leg straight out. The partner pushes the athlete's shin to his chest. Communication is vital; do not force this action. Switch to the other leg.

Athlete now places both knees to the chest. Partner pushes both shins to the chest. Hold for 8 to 15 seconds.

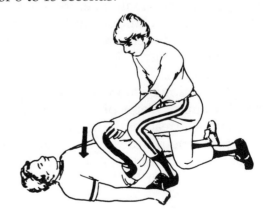

LAT STRETCH

Another problem area for pitchers is the latissimus muscles, which are located on the sides. Both athletes bend sideways at the waist, joining hands under and over their heads. They pull against each other for a count of 8 to 15 seconds, then switch directions.

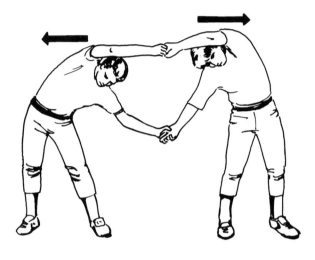

Strength Training

Strength training for pitchers can take many forms, including weight training, plyometrics, and exercising. The pitcher's first experience with strength training should be an exercise program using his own body weight as resistance. He can start this program any time and continue it throughout his career. As the pitcher grows, so does the resistance; therefore, his strength level grows. All types of strength training are good as long as the coach monitors each athlete to ensure proper technique and progress; coaches also need to ensure that athletes follow a good flexibility program and adhere to safety guidelines.

Weight training is a more advanced type of strength training that a pitcher should not attempt until he reaches the age of 15 or starts shaving. Plyometrics can begin at almost any age, but a coach must closely monitor a plyometrics program because technique is so important for safety and development.

Intensity levels of strength training can differ at different times of the year. An off-season program can be much more intense than an in-season program. During the off-season the pitcher might try to make greater gains, and he doesn't have to worry about pitching.

The muscles involved in throwing are divided into two groups. The *accelerators* are the muscles that bring the arm forward into the release position, and the *decelerators* are the muscles that slow down the arm after the ball is released. Both groups of muscles need to be trained at the same level to ensure that they work together during the throw and to prevent injury.

The main accelerator muscles are the pectoralis major and minor (chest muscles), anterior deltoid (front of the shoulder), and triceps (back of the upper arm). These muscles work together along with the rotator cuff muscles to bring the ball from the position of full extension behind the body to a point of full extension up from and in front of the body (release point). Strength training for these muscle groups helps increase athletes' throwing velocity as long as they maintain full flexibility.

The main decelerator muscles are the latissimus dorsi (lats), posterior deltoid (back of the shoulder), the biceps (front of upper arm), trapezius (major back muscle), and rotator cuff muscles. These muscles work together to slow down the arm after release and keep the arm from coming out of the shoulder joint.

Recent studies reveal that almost two-thirds of pitching-arm injuries occur during the deceleration phase. This is due mainly to imbalance between the accelerator and decelerator muscle groups. The accelerators are usually trained more than the decelerators, causing a strength imbalance in favor of the accelerators. Basically, the throwing arm is building up too much momentum during the throw, and the decelerators are not strong enough to prevent injury. This phenomenon is comparable to sprinters' strength imbalance between the quadriceps and hamstring muscle, which results in a pulled or torn hamstring.

The bottom line is that when the body is submitted to a strength program for developing the throwing arm, both muscle groups must be worked to prevent an imbalance and thus a decelerator injury such as a torn supraspinatus (rotator cuff muscle) or a biceps tendon tear. The body also has a built-in protective system—the body tries to limit or balance the action of antagonistic muscle groups to prevent injury. Strength training upsets the body's natural preventive system when it makes one group of muscles stronger than the opposing group of muscles. This affects the performance of the antagonistic muscle groups. For a baseball throw, the body naturally tries to prevent the accelerators from gaining more force than the decelerators can handle. It makes sense, then, to train the decelerator muscles: The stronger the decelerators, the more force the body allows the accelerators to produce, which in turn leads to greater hand speed and more velocity on the baseball.

Strength Training Without Weights

A good strength program that does not include weights is important for several reasons:

- Youngsters should not be allowed to lift weights until they are about 15 years old, so the coach needs some type of strength training for his pitchers that does not include weights.

- Weight training is time consuming, and during the season athletes often do not find the time to get to the weight room. A weight-free strength program saves time and is more convenient because it can be performed at the field.

- A strength program without weights is very convenient for teams that travel often. Weight rooms are hard to find on the road, and a few missed workouts may be detrimental to a pitcher's performance.

- Pitchers often run out of things to do during practice because they must not overdo throwing or running. If they have a strength-training program that excludes weights, they can use their free time during practice to gain strength.

Using body weight as resistance makes an athlete only as strong as the strength needed to lift his body weight. Is this type of strength training adequate for a pitcher?

Throwing a baseball is comparable to snapping a whip. The *pyramid theory* assumes, for such actions, that the legs need to be as big and strong as possible, the abdominals and lower back need to be strong with great endurance, and the upper body needs endurance and quickness. Based on these assumptions, a strength-training program using body weight as resistance is adequate for the top two thirds of the pyramid (the midsection and the upper body). Depending on the leg strength of the individual pitcher, a program using body weight may or may not increase size and strength of the legs. If the pitcher has worked very hard in the weight room in the off-season to build mass and power in his legs, then the best a body-weight resistance program can do is help maintain that strength during the baseball season.

The body-weight resistance program can be very intense, with many exercises, or very simple, with a few key exercises. Some of the exercises require equipment that can be constructed at the field at a very cheap price; others require no equipment.

Upper-Body Program

The upper-body program consists of exercises to develop the upper arms (including triceps and biceps), the pecs (pectoralis major and minor), the shoulders (deltoids), and the back (latissimus dorsi). All exercises should be performed through a full range of motion for greatest benefit.

FULL-RANGE PUSH-UPS

Three chairs are required to support the body. Starting with arms extended, slowly lower the body down to a point as far as possible below the hands. Then quickly push the body back up to the extended position. The full-range push-up allows an invaluable extra stretch compared to a conventional push-up. This exercise primarily works the pectoralis muscles, frontal deltoids, and triceps.

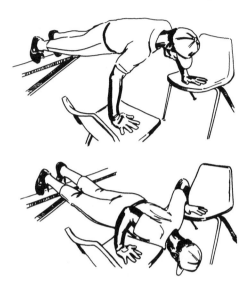

INVERTED ROWING

A bar three feet wide and suspended four feet off the ground is required. Prop the feet on a chair and lie down under the bar, facing up. Reach up and grasp the bar so that the body is now hanging from the bar. Keeping the body straight, pull up to the bar. The rise to the bar should be fairly quick. Then slowly lower to full extension of the arms. This exercise works the latissimus dorsi, posterior deltoids, and biceps.

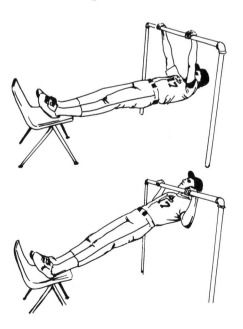

CHIN-UPS

A chinning bar is required. Reach up and grasp the bar with palms facing the body and hands shoulder-width apart. Feet should be off the ground. Quickly raise the body until the chin is over the bar. Then slowly lower to full extension of the arms. This exercise works the pectoralis muscles, deltoids, and biceps.

BEHIND-THE-NECK PULL-UPS

A chinning bar is required. Reach up and grasp the bar with palms facing away from the body and hands shoulder-width or slightly wider apart. Quickly raise the body until the back of the neck touches the bar. Then slowly lower to full extension of the arms. This exercise works the latissimus dorsi, posterior deltoids, and triceps.

DIPS

Dip bars are required. Perform conventional dips, rising quickly and lowering slowly. Never go lower than the point where the upper arm is parallel to the ground. This exercise works the pectoralis muscles, deltoids, and triceps.

Abdominal and Lower Back Program

The exercises in the abdominal program develop the rectus abdominis, transversus abdominis, and internal and external obliques, with some carryover to the hip flexors. The lower back program concentrates on the erector spinae groups, which aid in the deceleration phase of the pitch.

SIT-UPS, CRUNCHES, AND CURLS

An angled sit-up board is optional. Any type of sit-up, crunch, curl, or combination will improve abdominal strength. To avoid stress to the hip flexors and the lower back, bend the knees. Twisting is a variation that works the obliques.

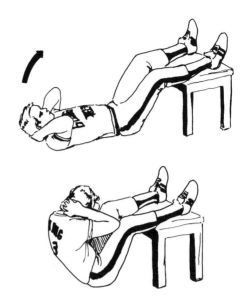

BACK EXTENSIONS

A bench and partner are required. Lie facedown on the bench with the upper half of the body extending over the end of the bench. The partner holds the legs. With hands behind the head, raise and lower the upper body from the ground to hyperextension of the back. This exercise works the muscles of the lower back.

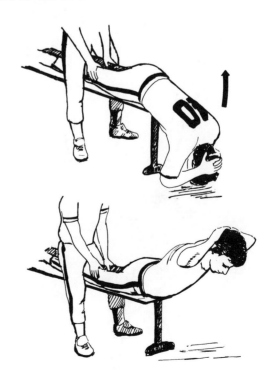

TWISTS

A heavy bar is required. Place the bar behind the neck, with hands atop the bar at each end. Stand upright with feet shoulder-width apart. Twist the body in one direction to its limit, then rotate in the other direction. Upon reaching the extreme twist, immediately start in the other direction using the stretch-reflex action of the muscles. This exercise works the rectus abdominis, transversus abdominis, internal and external obliques, and lower back muscles.

Lower-Body Program

The exercises of the lower-body program develop the upper legs (quadriceps and hamstrings), lower legs (calf muscles), hip flexors, abductors, and adductors. Many of these workouts also produce cardiovascular training.

JUMPING ROPE

The key is to use a soft surface to prevent shin splints. Depending on the style of jumping, this exercise works either the calf muscles exclusively or all the leg muscles.

STEP-UPS

A bench is required. Facing the bench, step up with one leg and follow it with the other. The same leg that started the step up also

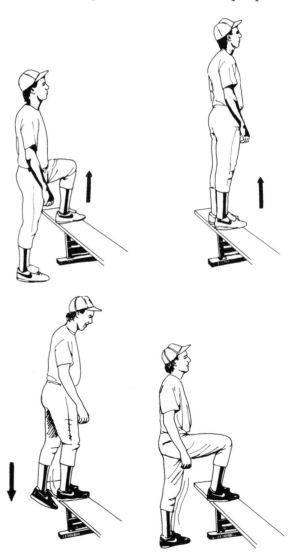

starts the step down, followed by the other leg. Do an equal number of repetitions with both legs. This exercise primarily works the quadriceps.

BENCH BLASTS

A bench is required. Facing the bench, step up with one leg, and, using only that leg, explode up and away from the bench. Perform this exercise in one continuous motion and with the same number of repetitions for each leg. This exercise works the quadriceps, hamstrings, and calf muscles.

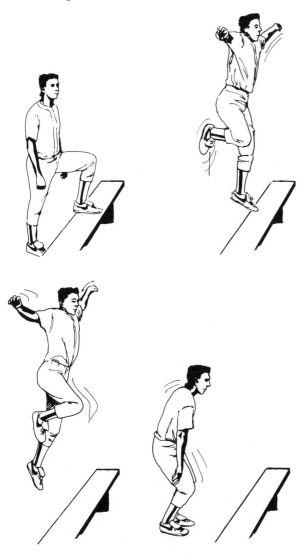

WIDE-BASED SQUATS

Stand with feet twice shoulder-width apart. Squat over one foot while keeping the other leg straight and to the side. In a squat, the

knees should never go in front of the toes and the upper leg should not dip below a parallel position to the ground. Heels should remain on the ground throughout the exercise. This exercise works the quadriceps, abductors, adductors, and hamstrings.

Body-Weight Resistance Repetitions

The number of repetitions in the body-weight resistance program varies from exercise to exercise. The beauty of this program is that if the exercise is executed properly and through the full range of motion, it is almost impossible to do too much. Table 5.1 lists the goals of the body-weight resistance program.

Plyometric Training

Plyometrics is the name of a group of athletic training exercises that exploit the *stretch-reflex* action of a muscle or muscle group. Plyometrics develop explosive power, which is very important in baseball. Throwing, hitting, and running all require some degree of explosive power. However, pitchers seldom hit or sprint, so the plyometric drills in this book are geared toward throwing, or, more accurately, pitching. To better understand the stretch reflex, let's look at a couple of power moves in baseball.

Table 5.1 Body-Weight Resistance Program Guide

Area	Exercise	Repetitions
Upper body	Full-range push-ups	30
	Inverted rowing	30
	Chin-ups	12
	Behind-the-neck pull-ups	12
	Dips	30
Abdominals and lower back	Sit-ups, crunches, or curls	50
	Back extensions	25
	Twists	50
Lower body	Jumping rope	Unlimited
	Step-ups	30 (each leg)
	Bench blasts	30 (each leg)
	Wide-based squats	30 (each leg)
	Plyometrics (see following section)	

A batter cocks or triggers the bat an instant before he starts to swing. The result of this cocking is a quicker swing. The cocking phase of the swing prestretches the muscles involved in the swing, helping those muscles to respond more quickly. When the muscles change directions from the cock to the swing, this is a stretch reflex; the muscles prestretch and then contract when changing direction.

Similarly, in throwing a baseball, the arm is first extended behind the body; when the arm is fully extended in back and has not yet started forward, it is in the prestretch position. When the arm changes directions and starts forward, this is a stretch-reflex action.

Plyometrics are designed to train stretch-reflex actions, in most cases using body weight and gravity as resistance. This training reduces the time needed for changing direction and therefore increases speed and power. Plyometric exercises include bounds, leaps, hops, ricochets, jumps for the legs and hips, and swings and twists for the abdominals.

Because the act of throwing is plyometric in nature, there is no need to train the upper body with plyometrics. The legs and hips supply the power, and the abdominals transfer this power, transforming it into speed. The arm is the benefactor of this speed and whips through the throw.

Athletes should follow certain precautions when doing plyometric exercise:

- Warm up and stretch thoroughly before training to avoid injury.
- Train two or three times per week.
- Do not do plyometrics after extensive weight training because fatigued muscles are easily injured.
- Follow the recommended number of repetitions and sets for each particular exercise, emphasizing quality exercise rather than quantity.
- Progress at a reasonable rate, avoiding the premature overloading that can cause injury.
- Land on the balls of the feet rather than flat-footed or on the heels.

Plyometric exercises should be a part of any pitcher's training regimen. The seven plyometric exercises in this chapter are just a few of many plyometric drills. These particular exercises were chosen because of their specificity to pitching. Used correctly, these drills will help the pitcher generate more power with his legs and hips and transfer this power, in the form of speed, to the upper body with more efficiency. Plyometrics make a great in-season lower-body and abdominal workout to ensure optimum power and speed throughout the season.

The following plyometric exercises develop the legs, hips, and abdominal muscles to improve their function in pitching. The exercises can be grouped together or performed individually. Safety should always be stressed for any plyometric exercise.

DEPTH JUMPS

Depth jumps develop the muscles of the legs, buttocks, hips, and lower back.

Stand on a bench or similar platform that is at least 18 inches high and no more than 40 inches high. Stand with legs straight and shoulders relaxed. To begin the depth jump, fall to the ground, landing on the feet (a soft surface is recommended). Do not jump from the bench; simply fall forward. Upon landing, bend the knees to absorb shock and, using the arms for momentum, jump as high as possible. Reach up with the hands. Try to jump both as high and as far as possible.

Start with two sets of 8 to 10 repetitions, and work up to six sets of 8 to 10 repetitions. Allow 30 to 60 seconds of rest between jumps. As the number of sets is increased, the height of the bench should be increased.

SPLIT JUMPS

Split jumps develop the muscles of the legs, hips, buttocks, and lower back. Split jumps simulate the action of the stride in the pitching delivery.

Assume a position with one leg bent at a 90-degree angle in front and one leg extended behind. The trunk should remain in a vertical position at all times. Jump as high and as straight up as possible, switching legs in midair and landing in the starting position with the legs reversed. The front leg should

land slightly bent and collapse to 90 degrees to absorb and prestretch the muscles. Continue the motion.

Start with one set of 8 to 10 repetitions of each leg, and work up to three sets of 8 to 10 repetitions. Allow 30 to 60 seconds between sets for recovery.

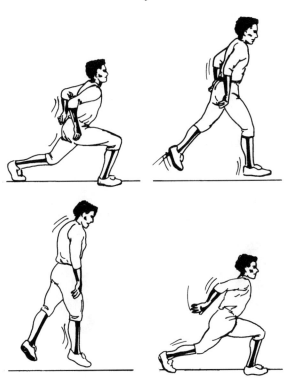

SIDE JUMPS

Side jumps develop the muscles of the lower legs, hips, buttocks, lower back, and, most important, the abductor muscles of the upper legs. A large part of the pitching delivery is performed with the body sideways to the plate; therefore, strong abductor muscles are important.

Set two rubber cones or tackling dummies approximately three feet apart. (Cones or dummies should be used for this drill to prevent injuries.) Stand in jumping position with a cone to the side. Side-jump over the first cone and land between the two cones. Without hesitation, side-jump over the second cone. Upon landing, change direction and jump back over the cones.

Start with two sets of 8 to 10 repetitions, and progress to six sets of 8 repetitions. One repetition is four jumps.

INCREMENTAL VERTICAL JUMPS

Incremental vertical jumps develop the muscles of the legs, hips, buttocks, and lower back. This drill is also valuable because it is a tool for measuring the height of jumps.

Secure one end of a 15-foot rope to a fence at a height of 4 feet. Attach the other end to something movable, such as a car tire lying flat on the ground. The movable object lets the rope "give" if it is hit. Start at the bottom of the inclined rope and jump back and forth over the rope, going higher up the rope with each jump. When you can jump over the highest point, the set is over. Start with two sets and work up to six sets.

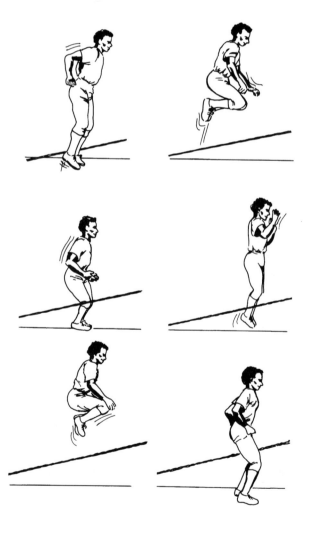

INCLINE RICOCHETS

Incline ricochets develop the ankle stabilizers as well as the muscles of the upper leg and the lower leg. Ricochets develop quickness of the feet, which is very important in fielding and pickoff moves.

Stairs are needed. Start at the bottom of the stairs with feet together, and move rapidly up each step. Emphasize quickness. Remember to land on the balls of the feet. Ricochets can be done with two legs or one leg, straight up or at angles. Start with one set of 12 to 15 steps, and work up to three sets.

BAR TWISTS

Bar twists develop the entire trunk and emphasize the muscles involved in trunk rotation. As the pitcher comes out of his windup, the trunk rotates, transferring power to the upper body.

A weighted bar is needed. It can be a standard weightlifting bar and can weigh up to 45 pounds (e.g., an Olympic bar). Stand with feet shoulder-width apart, with legs slightly bent. Hold the bar behind the neck with the hands as far apart as possible. Twist in one direction, then change direction before the trunk is fully rotated. Use only the trunk muscles to stop the momentum of the bar— using the shoulders cheats the trunk muscles of their development. Start with two sets of 30 repetitions, and work up to six sets.

Strength Training With Weights and Machines

Throwing a baseball has been compared to snapping a whip. Think of the pitcher's body as a whip divided into three sections. The handle of the whip represents the pitcher's legs and hips; the middle section represents the pitcher's abdominal and lower back region; and the end section represents the upper back, shoulders, arms, and hands. With this in mind, a weight program designed specifically for pitchers should include three separate phases of weight training that are tied together to maximize the power, speed, or mass needed in each respective area of the body.

A pitcher's legs and hips should have mass and power. Just as the handle of the whip is much bigger than the end, the pitcher's legs and hips should have more mass than the upper body. The whip's power is supplied by the arm of the person using the whip; the pitcher's power is generated by his legs. Thus, the weight training of the legs and hips emphasizes building power and mass.

The abdominals and lower back transfer the power developed in the legs and hips to the pitcher's upper extremities, just as the middle of the whip transfers the power of the thrust to the end of the whip. The weight training of the abdominals includes exercises to develop both power and speed. The weight training of the upper body includes exercises to develop overall strength, speed, and, through repetition, endurance to handle the power generated from the body and the rigor of the throw.

To prevent injury and produce ultimate gains, all athletes should adhere to the following guidelines when working with weights:

- **Use proper technique.** Proper technique is important for preventing injury, especially with the use of free weights. Never alter technique to lift more weight.

- **Start with appropriate weight.** Start out with a weight that can be easily lifted 8 to 12 times.

- **Warm up appropriately.** To prevent injury, warm up the body before weightlifting. (See the opening section on flexibility in this chapter.)
- **Breathe normally.** Exhale during the lift and inhale when bringing the weight back to the starting point. Do not hold the breath during a lift.
- **Work with a partner.** Always use a partner when performing heavy lifts and whenever possible for regular lifts; partners supply needed help and can offer encouragement for greater gains. When using free weights, always have a partner when doing squats or any other lift that may require help.

Lower-Body Program

The goal of the lower-body program with weights is to build power and mass. The following exercises, if done with proper technique and the appropriate repetitions and weight, build power and mass in the legs and hips.

SQUATS

Squats work all of the leg muscles, the hip flexors, and the gluteal group, with added benefit to the quadriceps. Because squats work some of the biggest muscles in the body, this single exercise develops mass more than any other exercise. Proper technique is a must during squats, so athletes should use a light weight until they master the technique.

Stand with feet shoulder-width apart, toes and knees pointed slightly outward. The eyes and head should be up, and the back should be straight. When lowering the weight, do not let the thighs go below parallel to the floor. Going beyond parallel greatly increases the chance of knee injury. Breathe deeply and normally, exhaling on the way up. Always squat with a partner to prevent accidents. When using a machine, do not lock out the knees at the end of the lift.

LEG EXTENSIONS

Leg extensions primarily work the quadriceps. Each athlete must adjust the seat of the leg extension machine for his body dimensions so that he can follow proper technique.

Adjust the machine to the proper setting. Maintain good posture throughout exercise. Lift slowly to extension and slowly back to starting position. Breathe normally, and exhale when lifting toward extension. (Do not hold breath.)

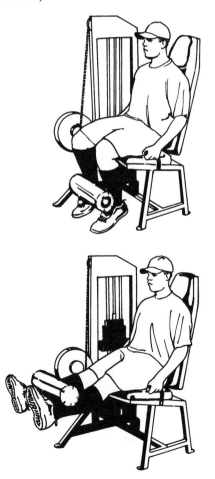

LEG CURLS

Leg curls primarily work the hamstrings (the muscles on the back of the legs). Proper technique includes going through the entire range of motion and not arching the back.

When curling weight toward the body, do so in a slow movement. Return weight to starting position with slow movement. Breathe normally, and exhale while lifting weight toward the body.

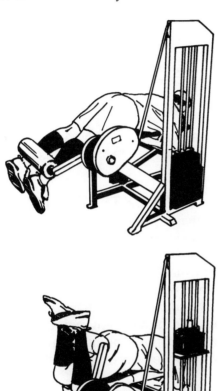

LEG ABDUCTION

This exercise works the muscles of the outer thigh, also known as the abductors. Abduction work is very important for pitchers because most pitching is done sideways to the plate, requiring abductor use.

Sit with good posture in the abduction machine, with back flat against the pad. Breathe normally, exhaling when the legs start away from the body. Push out away from the body with control; pause, and return to the center with control.

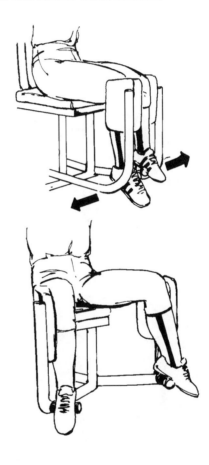

LEG ADDUCTION

This exercise works the muscles of the inner thigh, also known as the adductors or groin muscles. This is a great exercise for pitchers because adductors are also involved in the sideways pitch delivery.

Sit with good posture in the adduction machine, with back flat against the pad. Breathe normally, exhaling when starting to squeeze the legs together. Squeeze the legs together with control; pause, and slowly let machine back out.

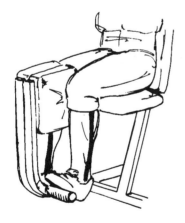

HIP FLEXORS

This exercise works the muscles involved in hip flexion, which is very important in the pitching delivery.

Using a machine or Velcro weights attached at the knee, start with the knee behind the center line of the body and move it down and up in front of the body. Upon reaching the apex, pause; then return the leg in a slow, controlled fashion to the starting point. Breathe normally and exhale when starting the lift toward the apex.

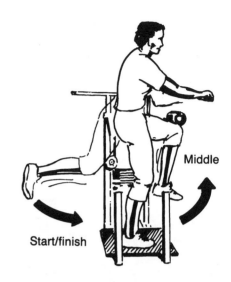

HIP EXTENSION

This exercise works the muscles involved with hip extension, also very valuable to the pitcher during delivery.

Using a machine or Velcro weights attached at the knee, start with the knee up in front of the body and move it down and up in back of the body. At the stopping point, pause, then return to the original point. Breathe normally, and exhale when starting to push the weight down.

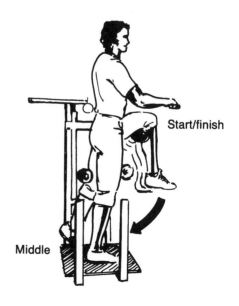

CALF RAISES

Calf raises work the calf muscles, which comprise the soleus and the gastrocnemius. The first movement in any activity involving the legs is plantar flexion (when the heel comes up from the ground and the athlete pushes off with the ball of the foot). With this in mind, it makes sense to develop these muscles for better athletic performance.

Calf raises can be performed while the athlete is lying down in a leg press machine, standing up using a machine, or holding weights. Regardless of the method used, place the feet so that the pressure is on the balls of the feet and the heels are over the edge. Slightly more than half of the foot should be off of the pad. A full range of motion is required, so the heels must rise as high as possible and, when lowered, go well below the push pad. Breathe normally during the exercise.

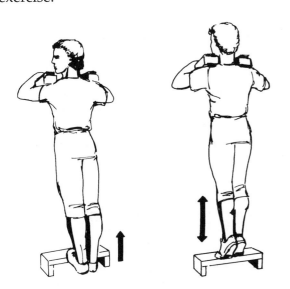

Abdominal and Lower Back Program

The goal of the abdominal and lower back program is to build strength while retaining full range of movement. Abdominal flexion occurs in the pitching delivery during the transition of power from the lower body to the upper body. The lower back muscles aid in the deceleration of the arm and body after the ball is released.

CRUNCHERS

The cruncher develops the upper abdominals; if side twists are added, the obliques also come into play.

Lie on the floor with the legs at a 90-degree angle and feet up on a bench. Inhale before starting and exhale during flexion. Start with the hands behind the head, and curl the upper body toward knees. The lower back should remain flat on the floor. Touch the elbows to knees. Alternating elbows to opposite knees works the oblique muscles.

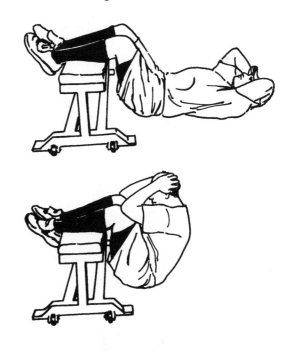

LEG RAISES

Leg raises work the lower abdominals and hip flexors. The quadriceps also get some work.

While standing, place hands and elbows on the padded bars. Breathe normally, inhaling before exercise and exhaling during the leg raise. Raise the legs straight out in front (keeping them straight) while supporting the body with the arms.

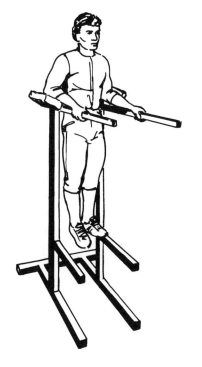

TWISTS

Twists primarily work the internal and external obliques, but all the abdominals come into play as well. As the body rotates from the gathered position to the acceleration position, the obliques come into play.

Hold a weighted bar behind the body with the arms. Twist first in one direction to full rotation and then back through the starting point to full rotation in the other direction. Breathe normally throughout the exercise.

BACK HYPEREXTENSIONS

Back hyperextensions work the muscles of the lower back, which are necessary for the deceleration phase of the pitch as well as for general posture.

Lie on a bench face down with the upper body off the bench. Start with the head and shoulders toward the ground so that the body is at a 90-degree angle to the floor. The hands should be together behind the neck. Raise the upper body parallel to the floor. (Use extreme caution during this exercise. Do not pass parallel into an extreme extension.) Breathe normally. Do not hold the breath. Do this exercise under the guidance of a coach.

Upper-Body Program

The shoulders and arms represent the end of the whip. Their function is to transfer to the ball all power, momentum, and speed developed in the windup. Therefore, when training the shoulders and arms we want general strength, durability, and most important, speed. Hand speed is what determines the velocity of the baseball, not the amount of weight that can be bench-pressed. The weight program for the shoulders and arms is designed to give general strength but not power, durability but not great mass. (Speed is developed by throwing or quickness-related exercises, without weight training. When we mention that we want to attain hand speed through our weight program, we really mean that we don't want to inhibit hand speed by developing power and mass as we would in the legs. The legs have to start and stop the pitching motion and stabilize the total body weight—and therefore must be very powerful. The shoulders and arms merely have to support themselves plus the weight of a baseball.)

Some experts believe that greater mass in the arms is one reason for arm injury—as the arms get bigger and stronger, the shoulders are under greater pressure when they support the arms through the throwing motion. One of the biggest problems facing the coach today is to convince his players that bigger is not better. Too many young pitchers want to bulk up and look good; they mistakenly think that this will make them throw harder. Our goals in a shoulder and arm strength-training program should be durability for a great number of throws and hand speed for greater velocity.

Our strength-training program also attempts to balance the muscles of the chest and biceps with those of the back shoulder area. Ninety-nine percent of all arm use is in front of the body. This creates a terrible muscular imbalance that is to blame for the round-shouldered athlete. This is also to blame for many throwing injuries. Therefore, this shoulder and arm program includes many exercises that work the back of the shoulder.

BENCH PRESS

The bench press works the chest and shoulder muscles (the pectorals and the frontal deltoids in particular). The triceps muscles of the upper arm also get some work. These muscles aid in the acceleration phase of the pitch.

The back should be flat against the back pad (if a bench press machine is used) or flat against the bench on the conventional bench press. The hands should be slightly wider than shoulder-width. On a machine the handles should be in the area of the armpits, so make any necessary adjustments with the seat. Inhale before starting, exhale while lifting weight, and inhale again when returning

weight to starting position. Lift the weight quickly but under control; pause at the top of the lift and then let the weight down slowly. Maintain full range of motion in the movements.

SEATED ROWS

Rows develop the posterior deltoids, the upper back muscles, and the biceps. These muscles are used during the deceleration of the arm and body after the ball is released.

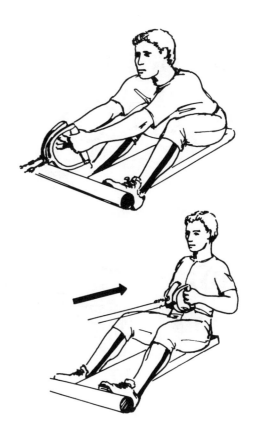

Hands should be palms down. (When the palms are up, the exercise becomes more of an arm curl working the biceps.) Breathe normally and do not hold the breath. Using good posture, pull the bar back to the chest, with the elbows going behind the body as far as possible. The pull should be quick but under control, with a pause at the top and a slow return to the starting point. Full range of motion is important.

FLYS

Flys mainly develop the pectoralis muscles, but the frontal deltoids also pick up a little work. These muscles are used in the acceleration phase of the pitch.

The back should be flat against the back pad if a machine is used or flat against the bench during conventional flys. Adjust the machine or the dumbbells so that the upper arm is at a 90-degree angle with the torso during the exercise. Do this exercise slowly and with control because of the extreme stretch to the pectoralis muscles. Many machines have foot bars to help start the weight forward without too much stretch. After the first stretch, attempt to use a full range of

motion to develop strength and flexibility. Press the elbows together in a controlled fashion and return to the starting position. Breathe normally for the entire exercise.

REVERSE FLYS

Reverse flys work the posterior deltoids and the upper back muscles, both of which are prominent in the deceleration of the arm after the pitch. To date there are no machines that aid in reverse flys, so a bench and dumbbells are necessary for this exercise.

Lie face down on a bench while holding dumbbells with the palms down. Using normal breathing, lift up the dumbbells with the palms down. When the lifting movement stops, turn the thumbs down and continue the lift through full range. Lift the weights slowly and with control, maximizing full range of motion.

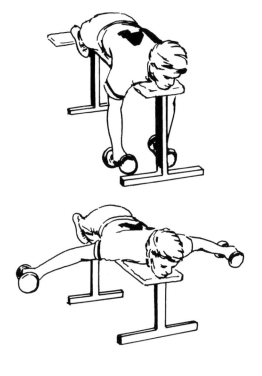

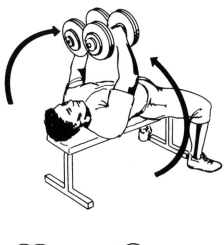

SUPRA LIFT

The supra lift works primarily the supraspinatus muscle (one of the rotator cuff muscles), but the deltoids also get some work. The supraspinatus is one of the most frequently injured parts of the shoulder because it acts as a decelerator in the throwing motion.

Locate the supra position: Using no weight, raise the pitching hand straight out in front of the body; now move the hand away from the front to a point halfway between the front of the body and out to the side. This is the supra position. Perform the exercise with a dumbbell or weight plate, increasing weight as needed. Lift the weight in a supra position, with thumb pointing down, to shoulder height. Pause, then slowly lower the weight. Breathe normally throughout the exercise.

TRICEPS EXTENSIONS

Triceps extensions work the triceps muscles exclusively. The triceps muscle is very active in the acceleration phase of the throwing motion. The rotator cuff also gets some benefit from this exercise when a dumbbell is used.

Triceps extensions can be performed with either a dumbbell or a weight machine. Both methods are excellent if executed correctly. With a dumbbell, start with the arm in the cocked position of the throw with the elbow slightly higher than the shoulder. The dumbbell hand should be palm up behind the body, and the other hand should be supporting the elbow. Lift the dumbbell up toward full arm extension in an inside-out fashion so that in full extension, the palm of the hand has rotated to the side. Using a controlled motion (do not snap the arm into hyperextension), work the full range of motion. Breathe normally throughout the exercise.

ARM CURLS

Arm curls develop the biceps, with some benefit to the frontal deltoids and muscles of the forearms, wrists, and hands. The biceps muscle slows down the arm during deceleration in the delivery.

The arm curl can be performed with a machine, bar, or dumbbells. All three methods are excellent when performed correctly. The arm starts in full extension with the palm facing away from the athlete. As the arm curls toward the body, the palm faces up and eventually faces the body. In a variation of this exercise, start with the palm facing down (reverse curls). Reverse curls develop the biceps but also work the forearm muscles. When doing curls, breathe normally and work in a controlled manner without hyperextending the elbows at the starting and stopping position.

LATERAL RAISES WITH ROTATION

Lateral raises with rotation are excellent for the external shoulder (deltoids) and internal shoulder (rotator cuff) muscles. The lateral raise works the deltoids, and the rotation works the cuff muscles.

Use only light weights for this exercise. Start with dumbbells hanging down by the sides with a palms-in grip. Raise the dumbbells to shoulder level (palms down). At this point, the palms rotate thumbs-up to a palms-up position. Continue up with the dumbbells until the weights are over the shoulders. Reverse the process on the way down. During

the rotation, stabilize the hands until rotation is completed. Breath normally throughout the exercise.

PRONATION-SUPINATION TWISTS

Pronation-supination twists work the rotator muscles of the shoulder and the forearm and hand-grip muscles. Throughout the course of a career, a pitcher throws many different pitches, each requiring him to do different movements with the arm, hand, and fingers. For instance, a fastball requires extension and flexion of the forearm, but a curveball or slider requires some degree of supination in addition to extension and flexion. Some forms of sinkers and change-ups require pronation—the entire arm pronates in the deceleration phase of the pitch to prevent injury to the arm.

Sit on a chair or stand, leaning over with the arm hanging straight down in front. Using light weight, hold the dumbbell with the palm of the hand facing the body. Rotate the entire arm back and forth from pronation to supination, feeling a slight stretch with each repetition. If executed with full range of motion, this exercise also may cause some stretch in the elbow.

WRIST FLEXION AND EXTENSION

The last major actions that occur before the release of the ball are wrist extension (which is gradual) and wrist flexion (which is the final action of the arm during the throw). This snapping of the wrist simulates the snap of the whip when all of the speed and power generated are transferred to this single movement.

A spring-loaded door is necessary for this exercise. Hold the arm by the side with the elbow at a 90-degree angle. Wrist and hand should be hyperextended as far as possible, holding the door open. Quickly flex the wrist with as much speed and power as possible. The door will open up and return slowly to the beginning position of wrist hyperextension. Catch the door, letting the force of the door stretch the hand back into hyperextension before flexing. This exercise works on the same principle as plyometrics and works the stretch-reflex action of the muscles, resulting in quicker wrist flex and more ball speed.

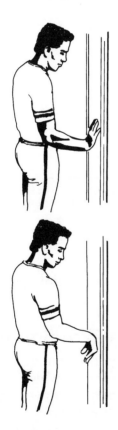

HAND GRIPS

Hand grips work the muscles of the hand and forearm, which help the pitcher with the various spins required when throwing breaking balls.

Use conventional hand-grip squeezes, increasing the number of repetitions as the grip gets stronger. As the grip becomes stronger, use only the first two fingers and the thumb.

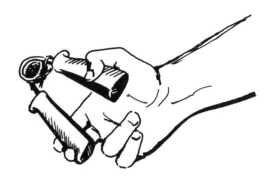

RICE BUCKET

The rice bucket works hand and forearm muscles for greater grip strength.

Submerge the hand and wrist in a bucket of dry rice. Open and close the hand, pronate and supinate the forearm, and work the fingers in flexion and extension.

Strength-Training Schedules

A pitcher's strength training regimen should be divided into three categories: off-season, preseason, and in-season. Each period has different requirements for strength, mass, and power.

Off-Season Strength-Training Program

Off-season training is the time for a pitcher to make great gains in strength as well as gains in mass and power to increase quickness and agility. Because it is the off-season, the pitcher has more time to work extra hard and build a good foundation for the upcoming season.

Pitchers can achieve this by working six days a week; they can use three days to work on strength, power, and mass and alternate days to work on overall quickness and agility. All throwing during the off-season should precede weightlifting. Throwing before weight training helps eliminate arm injuries that could occur from throwing with a body fatigued by weight training; this also gives the body two days to recover from training before throwing again. The stretching program should be performed before and after any off-season workout to prevent injury and promote flexibility. Table 5.2 presents an ideal off-season strength-training program.

Preseason Strength-Training Program

Preseason strength training is slightly different from off-season training in that the pitcher starts to prepare for the upcoming season by working on more baseball-related skills to get the body ready to pitch. Strength gains now cease and maintenance takes over. During the preseason, the pitcher stops increasing weight for upper-body resistance, but he increases repetitions to build endurance. The preseason includes more cardiovascular, agility, and throwing activities than the off-season, so there is less emphasis on and less time for strength training. The pitcher begins to fine-tune his body for the upcoming season: In daily workouts, throwing, fielding, and running drills gradually replace muscle-building exercises.

As with the off-season program, the athlete should pitch from the mound only before lifting to ensure arm safety. Pitchers should perform the entire stretching program both before and after the preseason strength-training program to prevent injury and pro-

Table 5.2 Off-Season Strength-Training Chart

Exercise	Sets	Repetitions
Squats	3	10-8-6
Leg extensions	3	10-8-6
Leg curls	3	10-8-6
Calf raises	3	10-8-6
Abduction	3	10-8-6
Adduction	3	10-8-6
Hip flexors	3	10-8-6
Bench press	2-3	15
Rows	2-3	15
Triceps extensions	2-3	15
Curls	2-3	15
Flys	2-3	15
Reverse flys	2-3	15
Pronation-supination	1	30
Wrist flexors	1	30
Hand grips	1	Until fatigued
Rice bucket	1	Until fatigued
Crunchers	3	25
Twists	3	25
Back extensions	3	8-10
Leg raises	3	8-10

Note: When starting a weight-training program, use a weight that you can handle easily for the required repetitions. Do the program three days per week.

mote flexibility. Table 5.3 presents an ideal preseason strength-training program.

In-Season Strength-Training Program

In-season strength training is merely a maintenance program in which players try to maintain the strength, power, and mass levels developed in the off-season and preseason strength-training programs. The pitcher now lifts only two times per week, with no increases in weight and more repetitions to build endurance. The athlete should be aware that overtraining may cause a performance letdown and that he should only perform in-season training after pitching from the

Table 5.3 Preseason Strength-Training Chart

Exercise	Sets	Repetitions
Squats	3	10-8-6
Leg extensions	3	10-8-6
Leg curls	3	10-8-6
Calf raises	3	10-8-6
Abduction	3	10-8-6
Adduction	3	10-8-6
Hip flexors	3	10-8-6
Bench press	1	15-20*
Rows	1	15-20*
Triceps extensions	1	15-20*
Curls	1	15-20*
Flys	1	15-20*
Reverse flys	1	15-20*
Pronation-supination	1	15-20*
Wrist flexors	1	15-20*
Hand grips	1	Until fatigued
Rice bucket	1	Until fatigued
Crunchers	1	25
Twists	1	25
Back extensions	1	8-10
Leg raises	1	8-10

*No increases in weight during the preseason for the upper body. Lift approximately 80 percent of maximum weight in the off-season. Do the program three days per week.

Table 5.4 In-Season Strength-Maintenance Chart

Exercise	Sets	Repetitions
Squats	2	15
Leg extensions	2	15
Leg curls	2	15
Calf raises	2	15
Abduction	2	15
Adduction	2	15
Hip flexors	2	15
Bench press	1	15-20*
Rows	1	15-20*
Triceps extensions	1	15-20*
Curls	1	15-20*
Flys	1	15-20*
Reverse flys	1	15-20*
Pronation-supination	1	15-20*
Wrist flexors	1	15-20*
Hand grips	1	Until fatigued
Rice bucket	1	Until fatigued
Crunchers	1	25
Twists	1	25
Back extensions	1	8-10
Leg raises	1	8-10

*The body-weight resistance program can be substituted for these exercises. Do the program two times per week.

mound. The baseball season is a long one, so the pitcher must be consistent in training during this time.

To prevent injury and promote flexibility, pitchers should perform the entire stretching program both before and after the in-season strength-training program. Table 5.4 presents an ideal in-season strength-training program.

Strengthening the Throwing Arm

Pitchers use three methods for strengthening the throwing arm: proper throwing mechanics, a physical development program, and the long toss. Each of these three methods will be discussed in full. To make the greatest gains, pitchers must use all three methods. Proper form, strength, balance, quickness, rhythm training, and overload throwing will develop the arm to its fullest capabilities.

Proper Throwing Mechanics

Proper mechanics provide definite physical advantages in throwing. The younger a pitcher can learn these mechanical advantages, the better off he will be. And the sooner a pitcher can learn the basic mechanics, the sooner he can start to work on the second and third methods. (Without the proper mechanics, the other two methods will have limited effectiveness in building strength in the throwing arm.)

In all sports, the most important phase of self-improvement is establishing a good foundation to build on. Good habits, when practiced, improve performance. When a pitcher builds on bad habits, he may be successful on a temporary basis, but eventually pitchers with the good habits will pass him by. A good example is the Little Leaguer who has such a good curveball that he never really develops his fastball, which he should have developed first. Sure, he will win in Little League and maybe in high school; but when it comes time to play college or professional ball, he won't be heavily recruited because he can't throw very hard. On the opposite side of the coin, the pitcher who mastered his fastball and refused to throw breaking pitches until he was in high school may be going to college or signing a professional contract. He practiced good habits, built a good foundation, and eventually came out ahead. A pitcher needs to learn the basics and stick with them. When the mechanics are solid, then he can work on the other two methods to fully develop the arm.

Physical Development

Strength training can include exercising, plyometrics, or weight training. All of these will build strength. Generally speaking, strength training improves the weaker athlete much more than the physically fit athlete.

Strength training will help a pitcher develop a stronger throwing arm, not necessarily a faster one. Throwing is a ballistic movement, not a power movement. Weight training creates power, but to make the ball travel faster we must concern ourselves with hand speed. Power and speed are two separate concepts, and more power does not necessarily mean more speed. A pitcher should start an intensive weight program with the sole purpose of creating a stronger throwing arm and not expecting to increase speed.

Because throwing is a ballistic movement, a pitcher will benefit most from workouts that emphasize balance, speed, and rhythm rather than straight weightlifting. The ideal training program consists of a combination of the two. (This is another reminder that a training program only reinforces and strengthens the basic throwing mechanics.)

Long Toss

The *long toss* involves throwing long distances for many repetitions. The key to having a great arm is to practice throwing by using the arm to its fullest capabilities. Notice how those players with great arms always seem to show off by throwing hard and long distances. It could just be that the reason they have great arms is that they do throw hard and at long distances. This is the most effective way to build strength in the throwing arm. (A good rule of thumb is to throw twice the distance of the baselines. A Little Leaguer's baseline is 60 feet, so he should throw at least 120 feet. High school and college pitchers should throw at least 180 feet.)

How many throws are enough? This depends on a lot of factors, including the pitcher's condition, the condition of his arm, and whether he will pitch soon. As with all phases of strength training, the time to build strength is when the arm is tired. By throwing a few more times after the arm has tired, the pitcher builds strength and endurance, pushing himself past his previous limits to make gains. The key to this form of training is to know the difference between fatigue and pain. If the arm is simply fatigued, the pitcher should do a few more repetitions to build strength and endurance. If the arm is injured and in pain, the pitcher should stop all throwing and see the trainer or doctor. One reason there are not as many good arms as there used to be is that today's young pitcher has trouble discerning between pain and fatigue.

A player cannot throw long and hard on a daily basis without hurting the arm, so a pitcher should train every other day to ensure rest between sessions. The ideal time for high school and lower levels to have a training routine for arm strengthening is in the fall. With few baseball games to work around, a continuous two- or three-month routine can be set up. If all three of the training methods described here are combined, all who participate are likely to increase their velocity and distance.

Energy Fitness Program

A correct energy fitness program is just as important as a good throwing, strengthening, and flexibility program. Without it, the athlete won't have the energy he needs for success.

The body has two types of energy systems: anaerobic and aerobic. When the body demands instant energy for sudden movement, the energy is supplied by the *anaerobic* system. During sudden movements such as sprinting, jumping, or pitching, the body uses 100 times more energy than when at rest, so a pitcher must train his body anaerobically to accommodate the energy surge. During long, continuous exercise, the *aerobic* system produces energy. Only 25 times the body's resting energy rate is needed during aerobic training, but aerobic workouts take more time than anaerobic workouts.

The anaerobic system supplies energy for activities that require maximum effort for up to four minutes. Energy for muscle contraction comes from two compounds stored in the muscle. After 8 to 12 seconds of maximum activity, these compounds are depleted, and the muscle then starts to use glycogen to produce more of these compounds. This process creates lactic acid as a by-product. Lactic acid buildup can have an adverse effect on energy production and is responsible for stiffness after exercise.

The aerobic energy system supplies energy for activities that take longer than four minutes. Hard breathing and increased heart rate supply oxygen to burn carbohydrate, and eventually fat, to produce more energy.

Pitching: Aerobic or Anaerobic?

Pitching, like most exercise, uses a combination of the two energy systems. There is no exact formula for figuring out how much each system is used, but a good estimate is 85 to 90 percent anaerobic and 10 to 15 percent aerobic.

A complete pitch takes two to three seconds, fitting the anaerobic profile; but a series of pitches requires a percentage of aerobic energy. The longer a pitcher stays in the game or the more pitches he makes, the more aerobic energy he needs. If the pitching staff is divided into three groups—starters, long-relievers, and short-relievers—each pitcher will be able to develop a workout routine with percentages of anaerobic and aerobic exercise appropriate for his specific pitching role.

Starting pitchers. Starting pitchers are expected to pitch six to nine innings or throw 75 to 135 pitches every four or five days during the season. Each individual pitch is anaerobic, so the training of the starting pitcher must include a large portion of anaerobic training. However, the high number of repetitions (75 to 135) requires aerobic training. Therefore, the starting pitcher's energy fitness program should include both anaerobic and aerobic training to meet the demands of that pitcher's role on the team. A formula consisting of 70 percent anaerobic training and 30 percent aerobic training is effective for a starting pitcher.

Long-relief pitchers. Long-relief pitchers are expected to pitch three to five innings or throw 45 to 75 pitches every three to five days. The long-reliever doesn't have as many repetitions as the starter and therefore doesn't need as much aerobic training. A formula consisting of 85 percent anaerobic training and 15 percent aerobic training is effective for a long-reliever.

Short-relief pitchers. Short-relief pitchers are expected to pitch one to three innings or throw 15 to 45 pitches every one to three days. Short-relief pitchers' training should be 100 percent anaerobic.

Heart Rate

The heart rate is a good tool for measuring the state of training. By placing his index finger lightly along the throat near the windpipe, the athlete can feel his heartbeat. The athlete should count the beat for 10 seconds and multiply by 6 to determine his heart rate.

Resting Heart Rate

The resting heart rate is the number of heart-beats per minute (bpm) during rest. A person can get the most accurate resting heart rate in the morning immediately after waking up. Resting heart rate declines as the athlete gets in better shape.

Maximum Heart Rate

The maximum heart rate is the highest rate at which the heart will beat. Here is the formula for finding a maximum heart rate:

$$\text{maximum heart rate} = 220 - \text{age}$$

Maximum heart rate is an important tool in aerobic and anaerobic training. By using the maximum heart rate in certain formulas, coaches and athletes will be able to determine the intensity of a workout, thus determining its worth in aerobic or anaerobic training.

Aerobic Training Program

All pitchers should create an aerobic base before getting into an anaerobic program. The aerobic base gets the body prepared for the strenuous anaerobic program that lies ahead. Starting from day one with a rigorous anaerobic workout would cause many problems and injuries.

Guidelines for an Aerobic Training Program

1. An aerobic base program should last three to four weeks (exercising two or three times per week, for a minimum of 30 minutes at a time).
2. When the athlete is building an aerobic base, his heart rate should be at 60 to 80 percent of his maximum heart rate.
3. Two to three hours per week of aerobic training is sufficient.
4. An athlete can build an aerobic base in any number of ways; aerobic dancing and running are the most specific to baseball.

Anaerobic Training Program

After an athlete forms an initial aerobic base, the anaerobic training program begins. How the anaerobic program works in with the aerobic depends on the role of the pitcher. All pitchers should train anaerobically at least 50 percent of the time, and usually more.

Guidelines for an Anaerobic Training Program

1. Anaerobic training begins after the initial aerobic-base phase and continues throughout the season.
2. When the athlete is training anaerobically, his heart rate should be at 80 to 100 percent of his maximum heart rate.
3. Exercise intervals should last from 30 to 60 seconds.
4. Recovery time should be twice the time of the exercise interval. For example, a 30-second sprint requires a 1-minute recovery time.
5. The number of repetitions of exercise intervals should increase as the season progresses.
6. Anaerobic training should be executed two or three times per week.

Designing Training Programs

When designing training programs for pitchers, coaches and athletes must stay within the guidelines for aerobic and anaerobic training. However, they can use a variety of exercises to prevent boredom and encourage maximum effort. For example, a variation on straight sprints is to run football patterns with the coach throwing passes. When working on an aerobic base, the athletes may do a three-mile run. Change the route every so often, and include some obstacles, such as stairs, hills, or trees in the woods, to keep the run interesting.

Peaking

When designing an energy fitness program for the season, keep in mind that the end of the season is usually the most important. At this time the pitchers should be in ultimate condition. Baseball seasons last from four to seven months, and the energy fitness program should be designed so that the athlete can use the season to build. Too many coaches get their athletes into prime condition to open the season and then let them slip until they are out of shape at the season's end. It is nearly impossible for an athlete to stay in top physical shape for four to seven months, so the coach should gradually build his athletes' fitness level so that they are in top shape for the last month of the season. It is in the last month that league races are settled and tournaments begin. In most cases, the team that plays well down the stretch will finish victorious.

Treating Injury and Fatigue

Discerning the difference between injury and fatigue often is not easy for the pitcher and coach. Many times only a trained medical eye can recognize the difference.

Injury and fatigue should be treated differently, so the pitcher must recognize the symptoms of pain caused by injury and discomfort caused by fatigue. Any time a diagnosis of injury or fatigue is questionable, the athlete and coach should seek the help of a professional trainer, therapist, or doctor.

Fatigue of the Pitching Arm

Fatigue is the normal exhaustion, stiffness, minor muscle ache, and general soreness that follow pitching. Throwing a baseball is a very unnatural, violent action involving high-speed muscle contractions and unorthodox arm angles requiring great ranges of flexibility. With this in mind, let's look at treatments for fatigue.

Treating Fatigue With Ice

Applying ice to the shoulder or elbow after throwing has become the "in" thing to do among pitchers. Coaches, beware that this phenomenon is growing daily and with no scientific grounds. Ice is for injuries and has no place in the treatment of fatigue.

There may be some psychological effects of icing the arm if a pitcher thinks that past successful performances have been the result of icing. However, pitchers often become addicted to ice and believe that without icing the arm they could not possibly pitch well.

Any pitcher who ices after pitching must be sure to follow the ice treatment with a mild stretching program. This is especially important for the relief pitcher because he might be called on to pitch the next day—the administration of ice will make the muscles in the treated area stiff and sluggish the following day.

Treating Fatigue With Warm-Down

Immediately after a pitching stint, the pitcher should play easy catch in the bullpen for 20 to 25 pitches, then follow this with a light resistance workout using surgical tubing or dumbbells. Swimming laps after pitching is an excellent passive-resistant exercise. A 15-minute total-body aerobic workout should be followed by a total-body stretching program.

Relief pitchers who throw only a few pitches may want to deviate from this program by eliminating certain phases of the warm-down. A good rule of thumb is to perform the warm-down to the degree of workload in the pitching stint. A relief pitcher who throws for one inning may warm down simply by playing catch, but the starting pitcher who threw 100 pitches would go through the entire program.

Injury to the Pitching Arm

Baseball injuries are of two major types: traumatic (or acute) and overuse. The *traumatic* injury occurs in a specific, sudden manner and may require emergency care. In contrast, the *overuse* injury is caused by a series of ongoing stresses and strains that finally cause functional problems. This type of injury often occurs in the pitcher's arm, usually in the shoulder or elbow, and often has no specific moment of onset. The coach's role in injury care is threefold. First, the coach should be prepared to deal with the on-field injury. In view of today's medical and legal liability atmosphere, every coach should undergo a course in basic first aid and CPR (cardiopulmonary resuscitation). Second, the coach is frequently the person most able to see that the athlete is referred to the most knowledgeable medical professional possible. After a physician diagnoses the athlete, an athletic trainer or a physical therapist should supervise the athlete's treatment and rehabilitation. Third, the coach is the key to modifying and restricting the athlete's activities during the recovery period. Inappropriate activity levels will slow healing time and may cause reinjury.

Most pitching-arm injuries occur either early in the game because of improper warm-up or late in the game when the pitcher is tired. The best way for a coach to treat an injury is to prevent the injury by ensuring that the pitcher is properly rested, warmed up, and not overused in the game.

Injured or Fatigued?

A coach must consider several things when trying to determine whether a pitcher is tired or injured. But to make this determination, the coach must know each of his pitchers. This means that the coach must observe the pitchers constantly.

The number one area of concern is control. Suppose a pitcher starts the game throwing good, low strikes. If his throws edge higher and higher after a few innings, the chances are that he is getting tired. Of course, if the pitcher is throwing high from the outset, then the problem lies elsewhere.

Obvious Indications of Fatigue

- The pitcher takes more time between pitches.
- The pitcher bends over on the mound.
- The pitcher breathes more heavily than normal for a longer time.
- The pitcher's elbow drops during the delivery as fatigue increases.

General Guidelines to Arm Care

1. Wear sleeves below the elbow.
2. Do not warm up while wearing a jacket.
3. Between innings, wear a jacket.
4. When sleeping, wear a long sleeve over the pitching arm (especially in air conditioning).
5. Do not apply ice unless
   - you have swelling or pain, or
   - you have thrown more than five innings.
6. Do not pick up a baseball at any time until
   - you have warmed up the joints,
   - you have stretched the arm, and
   - you have warmed up and stretched the total body.
7. Do not attempt to throw when another body part is injured and affecting the delivery. (Many a pitcher has ruined his arm by changing his motion to protect another injured body part.)
8. Find your natural arm groove (overhand, three-quarter, or in-between) and stay with it. Throw all pitches from one angle.
9. Follow through. The follow-through is the body's way of protecting itself.
10. Learn to read the body's warnings and know when to quit throwing. There is a fine line between pain and fatigue. It is inadvisable to throw with pain, but with supervision it is possible to gain arm strength when throwing while fatigued.

Obvious Indications of Injury or Soreness

- The pitcher shakes or moves his arm between pitches (an indication that the arm is sore).
- Between innings the pitcher does excessive stretching exercises (an indication that the areas being stretched are sore).
- The pitcher decreases his use of a certain pitch and may even completely eliminate the pitch (an indication that he feels pain during that pitch).

Overuse of Pitchers

The hardest decisions a coach ever has to make are those that weigh the welfare of the individual against the success of the team. The pitcher seems to be the player who gets caught in the middle. Many championships, from Little League to high school, have been attained by the overuse of one pitcher, just as many pitching careers have gone down the drain for the same reason. What is more important, a league title or preserving the health of a young pitcher's arm? Unfortunately, many think that winning is paramount. Others sincerely care about the welfare of the individual but don't realize the danger in overusing a pitcher. Winning is wonderful, but winning at all costs is not.

There are many common examples of overusing pitchers. For instance, high school baseball teams often ride the good arm of a pitcher into the state championship. If this pitcher is good enough to take a team to a state championship, he probably has enough

talent to go on to play college or maybe even professional baseball. Why take the chance of cheating a young man out of a college education or a professional contract? It takes exactly one throw too many from an overused pitcher to end his career. Occasionally such a pitcher may be lucky enough to get through the overuse, but he may still lose a college education because he is throwing five to six miles per hour slower than if he were well rested.

Another example is the Little League coach who uses his best pitcher whenever possible to win as many games as possible. How many of these Little League phenomena go on to become successful high school, college, or professional players? A recent survey of college pitchers found that the majority didn't even pitch until high school. (Another interesting fact revealed by the survey is that, of those who did pitch in Little League, the majority did not throw a breaking ball until high school.)

Preventing Overuse of Pitchers

Wise coaching can prevent overuse of pitchers. The following tips will help ensure that pitchers stay healthy.

- Make sure your pitchers get sufficient rest. A complete game requires three to five days of rest from pitching in a game. (A complete game is the length of a regular game at a given level. See table 5.5.) Pitchers should do some

Table 5.5 Protective Pitch-Count Chart for Games

Age	Bullpen pitches[1]	Game pitches[2]	Days of rest[3]	Type of pitch
Under 12	25	5 IP × 15 pitches = 75 total	3-4	FB only
12-13	35	6 IP × 15 pitches = 90 total	3-4	FB and CH
14-16	50	7 IP × 15 pitches = 105 total	3-4	FB, CH, and/or CB
17 and up	50-60	9 IP × 15 pitches = 135 total	4-5	FB, CH, CB, and/or SL

Note. FB = fastball; CH = change-up; CB = curveball; SL = slider; IP = innings pitched.

[1] Bullpen pitches are pitches from the mound, not including playing catch to loosen up.

[2] Game pitches are pitches in any type of competition including regular, practice, or intrasquad games.

[3] Days of rest are days between game appearances and do not include general throwing or between-starts bullpen workouts.

nongame throwing every day, with some normal work between starts to stay sharp.

- If possible, avoid playing pitchers at other positions between starts. If you must play a pitcher, then choose a position with limited throwing (first base) or a position that requires the same throwing motion (outfield). Switching back and forth from a short-arm position (catcher) to a long-arm position (pitcher) is very hard on the arm.

- Safeguard the pitcher's arm by doing the following:
  1. Make sure the pitcher is taking proper care of his arm.
  2. Remember that the better shape the pitcher is in, the more resistance he will have to injury.
  3. Encourage and enforce proper mechanics.
  4. Guard against too many breaking balls.

chapter 6

Creating a Winning Mental Approach

Pitching is an attempt to make the appropriate pitch to the appropriate location at the appropriate speed using knowledge of a hitter's swing, any other pertinent information, and belief in the law of averages to get the batter out. Mental toughness allows the pitcher to remain focused on these things regardless of all the chaos going on around him. The pitcher can focus on the things he can control and not let the things out of his control distract him.

The pitcher with a winning mental approach will appear to rise to the occasion in big games, when in reality he is the one who successfully keeps his head while others around him are distracted by the moment. Many say that mental toughness is an ability that is born into a pitcher, but with some work and effort all pitchers can create a winning mental approach. In this chapter we will look at identifying problems and then offer advice, drills, and practice ideas to help pitchers create a winning mental approach.

Factors the Pitcher Can't Control

The first step to becoming mentally tough is to figure out the factors you can control as a pitcher and those things that are out of your control. The list of things out of your control is much longer than the list of things within your control. First you determine those factors out of your control and then you learn to deal with them.

- **Weather conditions.** These include wind, rain, sun, cold, and heat. You can dress appropriately, but you cannot do anything to control the weather.
- **Field conditions.** These include wet field, dry field, poor field, dimensions of the field, poor lighting, and the height and condition of the mound.
- **Teammates.** A pitcher cannot control his teammates and their play. They may score 0 runs when you pitch; they may

© Yelman/Photri

A pitcher with mental toughness focuses on the pitch and blocks out distractions.

score 10 runs. This is true of errors too. Your team may field great when you pitch or they may make several errors. You can't do anything about errors or run support.

- **Umpires.** Umpires determine their own strike zone, and the pitcher will need to adjust to that zone for the day. A pitcher can't control whether or not the umpire makes all the correct calls during a ball game.

- **Unruly fans and bench talk.** Fans or opponents will try to disrupt a pitcher by verbally abusing him. You can't control fans; when you acknowledge their remarks, it gets even worse. Sometimes opposing teams will try to get a pitcher out of his game by bench talk.

- **The batter.** Once the baseball leaves a pitcher's hand, the batter has the control. The batter decides to swing or take. The batter will determine whether to hit the ball hard by his swing.

The pitcher may affect some of the factors with his performance, but he cannot control them. So he should not worry about them. A pitcher cannot focus on or spend time and energy on things out of his control.

Factors the Pitcher Can Control

A pitcher with a winning mental approach knows that there is only one thing a pitcher has complete control over, and that is himself. Mental toughness starts with the realization of this concept. Be concerned with those things and only those things that a pitcher can control: himself and his actions. A pitcher must first learn to be responsible for himself and his actions.

- A pitcher cannot control the weather, but he can pitch accordingly and give himself a better opportunity to be successful.
- A pitcher cannot control the condition of the field, but he can pitch accordingly and give himself a better opportunity to be successful.
- A pitcher cannot control the play of his teammates, but he can help himself by playing good defense and being positive in the dugout; he can pitch accordingly to ensure his own success.
- A pitcher cannot control umpire decisions; but he can make adjustments to different strike zones, affect umpiring decisions by his actions, and pitch accordingly to ensure his own success.
- A pitcher cannot control what is being said about him or to him from opposing teams or fans, but he can choose whether to let them affect his game.
- A pitcher cannot dictate what the batter will do with a certain pitch; but by studying hitters and learning weaknesses, he can pitch accordingly and ensure his own success.

Instead of focusing on things out of his control, a pitcher must take each set of circumstances and pitch or act accordingly to make himself succeed. Each pitch and each situation involve a new set of circumstances.

How he reacts to each new set of circumstances or situations is within his control, and this is where he can start to make a difference.

Assess the situation, make the appropriate decisions, make the appropriate pitch or play accordingly, and then accept responsibility for the result. Understand that the pitcher starts and affects the action of the game with each pitch more than any other single event in the game; this is crucial for a winning mental approach. The pitcher is the only player on the field who has the power to act. All other players on both teams only have the power to react. Use this power and act accordingly to each new set of circumstances and each new situation to help ensure your own success.

The key to a winning mental approach is not to focus on the things a pitcher cannot control but to be consumed by the things a pitcher can control. Telling a pitcher not to worry about the fan in the fourth row who is riding him hard or not to worry about the umpire whose strike zone appears to be on wheels and is moving around is as effective as telling someone not to think about an elephant that's standing in the room. Instead, create a pitcher who is consumed with the next pitch and is focused on what he can do in the next set of circumstances, no matter the current situation.

Between-Pitch Routines

A routine is something that, when done so many times, becomes automatic and can be executed without thought. A pitcher's routine is his safe haven, a place to go when things get tight. A pitcher should develop a consistent routine for pitching every time he throws a baseball off a mound both during bullpen work and in game situations. He should have a full windup routine and a routine he performs with men on base.

The majority of pitchers have a routine whether they admit it or not. The great pitchers are so into their routines that they are not distracted by the current circumstances and can stay in that routine even when things get exciting. Staying in your routine is a major step toward having a winning mental approach.

Starting the Routine

Upon receiving the ball from the catcher after a pitch, the pitcher starts his routine. As he catches the ball he assesses the current situation—the score, the inning, and runners on base—on his way back to the pitching rubber. On many occasions these things remain the same, and the pitcher can then start to fine-tune his thoughts to the next pitch or in some cases a pickoff attempt. (As the pitcher is walking back to the rubber and facing second base, this is the proper time to give a sign to put on a pickoff play. The runner is going back to the base, the coach at third base is giving the batter his next set of signals, and in most cases no one will notice the signal between the shortstop and the pitcher.)

As the pitcher prepares to step on the rubber to get his signal, he should assess the situation in finer detail. Examples of detail include the speed of the runner on base and the speed of the batter and whether it is a hit and run, stealing, or bunting situation. The coach, the catcher, and even a mentally alert infielder may be of help to alert the pitcher to possibilities and put on a special defense at this time. As long as no pickoff or bunt defense exists, the pitcher is ready to step on the rubber and go to work on the batter.

Preparing for the Pitch

The most important part of a pitcher's job is to focus on getting the batter out. Many pitchers who do not seem to be mentally tough simply have their priorities out of order and tend to concern themselves with the runner or runners and fail to get mentally prepared for the next pitch.

Breathing and Relaxation

Before stepping on the rubber to get the sign, the pitcher will take a deep breath and at the same time relax his shoulders. Many athletes who appear to be lacking mental toughness will simply fail to breathe appropriately and take short, shallow breaths. Deep breathing helps to calm the pitcher and assist with relaxation and focus. During inhalation, the shoulders should rise; the shoulders should drop during exhalation, which will relax the shoulders in preparation for the pitch.

Getting the Signal

When the pitcher has assessed the situation and has an idea what the batter is planning (moving the runner, bunting, or hitting away), the pitcher, with help from the coach or catcher, will determine the pitch and location. Remember to watch the entire set of signals so that the opposing team doesn't try to steal your signs. Finally, make sure that the pitcher is sold on the pitch. If the pitcher does not believe in the pitch, chances are it will not be a quality pitch.

Visualizing the Perfect Pitch

Once all parties concerned (pitcher, coach, and catcher) agree on the pitch, the pitcher will visualize the last five feet of the pitch successfully landing in the exact location with positive results. If the goal of the pitch is to get the batter to swing and miss, then that should be the visualization. Should the pitcher want the batter to hit a groundball to entice a double play, then that should be the visualization. Many times the pitch is simply designed to be out of the strike zone to set up the next pitch. Whatever the desired result, the pitcher should see with his mind's eye the final five feet of the successful pitch.

In essence, the pitcher is throwing each pitch twice: once in his mind and, of course, the real pitch that follows. If at any time the visualization is interrupted (for example, the batter steps out or the pitcher cannot see the perfect pitch in his mind), he should step off the rubber and try again. Thinking negatively and visualizing poor pitches will lead to poor results.

Throwing the Pitch

After the pitcher assesses the situation, determines the location and type of pitch, prac-

Many pitchers perform between-pitch routines that include visualizing a perfect pitch.

tices deep breathing and relaxation, and visualizes the perfect pitch, it's time to pitch the ball. The pitcher must stop thinking at this time and let all his preparation work for him.

Starting Over: The Next Pitch

The pitcher will receive the ball from the catcher or from a position player and begin preparation for the next pitch. The situation and circumstances may have changed a lot or very little. Regardless of the results of the last pitch, this is the next pitch and it is all that matters at this moment. Whatever happened on the previous pitch, it is over and done. Each pitch requires full attention. When a pitcher lets the previous pitch affect his next pitch, the results are usually poor and it may be time to talk to him or remove him from the game.

Working Quickly Between Pitches

The between-pitch routine is an important aspect of creating a winning mental approach.

Close observation of major league pitchers will verify that the best pitchers in the world all practice a between-pitch routine. A pitcher's individual routine must be complete but executed in a 10- to 15-second interval of time. The pitcher who works quickly between pitches has many advantages.

More Alert Defense

When a pitcher works quickly, his defense is more alert and ready to make a play. If the pitcher takes too much time between pitches, the defense tends to lose focus and actually get back on their heels, causing them to be passive and not charge a groundball. It is natural for the mind to wander, and taking too much time between pitches creates more opportunities for the defense to lose focus on the situation.

Shorter Batter Adjustment Time

Batters, just like pitchers, use the time between pitches to make adjustments in their swings. Working quickly gives the batter less time to assess the situation and plan his at-bat.

Hitting is one of the toughest skills in sport; and when a pitcher works quickly, he makes it even harder for the batter to be successful.

Increased Feel for the Release Point

Successful pitchers often attribute good control to their heightened sense of feel of the baseball. Working quickly enables the pitcher to make adjustments between pitches because of the shortened time between pitches. When a pitcher's release point is slightly off, it will adversely affect his control. A short time between pitches helps the pitcher adjust his feel for his release point, which will enable him to command the strike zone.

Umpire Relations

Any umpire will tell you that he prefers calling the game behind the plate when a pitcher works quickly. Umpires get into a rhythm with a pitcher who works quickly and perhaps help that pitcher on an occasional marginal pitch.

Cat and Mouse

When a pitcher and batter try to upset each other's timing by stepping out of the batter's box or stepping off the rubber, this is known as *cat and mouse*. A good hitter will try to upset a pitcher's rhythm by stepping out of the batter's box and force the pitcher to work a littler more slowly. The pitcher must remain in control of the situation by going through his routine again so that he is prepared to pitch and not give in to the batter by getting upset.

A good pitcher will notice when he is facing an anxious batter who cannot wait to hit. The batter may be squeezing the bat exceptionally hard or taking practice swings that are short and choppy. Rather than play into the batter's hands and give him what he wants, the pitcher should choose to purposely slow down between pitches or step off the rubber to create more anxiety in the hitter.

Practicing the Routine

A pitcher should practice his routine every time he is throwing from a mound. This includes both bullpen work and game work. Pitchers have a tendency to rush through their bullpen work and, as a result, are not getting as much out of their bullpen. Young pitchers benefit from the bullpen routine because it gets them ready for the game—they work on signals with infielders and catchers as well as visualization and deep breathing practice.

Pitcher's Self-Assessment

To have a winning mental approach, a pitcher must constantly assess himself. A pitcher has to know his capabilities and his limits and develop his own style of pitching. By discovering what he can and cannot do, a pitcher creates his own identity, figures out how to stay within himself, and does not try to do more than he is capable of. With time a pitcher develops his own style that will follow him throughout his career. He may adjust his style now and then because of his increasing abilities, plateauing ability, or injury setbacks. Self-assessment is an ongoing process: Pitchers will continually try to improve by smoothing out their mechanics, getting stronger and more flexible, developing more velocity, and adjusting grips and release points for better movement and location. Also, the natural maturation process plays a large part in a pitcher's self-assessment and growth.

To Thine Own Self Be True

First and foremost, a pitcher needs to be honest when trying to make an assessment of himself and his abilities. A coach, catcher, and batter will help a pitcher in this process. All pitchers can be successful if they truly understand their strengths and weaknesses, work hard to create their own pitching style, and feed off the things that they do well.

Repeatable Delivery

A pitcher has to work many hours on his mechanics to create a delivery that is not only mechanically sound but also repeatable. A repeatable delivery looks and feels the same and is effective repetition after repetition. Mechanics do not have to be perfect, but they do have to be repeatable. A repeatable delivery leads to a consistent release point, which in turn leads to command. The first pitch of a game should be identical to the last pitch.

Without a repeatable delivery, a pitcher has difficulty assessing the other areas of his game because inconsistencies will lead to misinformation. The pitcher needs to establish a consistent arm slot and release point before he can do any serious work on control, movement, changing speeds, and changing velocity.

Command of Pitches

A pitcher's command of his pitches is the biggest factor in determining success. Command is the ability to throw a particular pitch to a particular location. The higher the level of baseball, the more important command becomes. A 10-year-old pitcher in Little League who can continually throw his pitches into the strike zone is thought to have command. A college pitcher who can just get his pitches over the plate will not be successful unless he has overpowering velocity or outstanding movement. To use an archery analogy, a beginning archer may be happy to hit the target, but an elite archer had better be able to hit the bull's-eye on a consistent basis.

Command does not improve unless a pitcher is accountable for his ability to hit his target. In bowling, archery, skeet shooting, and even basketball, the athlete's score is dictated by his ability to hit his target. In many cases a pitcher can get by with not hitting his target because of overpowering ability, hitter's weaknesses, or luck such as a line-drive hit right at a player. These things reinforce bad habits. A pitcher should be accountable for his pitches and their location. When a batter hits a good pitch (a pitch that would have hit the target), then a pitcher must accept this and tip his hat to the batter. When a pitcher misses his location and retires the hitter, the pitcher should acknowledge that he missed his target and was lucky to retire the batter. A great pitch and a bloop single have to be acknowledged as a good

thing while a poor pitch that is hit hard at a fielder for an out has to be acknowledged as poor performance with a little luck.

When a pitcher begins to understand the importance of hitting his target and judges his performance accordingly, he will begin to improve and create a winning mental approach. A pitcher cannot judge himself and his performance on the results of the at-bat. Over the long run a pitcher who thinks this way will become a better pitcher. When a pitcher has a lack of command, he depends on luck for success.

Staying Within Oneself

Once a pitcher starts to be honest in his self-assessment, he can then learn to pitch by staying within himself, or within the limits of his abilities. The sports world is full of athletes who have failed or have not done as well as they could because they try to do more than they are capable of doing. An example of this in pitching is when the pitcher with the subpar fastball continually tries to throw the baseball past hitters. In this instance perhaps the pitcher should throw his off-speed pitches for strikes and just miss with his fastball. In this way if a hitter chooses to swing at his fastball, at least it will be out of the zone, making it harder to hit.

Another example of going outside oneself is the smaller, faster batter who takes an upper cut and, instead of hitting the ball on the ground and using his speed, hits the ball in the air for easy outs. The sports world is full of successful athletes who have limitations but have learned how to stay within themselves and be successful by focusing their attention on what they can do to be successful.

Developing a Pitching Style

Once a pitcher makes an assessment of his capabilities and limitations and learns to stay within himself, he can then develop his very own style of pitching. The major leagues have the whole range of pitchers, from the classic power pitcher who comes right at the batter with overpowering stuff, to the finesse pitcher who, with a below-average fastball, relies on hitting his spots, changing speeds, and taking advantage of hitters' weaknesses.

The coach, the catcher, and of course the opposing hitters will help the pitcher develop a style to become successful. It merits repeating that all pitchers can be successful if they work hard to figure out what works for them and then put in the time to perfect that style.

As young high school and college pitchers mature they may have to change their styles. It is not uncommon for a physically maturing pitcher's fastball to go from average to above average. This jump in velocity may enable the pitcher to challenge more hitters and use less finesse. Sometimes this adjustment is difficult as a pitcher who has had success by pitching the corners and using finesse can suddenly throw the baseball by most hitters.

When a major league pitcher has an injury or reaches his mid-30s and has lost the pop on his fastball, he either makes an adjustment in his pitching style or gets out of the game. Many major leaguers change their style to survive, but one of the most dramatic changes was that of Frank Tanana, who had success with an overpowering fastball early in his major league career and, after arm problems, became a very successful finesse pitcher late in his career.

Adjustments to style can be mental or physical. Physical adjustments might include a new pitch, a new delivery, or a new arm slot. Pitchers who have a winning mental approach understand the need to develop a style that gives them success, and they make adjustments along the way to stay successful.

Pitching Confidence–Success Cycle

Confidence breeds success, and success breeds more confidence, which leads to more success. A pitcher steps into this cycle from his first pitch in Little League, and the cycle follows him until he puts the ball and glove

© Brian Drake/SportsChrome USA

Once a pitcher determines what combination of pitch, arm slot, and delivery works best for him, he can develop his own pitching style. High school and college pitchers often need to experiment to discover their best combination.

away at the end of his career. At each level of play, from Little League to the major leagues, a pattern develops.

As a pitcher moves up to a higher level, the cycle starts again. Can he continue to get batters out or will he eventually discover that he is no longer effective as a pitcher? When the successes of pitching outnumber the failures, the pitcher continues up the ladder. When the failures start to outnumber the successes, the pitcher either makes adjustments or continues to fail; either he is asked to stop pitching or decides to stop pitching. This is the natural order of things in athletics. A community's Little League may have several players at a young age but only one high school in town. Ultimately the strong survive and continue to play.

With understanding of the confidence-success cycle a coach can help his pitchers to move forward, have success, and create confidence. The good coach knows the rules and teaches skills; the great coach learns the game within the game and creates small building blocks of success so that confidence grows. Just as important is teaching pitchers to handle adversity and bounce back from failure. Pitchers want to succeed, and they will respond especially when they are not doing well. This is the time to teach and reach out to pitchers.

Building Confidence

Young pitchers need to build confidence for their future successes. Standing on a hill in the middle of the field with all eyes following every move is not easy. The hitter, the umpire, both teams, and (unfortunately) the fans grade every pitch. The hitter grades the pitch by swinging or not swinging, while the umpire determines the pass or fail grade rather loudly with the ball or strike call for all to hear. No do-overs are allowed. Inner confidence helps a pitcher to enhance his performance.

To create an environment that fosters improvement, the great coach teaches a pitcher the values of positive self-talk, visualization, acting confident, playing percentages, gauging success, and building a success pyramid.

Using Self-Talk

All psychologists agree that how a person talks to himself is so important in all walks of life. Self-talk is even more important in an activity like pitching because of the nature of the position and the time between pitches. In those 15 to 20 seconds between pitches, a lot of thoughts float around, which a pitcher can use in a positive way or in a harmful way.

There is a positive way of thinking or talking and a negative way of thinking or talking. Coaches, pay attention to what pitchers are saying not only to themselves but to others as well. Encourage positive talk among your team and especially from yourself. "Make the batter hit the ball" or "Go right at the hitter" is so much more positive than "Don't walk this batter." Focus on what you hope will happen as opposed to what you don't want to happen. "Work low in the zone to get a groundball" is a better way to say "Don't throw this batter high fastballs."

You are what you think about. When pitchers' self-talk becomes negative and the coach and his teammates compound that negative self-talk with negative communication, it creates a poor environment for success.

Using Visualization

Many studies by researchers and many testimonials from successful athletes have shown that visualization is a powerful tool for improving performance. Visualization that includes positive results helps to build confidence almost as efficiently as actual successes. Negative visualization obviously can drain confidence almost as efficiently as actual failures. Thinking positive thoughts and seeing success in the mind's eye are very beneficial. Coaches can lead pitchers through situations and coach players into visualization until the players learn to visualize on their own.

For baseball coaches with budget and time restraints, positive visualization is well worth the effort. It's free, it doesn't take much time, and it can be done anywhere and anytime. Take time to learn all you can about visualization and teach your pitchers to visualize success as often as possible.

Acting Confident

For those pitchers who lack confidence and are unsure about their ability to get the job done, coaches must first inform them that the look of no confidence acts as a deterrent to their team and fuels the fire of the opposing team. When a pitcher slumps his shoulders, walks with his head down, or looks unsure of himself, his team will start to take on the same traits and not play as well as they should. The batter's confidence soars when he sees a pitcher who is down on himself or looks beaten. The opposing batters become sharks at a feeding frenzy.

A pitcher must always look confident and in control when on the mound, even when things are not going well. His team will play better behind him, and even the umpires pick up on a pitcher's confidence. The opposing batters will be a little bit unsure of themselves when they are facing a pitcher with confidence.

A lot of research shows that when a person begins to act in a certain way, he begins to *be* that way. The opposing batters, fans, umpires, and his teammates will not know how the pitcher is feeling inside, only how he appears on the outside. Every time a pitcher is on the mound—either in a bullpen situation or in a game situation—he should practice looking confident and in control. When a pitcher has his head up and his shoulders back, he looks confident. When he works fast, doesn't show a lot of emotion about his own or others' poor performance, and doesn't whine or feel sorry for himself, he is acting confident and in control.

A pitcher will appear confident and, in time, will become confident. His performances will be better and he will begin to gain small successes that build his confidence level. Soon how he feels on the inside will match how he appears on the outside.

Playing Percentages

A pitcher can increase his confidence just by understanding the percentages of the game. For example, a good hitter will make an out 7 times out of 10. When a pitcher focuses on the 70 percent chance of getting an out as opposed to the 30 percent chance of a hit, he becomes more confident.

For those pitchers who are afraid to challenge hitters because they don't understand the percentages, have them chart batting practice. A batting-practice pitcher throws pitches right down the middle at greatly reduced speeds with little or no movement, and hitters still make outs 50 percent of the time. A young pitcher sitting behind the pitching screen watching hitters get themselves out in batting practice will grow in confidence. The pitcher can also begin to learn to read swings and look for hitters' weaknesses. This is a great teaching tool for the coach and learning experience for the pitcher.

Gauging Success

A pitcher's judgment of himself and his performance will affect his confidence level. Fans and the media judge pitchers by wins, losses, and saves. When pitchers begin to gauge their own success by these measures, that can begin to erode their true sense of pitching. A pitcher has to understand and believe that he can pitch poorly and win or pitch well and lose. A confident pitcher is concerned about one thing only: whether or not he made his pitch.

The game, outing, or bullpen must be broken down pitch by pitch. A complete game with 100 pitches should be thought of as 100 separate games. Why is it so important to think this way? The only thing a pitcher can control is the pitch. Everything else is beyond his control—what the hitter does with the pitch, whether the umpire calls the pitch correctly, or whether the fielders behind the pitcher make the play. This method of thinking encourages the pitcher to be responsible for each pitch, which encourages him to practice more efficiently, which helps him to become a better pitcher.

A successful pitcher knows that when he makes a great pitch and the fooled hitter hits a flair off the end of the bat for a base hit, he succeeded. A successful pitcher also realizes that when he makes a poor pitch and the hitter lines out to an outfielder on the warning track, he made a poor pitch. The results may be better with the poor pitch, but the pitcher has to realize he made a poor pitch and recognize that he was fortunate to get an out.

The bottom line is that a successful pitcher always gauges his success on one thing: whether he made the pitch, not the result of the pitch. A pitcher can practice acknowledging his success or failure after every pitch in the bullpen. A simple yes or no from the pitcher to the coach or catcher after each pitch will start the pitcher in the right direction of taking responsibility for each pitch. Another player or a coach can chart the success rate based on whether the pitcher hit his spot; then the pitcher can figure out his percentage. This percentage then becomes a teaching tool, a motivator, and a method of gauging success.

Building a Success Pyramid

Confidence does not happen overnight. It is formed gradually with many small successes that in turn lead to larger successes. Picture a pyramid with many small successes on the bottom. The successes get bigger toward the middle of the pyramid, and the top of the pyramid contains a large success. For a pitcher, the bottom of the pyramid (the small successes) represents bullpen workouts. The middle successes may be scrimmages or simulated games, and the larger successes at the top may represent actual games against outside teams.

The coach should always make sure that the pitcher leaves the bullpen with a small success. Small successes might be reaching a certain percentage of strikes, hitting spots, or first-pitch strikes. Pitchers will always have something to work on and a way to keep score for accountability, motivation, and confidence building.

Eventually, as a pitcher has more and more small successes, he should get the opportunity to experience some middle successes during a scrimmage or a simulated game. Depending on the type of pitcher he is, scrimmage successes might include getting ahead, increasing number of groundballs, and increasing number of walks or strikeouts.

When the pitcher is successful in the bullpen and in a scrimmage situation, he may be ready for some outside competition and an opportunity for a large success. The success of the pitcher at each level will determine whether he will move up or down in the pyramid and what his practices will involve. This cycle will continue from the time a pitcher starts pitching in Little League and through high school, college, and professional baseball.

Unfortunately, many pitchers don't get the opportunity to develop using the success pyramid. They are simply cast into large-success opportunities and either sink or swim. Those that succeed seem to keep pitching, and those that fail will eventually lose the desire to pitch or lose the desire to play baseball.

The success pyramid in baseball can be compared to a baby learning to crawl, walk, and run; this comparison shows that the success pyramid works. Each small success is encouraged along the way with positive reinforcement. Someone is always there to lend a hand, encourage the pitcher, and pick him up when he falls down. A baby isn't expected to skip the walking stage and go straight from crawling to running. Many coaches and pitchers expect to be able to skip the process and jump into large-success opportunities and be successful without doing the preliminary work. A pitcher cannot have a large success without a foundation of small successes on which to build.

Earl Weaver, former manager of the Baltimore Orioles, was excellent when it came to developing pitchers at the major league level. His young pitchers always started in middle relief, where he could choose opportunities for success. As they gained experience and small successes, they had opportunities for a spot start, eventually earning the job of starting pitcher.

Structure practices so that each pitcher can get the required repetitions and opportunities for success, and watch them grow and develop into confident, successful pitchers.

Handling Failure and Adversity

The confidence–success cycle will be interrupted from time to time with failure. Because of the uniqueness of baseball, failures will often be individual failures even though baseball is a team game. The baseball will eventually find everyone in the field, and a player either makes the play or he doesn't. The pitcher starts play with the pitch and is therefore more involved with the defense than any other player. For this reason the pitcher's failures are often magnified, and he must learn how to handle failure or he will not be in the game long. Each failure is a learning experience; the way to a successful game, season, or career is to keep failures in perspective, work through failures, learn from mistakes, and make adjustments.

Law of Averages

When a pitcher understands and accepts the law of averages, it helps to explain events that happen in a baseball game. Unlike many sports, baseball has many more opportunities for chance, and the law of averages becomes a greater factor over the long run. Because of the many external factors that affect baseball, the best teams will struggle to win 66 percent of their games. In football the best team will win close to 90 percent of its games. In basketball, the best team will win close to 80 percent of its games. Baseball teams will always have a lower winning percentage.

As a pitcher matures, he begins to understand that many things happen in baseball that are out of his control. The law of averages is the belief that it will all equal out over the long run. (For this reason, baseball is not a good tournament sport; and play-offs are at least in the double-elimination format or, as in professional baseball, a four-out-of-seven series.)

A pitcher must focus on his job and believe that over the course of a season the good-pitch flair hits will equal the poor-pitch line drives that are caught. Umpire calls will also even out over the course of the season. Weather, run support, bad hops, and great plays will also even out over the course of a long season. When a pitcher begins to understand the law of averages he will then begin to focus or refocus on his job of pitching and let the rest take care of itself.

It's What You Do, Not Who You Are

A pitcher must be able to separate what he does and who he is if he expects to play the game of baseball for a long time. The higher the level of baseball and the more that is at stake, the harder this is to do. Sometimes failures begin to snowball and begin to affect other areas of a pitcher's life, and before long that pitcher is failing at many things both on and off the field.

Each pitch is a ball game in itself. A pitcher either hits his spot or he doesn't. The pitch must remain the focus of a pitcher, not the result of the swing. (Percentages prove that if the pitcher makes the appropriate pitch he will be successful a majority of the time.) A pitcher can throw a great game and lose or he can miss his spots the entire game and win. Successful pitchers know this and don't base their self-esteem on the outcome of the game. Pitchers should learn to judge their performance on the pitches they make or don't make.

Sometimes Hitters Win

Pitchers believe that if they make the appropriate pitch with the appropriate speed, movement, and location, it will work 100 percent of the time. But sometimes a hitter will win the battle. In these instances when you did exactly what you wanted to do and the hitter still beat you, you must tip your hat to the hitter. You successfully made the pitch you wanted to make. You did your job and you shouldn't feel bad. Hitters sometimes win.

Comparisons are often made between pitching and other sports such as archery, bowling, and target shooting. These sports are similar in many ways; but in baseball a hitter waits at the other end trying to get the barrel of his bat on the pitch, and sometimes, regardless of how great a pitch it was, the hitter wins.

Turn the Page

The great pitchers know that the past cannot be changed, and they have learned how to turn the page and move on to the next pitch. *All* successful athletes have the ability to refocus after events (both good and bad) that occur during a game. A pitcher has one job to do: make quality pitches that will give his team the best chance to win.

The pitcher who finds himself in a situation where his team is up by several runs may have a natural tendency to relax a bit and lose focus on the next pitch. The focus should remain the same on the next pitch regardless of the score. The strategy may change, but the pitcher should still continue to focus as if the score is 0-0. Pitchers who lose focus in this situation may let the other team back in the game or begin to pitch poorly and be removed from a game before pitching enough innings to get the win. The pitcher who finds himself in a situation where his team is losing by several runs must turn the page and refocus on every pitch to keep the score where it is and give his team the opportunity to come back and win in the late innings.

Remember that baseball does not use a time clock. As Yogi Berra stated, "A baseball game is not over till it's over." History is full of games in which a team blew a big lead or came back to win a game that seemed unwinnable. In both these instances the pitcher on the winning team was able to turn the page, focus on the next pitch, and put his team in a position to win.

Damage Control

Big innings, when a team gives up three or more runs in a single inning, will more often than not determine who wins a ball game. In close to 70 percent of all baseball games, the team that wins scores more runs in one inning than the losing team scores in the entire game.

Very seldom is a big inning the result of the pitcher's giving up several hits in a row; it is usually a combination of events that take place on defense when a pitcher and his team begin to lose focus or try to do things they are not capable of doing. Big innings are usually the result of a combination of hits, walks, errors, and poor judgment.

The mentally tough pitcher is a master of damage control. He may give up a run or two; but he understands that sometimes getting an out—even if it means giving up a run—is more important than trying to do too much by making poor pitches or using poor judgment on defense. When a team is down by a run or two, they still feel as if they can come back and win. However, when a team gives up a big inning and is down by five or six runs, they begin to panic and either give up or try to get it all back at once and begin to play out of character.

When a runner has safely reached third base with zero outs, the percentages show that he is going to score a run 75 percent of the time. Knowing this, the pitcher should stay focused and get out of the inning with only one run. Many times the defense will try in vain to cut off the run at the plate and create more base runners instead of getting the next batter out. When the defense fails to get the runner at the plate, the batter is safe at first, and this is the beginning of a big inning. Instead, the defense should get the out at first base; now there is one out with no one on base.

Many big innings begin when, after a runner reaches base, the pitcher or defense fails to get an out on a sacrifice bunt. Always get an out in a sac bunt situation. Pitchers can become obsessed with base runners and either lose focus for the pitch and walk batters or make a poor pitch and give up a hit. The pitcher or defense will often rush in an attempt to make a great play to get out of a jam. Instead of getting an out, they create more base-running opportunities.

Keys to Stopping the Big Inning

1. Always get an out in a sacrifice bunt situation.
2. Make the batter hit the ball. *No walks.*
3. Stay within yourself.

4. Always make sure you get the first out of a double play.

5. Think ahead and know the situation.

6. Communicate on defense.

Mentally tough pitchers who are successful seldom give up the big inning. They practice damage control and stay focused on getting outs. They stay within themselves and don't try to do things they can't do. They pay attention to base runners but don't lose their focus on the batter and the next pitch.

Make Adjustments, Not Excuses

Taking responsibility for the pitch is a trait of successful pitchers who have mental toughness. Nobody likes excuses, especially from the pitcher who just may be the most important player on the field. Rather than make excuses for poor performance, a pitcher should take responsibility, learn from his experience, and make an adjustment. Here are some examples of poor performance and adjustments that pitchers need to make.

• **Not adjusting to the strike zone.** Each umpire determines his own strike zone. Rather than make excuses about an umpire's strike zone, the pitcher should figure out what his zone is and make an adjustment. Making excuses or throwing a fit will not help a pitcher to win. Getting ahead and throwing a large percentage of strikes is still the way to win regardless of a particular umpire's zone. Once the zone is established, pitch to that zone. The team will also benefit from the knowledge of the zone when they are on offense.

• **Hitters on the plate.** Many hitters stand very close to the plate and sometimes hang out over the plate with their hands. Many do this to create a better opportunity to hit an outside pitch, and some do it simply to distract the pitcher. The batter may have helped himself to hit the outside pitch by making this adjustment, but he has also created a weak spot on the inside part of the plate. Rather than whine or make excuses about the hitter hanging over the plate, the pitcher should make an adjustment and attack the hitter's inside weakness to either get the batter out or back him off the plate to expose his weakness on the outside.

• **Poor mound conditions.** The home team is responsible for taking care of the mound, and the pitcher is responsible for asking the umpire to request that the mound be fixed. On occasion the mound may be as good as it's going to get, and it's still not satisfactory. This instance may call for a move on the pitching rubber or another adjustment.

• **A mound that is too flat or too tall.** Occasionally, a pitcher will run across a mound that does not meet legal standards. Instead of making excuses, a pitcher should make adjustments in his mechanics to adjust to the mound.

When the mound is flat, the pitcher needs to focus on bending at the waist and reaching to the mitt to ensure his release point is still out in front. A tall mound creates the problem of rushing, and the pitcher has to keep his weight back a little longer to compensate. (A coach can build a couple of extra mounds with which to practice before the team goes on the road. In this way a pitcher can get comfortable with the differences before the game, not during the game.)

• **Inclement weather.** Whatever the playing conditions—cold, wet, or windy—the pitcher has to make adjustments and do the best he can. Excuses don't win games. Proper adjustments to the elements will help a pitcher to win.

Cold-weather adjustments include wearing the proper clothing, throwing between innings in foul territory to stay warm, and even pitching inside a bit more because hitters don't like to hit the inside pitch during cold weather. Wet-weather adjustments include requesting a dry ball before the pitch, placing the ball a little deeper in the hand to get a better grip, or having the home team add a drying agent to the mound to prevent slippage. Windy-weather adjustments include keeping an eye on the wind to establish its direction. When the wind is blowing in, the breaking pitch may not break as well, but the ball will not carry as much if a high fastball is hit. When the wind is blowing out, the breaking pitch will break better, and any fastballs up in the zone have a better chance to carry out of the park. Crosswinds will affect pitches as well, so pitchers must pay attention and make adjustments.

At a young age the pitcher will require help from the coach and the catcher to make the proper adjustments. As a pitcher matures, he should be able to better assess the situation and make adjustments on his own. Successful pitchers who are mentally tough make adjustments *before* the fact, not after the damage is done.

Aura of Success

Pitchers who are successful over an extended time develop an aura about them. These pitchers seem to stir the emotions of both the team playing behind them and the team who is trying to hit. This aura also reaches beyond the playing field to the fans at the game and even to the television audience at home.

At any given time there are always a few pitchers who give off this aura. Currently in major league baseball, Randy Johnson, Curt Schilling, Kevin Brown, Greg Maddux, Tom Glavine, Pedro Martinez, and Roger Clemens give off that aura. Several relief pitchers also give off that aura when they come into the game in the ninth inning.

The defense always plays better when that aura is on the mound because they know that they will have a greater opportunity to win. The umpires call more strikes when a pitcher with aura is on the mound. The team who has to hit knows that they will have a bad day before the game begins. When aura is on the mound, there are usually more opponents sick or injured who cannot play.

Opponents expect to fail when they face a pitcher with aura and consider themselves lucky when they win. The TV cameras are caught up in this aura and spend much more camera time on these pitchers. The cameras study the faces of aura, they follow them on and off the field, and watch them between innings as they prepare for the next inning.

Kevin Brown exudes an aura of success and confidence from the mound.

© G. Newman Lowrance/The Sporting Image

What is aura and where does it come from? Why do some pitchers have it and some pitchers with really good stuff don't have it at all? Why do some pitchers have aura their entire careers and some have aura for a season or two and then lose it altogether? Some pitchers have an aura about them in playoffs or big games but don't have it during the regular season. A closer look at the traits of those with aura will uncover more about the mystery of aura.

Inner Arrogance

Inner arrogance is a step above self-confidence. Through years of success, pitchers who have aura have that inner arrogance—that feeling that they are better than their opponents and that they will win every time they step on the field.

Inner arrogance is not to be confused with outward arrogance, which is considered a negative trait in our society. Pitchers who have had success and continue to work hard and have higher expectations for themselves will develop inner arrogance and feel that they are invincible when on the mound. These pitchers are not shaken easily and don't let an occasional bad outing affect how they feel about themselves. Pitchers with inner arrogance love to be in the spotlight and feed off of being called the ace or the stopper. When self-doubt starts to creep in, instead of giving in, they use these doubts to fuel their fire.

Inner arrogance is the belief in oneself and in one's pitches. These pitchers' confidence extends outward, is contagious to their teammates, and creates self-doubt in their opponents.

Ultracompetitor

An ultracompetitor believes that every pitch is a battle and every batter a war. These warriors thrive on the feeling of competition and will never quit or give in to a batter. The ultracompetitor, regardless of the situation, still believes that he can win and will win. Whether running wind sprints, playing a round of golf, or even playing checkers, ultracompetitors love to compete and love to win.

Ultracompetitors at a young age have trouble controlling themselves after setbacks, but with time they learn to control this competitiveness and channel their emotions into preparation for the next competition. These pitchers never want to come out of a game and sometimes are quite put off when a coach or catcher comes out to the mound for a visit.

Baseball has many competitors and even ultracompetitors. The pitcher with aura is the ultracompetitor who has learned to use his competitiveness to his advantage and not be consumed by it.

Amazing Work Ethic

Preparation helps create confidence; pitchers who have aura have learned that good old-fashioned hard work correlates into successful games, seasons, and careers. Many pitchers who have a big year or two but couldn't sustain that success rate simply stop preparing mentally, physically, or nutritionally to stay on top.

Physical Preparation

Pitchers who have aura work year-round on their physical preparation to understand what their body needs for success. This pitcher's body is a machine that he continually fine-tunes for better performance. The physical preparation of the pitcher with aura is a priority, and he realizes the importance of having a routine and sticking with that routine throughout the year. Pitchers who have aura are seldom not physically ready to pitch.

Mental Preparation

Pitchers who have aura mentally prepare for their opponents. They keep journals on the opposing batters and teams and prepare a game plan for success. These pitchers also have a grasp of their own strengths and weaknesses and find a way to be successful. Pitchers with aura have done their homework and, on test day, give themselves every opportunity for success.

Ability to Adjust

Pitchers with aura have learned how to make adjustments. There are many forms of adjustment, and these pitchers are prepared to make the necessary decisions to be successful. Pitchers make tiny pitch-by-pitch adjustments between pitches as well as game-by-game adjustments to the delivery or mental approach to a batter or team. They may need to make adjustments in their physical preparation if the pitcher doesn't feel that he had a peak performance. Nutritional adjustments occur when the pitcher doesn't feel as if he had enough energy to be successful.

Occasionally a pitcher with aura will make adjustments in the off-season to stay on top of his game. A pitcher can tweak his delivery or come up with a new pitch. In many instances wholesale changes take place after an injury or surgery. In these cases the pitcher has to change his physical and mental and even his entire philosophy of pitching. Some power pitchers become finesse pitchers late in their careers when they lose their fastball to age or injury. Many pitchers never make the adjustment and move on to something else.

Pitchers who have aura have learned to make adjustments before they fail. They don't wait until they fail to make that small pitch-by-pitch adjustment or that major philosophy adjustment between seasons.

Defensive Responsibilities

Pitchers who have aura concern themselves with the little things that will help them be successful. These pitchers work hard on fielding practice and expect to make every play. It is no coincidence that the top pitchers in major league baseball have very high fielding percentages. These pitchers also understand the importance of holding runners and keeping runners from taking extra bases to help the team.

Pitchers with aura know where to be and get there on time, whether it's covering first base or backing up the bases in preparation for an overthrow. The mentally tough pitcher understands that once the ball leaves the hand, he is now one of nine defensive players and works hard to help himself and help the team.

Self-Awareness

The pitcher who has that aura is a master at knowing himself. He knows his body and his mind. Before a pitcher can truly be successful he must first understand himself and his body. He acquires this self-awareness through trial and error over an extended time.

For many natural athletes, self-awareness comes easy; however, the majority of mentally tough pitchers need hard work and attention to detail to really know their own bodies and minds. Several pitchers have learned to keep notes about what works and what doesn't work concerning their bodies, nutritional needs, workout programs, and recovery programs.

Successful pitchers leave as little as possible to chance or superstition by observing and taking notes. Eventually a pitcher will develop a plan for success and, through years of attention to detail, give himself the greatest opportunity to win.

When the mentally tough pitcher develops a winning routine for success, he has the fortitude to stick with his plan and make only minor adjustments in preparing himself for success. His belief in his system is a large component of his success, and he takes that aura to the mound with him whenever he pitches.

chapter 7

Choosing and Implementing a Game Strategy

Pitching strategy involves the decisions about which pitches to throw and in what locations. Pitch-by-pitch strategy, inning-by-inning strategy, and game strategy also come into play. Strategy is determined by the pitcher's strengths, the situation, and the hitter's weaknesses. Occasionally the weather, field, and pitcher's health are factors in determining a strategy.

This chapter covers successful strategies that pitchers can use to foil the opponent's attempt to score runs. A pitcher's talent is God-given, but even the least talented pitcher can win if he learns to use what he has in the right situation.

Pitch Strategies

The fastball, change-up, and breaking ball have distinct characteristics, and call for distinct situations.

Fastball

The fastball is every pitcher's basic pitch, and every pitcher must master control of it. There are tailing, sinking, and straight fastballs.

Here are some important concepts to remember when throwing the fastball:

- The number one concern of the pitcher when throwing the fastball is location. When the pitcher masters control, the next concern is movement. Velocity is the least important aspect.

- One inch of movement is worth two miles per hour. Generally speaking, when a pitcher throws his hardest, the ball tends to straighten out. The pitcher must find the fastball speed that has the most movement and stay with it.

- Changing speeds with the fastball is an art that helps make a pitcher successful. A pitcher who can take off some speed or add extra speed when needed will usually be very successful, as long as he has control.

Pitching Inside

"Pitch in to win." This is so important for a pitcher, but it is almost a forgotten art. A pitcher must control the strike zone to be effective. Many of today's hitters are taught to extend their arms when hitting and, because of the success of the slider, to stay in and hit the low-and-away pitch to the opposite field. The only defense a pitcher has today is to pitch to the inner third of the plate. The pitcher should make the batter respect the fastball on the inside corner and make him know that the pitcher will come inside five or six inches at any time to set up the low-and-away pitch.

To hit a good fastball in on the hands, the batter has to have a very quick bat, which most batters from the college level down do not have. Most balls hit on the inside are either handle-type hits or, if the batter is quick enough to get the barrel of the bat around, foul balls. Many young pitchers think that the better the hitter, the more he should be pitched away. In most cases just the opposite is true. Good hitters are good hitters because they extend their arms when hitting. Therefore, a pitch away from this batter will be easier to hit. A pitcher must make the hitter hit the inside fastball. If, after pitching inside to a hitter, it is clear he is turning on the fastball, then it is time to change speeds to take advantage of the quick bat.

Moving hitters off the plate is necessary for success. A hitter who crowds the plate or steps toward the outside of the plate should be moved back occasionally. Many times pitchers with good breaking balls should win, but they don't win because the hitters look for the breaking ball away from them. Throwing an occasional fastball inside will keep the hitter honest.

Facts About Pitching Inside

The following facts apply to inside pitching:

- All pitchers can and should pitch in. It doesn't take a 90-mile-per-hour fastball to pitch in.
- A pitcher who is afraid to pitch in will not be successful in the long run. He may have success initially, but eventually hitters will begin to catch on and will be ready for pitches out over the plate.
- Often a high-and-tight pitch is followed by a low-and-away breaking ball. Sometimes it is smart to come back with an-

other inside fastball. Hitters will discover a pattern, so pitchers should not become predictable.
- As a general rule, a four-seam fastball is easier to control than a two-seam fastball. (The two-seam fastball has a tendency to move.) Rather than take a chance on producing the wrong movement when throwing a brushback, a pitcher should use a four-seamer. Of course, a great pitch is a moving fastball that starts out over the plate and breaks into the hands.
- Pitching inside adds a couple of feet to the fastball. An 80-mile-per-hour pitch on the inside will seem like 82 miles per hour because of where the batter has to hit the ball. The batter must hit the inside fastball out in front of the plate to avoid getting jammed. This cuts down the distance between ball release and bat contact, giving the batter less time to react and swing at the pitch. Although it really doesn't give the pitch more velocity, pitching inside does make the pitch *seem* faster. This is why pitching inside is more important for a pitcher who doesn't have great velocity than for a pitcher with good velocity.

Many pitchers are afraid to throw a fastball at or around the hitter's hands. They fear hitting the batter, being hit by the batter, and, of course, walking the batter.

Fear of Hitting the Batter

Coaches and parents, through their reminders that a baseball can kill, often instill this fear in young pitchers. And some pitchers may indeed have hit and even injured a batter in the past.

Hitting the batter is a reasonable fear, but it has no place in the good pitcher's mind. A pitcher should *never* try to hit a batter intentionally, but one who frequently pitches inside will inevitably hit a few batters. A pitcher should never have to pitch more than six inches inside to be effective. If the batter can hit the pitch six inches inside, then it is impossible for him to hit it on the outside of the plate.

Technically, the batter can't get any closer than six inches to the plate because of the batter's box. The purpose of the batter's box is to keep the batter from standing on top of the plate. Should a batter lean into the six-inch dead space, then he is to blame for getting hit, not the pitcher.

Fear of Being Hit

Few hitters have bats that are quick enough to get around on an inside fastball. And should the hitter hit the inside fastball, he usually pulls it into foul territory.

The fastball over the inside corner of the plate is used to jam the hitter and works on most batters (exceptions are the rare hitter with an exceptionally quick bat and the batter who steps in the bucket). The fastball thrown six inches inside at the hands is used to set up a later pitch on the outside part of the plate.

Fear of Walking the Batter

If the pitcher doesn't throw inside because he lacks confidence and thinks that he should throw only strikes, then he needs to work on his control in the bullpen and should not pitch in a game until he has mastered control of his fastball.

Significance of Velocity

Hitting a round baseball squarely may just be the toughest skill in all of sport. The hitter has less than half a second to see the pitch and decide to swing. Obviously, the faster the pitch, the less reaction time a hitter has to decide to swing the bat. Having good velocity is a big advantage, but velocity without command is useless.

The pitcher with good velocity does not need the command of a pitcher with average stuff because of the hitter's decreased reaction time with a high-velocity pitch, but he still has to throw strikes. The less velocity a pitcher has, the more important location becomes.

Change-Up

Three important concepts are involved in the change-up, regardless of what grip is used. First, a change-up should always be low in the strike zone. Second, it should always be 10 to 12 miles per hour slower than the fastball.

When to Use the Change-Up

1. When the hitter takes a big stride
2. When the batter is considered a pull hitter
3. When the hitter's front foot pulls out
4. After the batter has pulled a fastball foul
5. As a first pitch when the batter is a first-pitch fastball hitter
6. Any time the hitter is sitting on a fastball because the pitcher is behind in the count (2-0, 2-1, 3-1, 1-0)
7. When there are no outs with a man on second and a right-handed hitter up

When Not to Use the Change-Up

1. When the pitcher is ahead of the batter (unless the change-up has a big break)
2. When an opposite-field hitter is up
3. When the hitter has two strikes (unless the change-up has a big break)
4. When there are fewer than two outs with a man on first and a left-handed hitter up
5. When there are no outs and a runner is on second with a left-handed batter up

If the change-up is fast, the hitter's timing will not be thrown off. If it is too slow, then the hitter can readjust his timing and take a good swing. Third, the change-up delivery must be identical to the fastball delivery. If the pitcher slows down his windup or his arm, then the hitter knows a change-up is coming.

Used wisely, the change-up can get a pitcher out of a jam. It can also make the fastball appear faster than it really is; and because it places less strain on the arm, it may prolong a pitcher's appearance in the game.

Breaking Ball

Both the curveball and the slider are breaking balls—both are designed to break away from the side of the pitcher's arm. Breaking balls can be used in a variety of ways depending on a pitcher's control and the speed and break of the breaking ball.

A pitcher must remember four concepts when throwing a breaking ball:

1. The amount of break and the location go hand in hand. The smaller the break, the more important location becomes; the bigger the break, the less important location becomes.

2. Breaking balls thrown waist-high usually get hit hard unless the batter is guessing that a fastball is coming.

3. Breaking balls are most effective when they are low and on the outside of the plate. The exception is when the batter is looking for the fastball (for example, when the pitcher is behind in the count).

4. Breaking balls do not have to be strikes to be effective. Often batters swing at breaking balls that are not strikes, and other times a breaking ball for a ball can be used to set up a fastball.

Command of Two or More Pitches

The pitcher who has command of two, three, or even four pitches is at a great advantage. Imagine the hitter's dilemma when he knows that the pitcher can throw any of his pitches in any situation.

When to Use a Breaking Ball

1. When the hitter pulls his head away from the ball
2. Any time the hitter is looking for a fastball (for instance, on the first pitch or on a count of 2-0, 2-1, or 1-0)
3. When a left-handed hitter who hits the ball to the opposite field is up to bat, because breaking balls will make him pull the ball
4. Right after a previous breaking ball, because many hitters guess fastball after a breaking ball, making three or four breaking balls in a row effective sometimes

When Not to Use a Breaking Ball

1. When the hitter is outmatched by the fastball (unless the breaking ball is thrown as an intentional ball)
2. When the hitter has a slow bat and is looking for off-speed pitches (unless the breaking ball is thrown as an intentional ball)
3. When the runner at first base is stealing, because a fastball gives the catcher a better chance to catch him (although sometimes a steal is inevitable and a breaking ball must be thrown)
4. To a left-handed hitter with no outs and a man on second base, because the batter will pull the ball

Lower-level pitchers who are first learning an off-speed pitch have no choice but to throw the off-speed pitch when they are ahead in the count (0-2, 1-2, or 2-2). Because they have not mastered the pitch, they are more than likely going to throw a ball. If the hitter swings, there are no problems. If the pitch is a ball, then again there is no damage because the pitcher was ahead in the count. The pitcher can always come back with his fastball.

In the upper levels of baseball—high school, college, and professional—this philosophy starts to backfire. The hitter now realizes that the pitcher can't control his off-speed pitches and throws them only when the pitcher is ahead. The hitter can look for an off-speed pitch, knowing, of course, that it most likely will be a ball. When the count gets even or the pitcher gets behind, the hitter knows that the pitcher will throw the fastball.

When the pitcher has mastered his off-speed pitches, he can throw them any time, no matter what the count. When the pitcher is behind in the count, the hitter is usually looking for a fastball. This is an ideal time for an off-speed pitch. Counts such as 1-0, 2-1, 2-0, and 3-1 are ideal counts for throwing something off-speed. The hitter is looking for a fastball and most likely will not hit the ball hard if the pitcher can throw an off-speed pitch for a strike.

As noted in previous chapters, the fastball is the first pitch that the pitcher should master and be able to throw when and where he wants. When the hitter is looking for an off-speed pitch, the fastball will catch him off guard, and he won't be able to catch up to the pitch.

In lower levels of baseball the tendency is to get ahead with fastballs and throw off-speed pitches to get the hitter out. In upper levels of baseball, just the opposite is true. When the pitcher is ahead in the count, he might throw fastballs to get the hitter out. When behind in the count, the pitcher might throw off-speed pitches because the hitter is looking for a fastball.

Control of two, three, or even four pitches allows the pitcher many more choices of pitches to throw to the batter in any situation.

More choices means that the hitter has more to think about, and decisions take time. The more decisions the hitter has to make, the greater the chance that he will fail.

Intangible Strategies

Intangible strategies include working fast, upsetting a hitter's rhythm, getting ahead of the hitter, establishing pitch location and consequences, getting hitters out with balls, and reducing walks that score. All of these strategies are important to the winning pitcher because he can use in his favor not only his pitching skills but also statistics and psychology.

Working Fast

Taking very little time between pitches can be very effective and may help the pitcher in several ways:

- Hitters tend to get upset and often are not ready to hit when the pitch is delivered. (To upset the pitcher's pace, hitters are instructed to repeatedly step out when a pitcher is working fast.)
- Pitchers who work fast usually have a better defense behind them. A pitcher who works slowly makes his fielders relax and lose their mental or physical readiness to make a play. Fielders are alert when playing behind a fast-working pitcher.
- Umpires like to call strikes when a fast-working pitcher is throwing. (This reason alone is enough to make a pitcher work quickly.)
- The faster a pitcher can get his team off the field, the sooner they can start scoring runs.
- Often a successful pitcher who is working fast has a hypnotic effect on the opposing team. Before they figure out what is going on, it is the eighth or ninth inning.
- With a fast-working pitcher, a team can play a game in a shorter time. This helps out everyone on the team.

Working fast should not be confused with rushing. When working fast, the pitcher uses his regular delivery; he just takes less time between pitches. (Young pitchers in particular tend to rush when trying to work fast.) After receiving the ball back from the catcher, the pitcher should simply check his fielders and any base runners, get the sign, and make the pitch. He makes absolutely no change in the delivery. (If a pitcher saves 10 seconds per pitch at 100 pitches per game, the game will be 17 minutes shorter. If both pitchers work fast, they can save up to half an hour.)

Upsetting a Hitter's Rhythm

Working fast is very important; sometimes it is necessary to play games with the batter. When an aggressive hitter steps into the batter's box and it appears as though he can't wait to hit, it may be appropriate to step back off the rubber and rub up the ball or talk to the catcher. Many times these mind games will make the hitter impatient, angry, or both. Of course, an impatient hitter is easier to get out. Hitters will try to shake the pitcher using the same tactics, so pitchers need to learn to ignore mind games and concentrate on getting the hitter out.

Getting Ahead of the Hitter

It is not uncommon to hear a coach yell at his pitcher, "Get ahead of the hitter." This means to throw strikes early in the count so that the hitter will have to hit the pitcher's pitch instead of the hitter's pitch. Statistics listed in table 7.1 show the importance of getting ahead of the hitter. (Notice that hitters who hit the first pitch hit only .228.)

Good hitters generally look for a pitch in a particular zone. Getting ahead of the hitter takes away this option—he now has to hit what is given him. Hitters basically become defensive when behind in the count.

Conversely, many pitchers are so obsessed with getting ahead in the count that they continually throw fastballs for the first pitch. *Pitchers must not become predictable.* Pitchers who repeatedly throw fastballs on the first pitch eventually get hit very hard. Hitters

Table 7.1 Batting Averages on Specific Counts

Count	Batting average*	Batting average**
0-2	.118	.170
1-2	.151	.182
2-2	.169	.205
0-0	.186	.228
3-2	.192	.253
0-1	.199	.215
3-0	.267	.286
1-1	.269	.276
2-1	.290	.288
3-1	.329	.355
1-0	.342	.338
2-0	.386	.392

*Division I college baseball 1983 to 1987 (308 games)

**Division I college baseball 1996 to 2000 (314 games)

will anticipate the fastball and be prepared to hit it. Of course, a fastball for a strike is better than a breaking ball for a ball.

Pitchers must learn to mix in a breaking ball on the first pitch to keep the hitter honest. Good hitters often take a breaking ball for a strike simply because they are waiting for a fastball. This is a great opportunity to get ahead of the hitter.

A change-up is not a good pitch to throw on the first pitch in most situations, particularly the first time around the order. However, there are times later in the game when it is effective.

It is important to note that, even if a pitcher throws the fastball on the first pitch and it gets hit, it is still better than throwing another pitch for a ball. Remember that first-pitch hitters hit only .228 on the count chart.

Establishing Pitch Location and Hard-Hit Balls

Pitch location, or control, is the most important aspect of pitching. The more control a pitcher has, the more easily he can exploit hitters' weaknesses. All hitters have specific locations that give them trouble, and a pitcher with good control can pinpoint those spots and exploit hitters' weaknesses.

Table 7.2 shows hard-hit averages for pitch locations along with certain tendencies for left- and right-handed batters. Obviously, the middle of the plate yields the most hard-hit balls for both groups. Right-handed hitters generally have more trouble with the low, inside pitch than do left-handers. The opposite is true for outside pitches—right-handers seem to hit the outside pitch harder than left-handers.

The dominant-hand theory offers an explanation of why left-handed batters hit the low, inside pitch so well. Many players who hit left-handed are otherwise right-handed. Their dominant hand is on the bottom of the bat when they hit, which may cause the swing to be an uppercut, pull swing. This theory also explains why left-handers generally have trouble with the high, inside pitch. It is hard to uppercut a high pitch.

Similar reasoning can explain why right-handed hitters hit the high, inside pitch so well. If a right-handed batter's dominant hand is the right hand, then the dominant hand is on top during batting. This causes the hitter to swing down on the ball, making it easier to hit the high, inside pitch.

When a pitcher doesn't know anything about the opposing team, he can pitch according to the dominant-hand theory: He can pitch left-handers up and in and low and away and pitch right-handers low and in and up and away.

Getting Hitters Out With Balls

Often the pitcher's best pitch is not a strike but an intentional ball. Many successful pitchers have said that to get hitters out, a pitcher must get ahead with strikes and get the hitter out with balls. This is an excellent philosophy, but once again, to do this a pitcher must have control of his pitches.

All hitters have a certain pitch they will chase. It is up to the pitcher to determine the hitter's weakness here. Many hitters like a high fastball because they can see it much more easily than a low pitch. When a batter swings at a high fastball, he must have liked it—so why not give him another one just a little bit higher? Many batters like inside fastballs and will swing at a fastball two to six inches inside.

A smart pitcher gets ahead of the batter and then nibbles the corners or continually works the baseball up on the hitter. The pitcher makes the hitter show him what he likes and then throws that very pitch, but he misses by just a couple of inches. Many times a pitcher knows that the hitter is a dead-fastball hitter and throws him only off-speed pitches. If the pitcher has excellent off-speed pitches, this strategy will probably work. On the other hand, the pitcher can take advantage of the hitter's love of the fastball by throwing him fastballs that are just off the plate. The hitter will swing, fearing that he may not get another fastball, and probably will not hit the ball with much authority because of its location.

Reducing Walks That Score

By going back through the scorebook after the season, a coach or pitcher can get a general idea of how bad walks are for a team. Table 7.3 shows the approximate percentage of walks that score over the course of a season. These statistics were taken from Division I college baseball, where double plays are standard procedure. The percentage would obviously be higher in high school.

Table 7.2 Hard-Hit Average Chart

Pitch location	Right-handed batter		Left-handed batter	
	*	**	*	**
Low and inside	2.13	2.41	3.62	3.05
Low and middle	3.72	3.86	2.89	3.16
Low and away	2.53	2.78	1.81	2.22
Belt and in	2.41	2.53	3.52	3.25
Belt and middle	4.12	4.19	4.21	4.28
Belt and away	2.61	2.93	2.14	2.52
Up and in	2.35	2.48	1.93	2.10
Up and middle	2.71	2.91	2.64	2.78
Up and away	1.92	2.16	2.08	2.21

*Division I college baseball 1983 to 1987 (308 games)

**Division I college baseball 1996 to 2000 (314 games)

Table 7.3 Percentage of Walks That Score

Total walks	2391
Walks that scored	694 (29%)
Leadoff walks	521
Leadoff walks that scored	198 (38%)
Ninth-hitter walks	148
Ninth-hitter walks that scored	58 (39%)
Leadoff ninth-hitter walks	46
Leadoff ninth-hitter walks that scored	20 (43%)

Note. Data gathered from 10 years of Division I college baseball.

About 20 to 40 percent of walks score, depending on how good the defense is at turning the double play. Notice that the percentage goes up when the leadoff man is walked, because three men are now behind him to hit him in. The percentage goes up a little more when the ninth batter is walked, because the top of the order is up behind him. (The ninth-place hitter is always the weakest hitter and should never be walked.)

Calling Pitches

Pitchers must consider three things when deciding what pitch to throw. First, the situation often dictates how a batter will be pitched. The situation is always changing, so it is best just to stay alert and know what is happening on the field. Second, the pitcher's strengths are equally important, because the pitcher must throw his best pitches. He can learn his own strengths by spending time with the pitchers in the bullpen and by talking with the catcher about what is working and what is not. The third is the hitter's weaknesses. The pitcher can pick up on the hitter's weaknesses through observation. Pregame batting practice or even the hitter's practice swings in the on-deck circle might tip something off.

Game Situation

Pitch selection and location are important in various game situations. The following are some examples.

A runner is on second base with zero outs. The pitch should be inside to a right-handed hitter and outside to a left-handed hitter. The pitcher hopes the ball will be hit to the left side of the infield so that the runner cannot advance to third base.

A double play is needed. The pitcher should try to throw a pitch at the knees with some kind of sinking movement to instigate the double play.

The field has a short fence. The pitcher should try to make the hitter hit the ball to the longest part of the park. If left field is short, the pitcher should work the right-handed power hitters away and the left-handers in.

The game is on the line. Any time the game is on the line, the pitcher should use his best pitch.

There is a definite bunt situation. In the definite sacrifice-bunt situation (close game, zero outs, runner on first base or runners on first and second base), the pitcher should throw fastballs. There is some controversy as to which fastball location—high or low—is the most difficult to bunt. Obviously, excellent out pitches, such as a great slider or hard curveball, would be difficult to bunt. However, most pitchers have more success throwing a fastball.

Often, by hesitating for a long time before pitching, stepping off the rubber, or trying an inside move to second base, the pitcher can get the hitter to square around early and tip off the bunt. When the hitter squares early, he might also tip off a weakness for a certain location of the fastball. If the hitter holds the bat low, a high fastball would be in order because the hitter will have to come up to get the ball, increasing his chances of popping it up. If the hitter starts the bat high, a low fastball would be in order, making the bat travel farther and making it harder for the eyes to pick up the ball.

Pitcher's Strengths

Whoever is calling the pitches—be it the coach, catcher, or pitcher—must know the pitcher's strengths and weaknesses. The person calling the pitch must know three things about the pitcher:

- What is the pitcher's best pitch?
- What are the pitcher's two or three pitches?
- What pitch is working and what pitch is not?

If the pitch caller doesn't know the pitcher, he may ask the pitcher to do things he is not capable of doing. The team must use the pitcher's strengths and make the hitter hit the pitcher's best pitches.

Hitter's Weaknesses

The art of calling pitches is to pitch to the hitter's weaknesses. The pitcher needs to watch the hitter, learn his habits, and study his mechanics. Does the hitter have a mechanical flaw? If so, the pitcher must try to exploit it. Pitchers should learn some habits of hitters and how to pitch to these types of hitters. Table 7.4 shows some hitter weaknesses and how to pitch to these weaknesses.

Here are some things to consider when calling pitches:

- Is the hitter a good fastball hitter, or does he like the slower stuff?
- Does the hitter frequently swing at the first pitch?
- Is the hitter aggressive? Will he swing at bad pitches?
- Does the hitter have any mechanical flaws?

Who Calls the Pitches?

Who should call the pitches has been the topic of many conversations in baseball circles. Many think that the pitcher should call his own game. Others think that the catcher is in a better position to call the pitches.

Table 7.4 Pitching to the Hitter's Weaknesses

Hitter's habits	Out pitch	Setup pitch
Sweeping bat	FB in	Miss outside
Loop in swing	FB in	Miss outside
Slow bat	FB in	Miss outside
Hitch in swing	FB up	Miss off-speed
Step in bucket	Breaking ball away	Miss FB in
Steps to ball	FB in	Breaking balls away
Lunges	Off-speed or FB up	Miss FB
1-2 count, on toes	FB in	Miss FB away
1-2 count, on heels	Away	FB in
Very aggressive	Change speeds, nibble corners	Same
Good FB hitter	Breaking ball, change-up	Miss with FB
Good CB hitter	FB	Miss with CB
2 strikes, goes opposite way	Bust FB in	Miss with CB away
Pulls everything	Outside corner	Miss in
Guess hitter	Mix up pitches	Mix up pitches
Stands away from plate—steps away from plate	Outside corner	Miss in
Stands away from plate—steps toward plate	Inside corner	Miss away
Golf swing	Pitch up	Miss low
Hits off front foot	CBs or FBs up	CBs or FBs up
Front shoulder starts down	Low in zone	Low in zone
Front shoulder starts up	Up in zone	Up in zone

Note: FB = fastball; CB = curveball.

Still others believe that the coach should call all or some of the pitches. The following is an examination of each of these claims.

Pitcher

Being a former pitcher, my choice is for the pitcher to call his own game. After all, who gets the win or loss? Who actually throws the pitch? The catcher catches, and the coach watches.

The pitcher should throw the pitch he wants to throw. For example, the count is 1-2. The pitcher wants to throw a fastball in on the hands. The coach signals to the catcher that the pitcher should throw a curveball low and away. The pitcher is thinking about jamming the hitter with a fastball while he's trying to throw a curveball low and away. The result is that the subconscious overrules the conscious—a hanging curve, which can be hit hard. All players and coaches have seen this happen. A classic example of this phenomenon is trying to shoot a basketball from the one spot on the floor where the shooter doesn't know whether to bank it or shoot it straight in. The result is the same. The ball goes somewhere between, and the shot is missed.

I would rather have the wrong pitch thrown with the pitcher's firm belief behind it than the right pitch thrown by a doubting pitcher. If the pitcher is expected to simply be a robot for his catcher or coach, he will never truly learn the art of calling a game.

Catcher

A good argument for the catcher to call pitches is that he is in the best position to see where the batter stands in the box. This would be of great value if the coach, pitcher, or catcher knew absolutely nothing about the hitter except where he stood in the box.

Another excellent argument for the catcher's calling the pitches is that only he can tell what pitch is working best for a pitcher on a particular day. For example, the situation might call for a fastball in on the hands. The catcher may realize that the pitcher's fastball has slowed down and straightened out and therefore it may be best to try something else.

Coach

The obvious argument for the coach to call the pitches is that he should be much more knowledgeable about pitch selection. In many cases this is true, but in some cases it is not.

Many coaches believe that if the coach calls the pitches, the pitcher and catcher can learn how to call games by osmosis. Still another view is that by calling the pitches, the coach takes pressure off the catcher and pitcher so that they may concentrate on other phases of the game. (Of course, even though the pressure is off, the pitcher still gets the loss!)

Any one philosophy cannot work all of the time. For example, a freshman catcher and a senior pitcher are on the field. The pitcher should be more experienced and knowledgeable. Reverse the situation and the opposite is true. Now suppose the catcher and pitcher are both freshmen. The coach needs to advise in this situation. There are too many variables for any one of these systems to be adequate.

Many coaches let the pitcher or catcher call the game until a crucial situation arises. This may work on occasion; but if the coach takes over every time the pressure is on, the pitcher and catcher never learn to take responsibility in choosing their moves. They have to learn to deal with adversity some time.

Scouting Hitters

When a team plays another team several times, a scouting chart can be a very good tool for learning about individual hitting patterns. Figure 7.1 presents a sample player chart showing some of the batter's hitting traits. (A blank copy of this chart is given in chapter 9.)

After facing this hitter a few times, the team noticed that (1) the hitter tries to pull all pitches, (2) the hitter has trouble with breaking pitches away, and (3) the hitter is susceptible to changing speeds. After tracking the hitter through several at-bats, they developed a plan of defensing him. It would be to the defense's advantage to play the batter four or five steps pulled. Of course, by keeping track of bunt attempts and stolen base attempts, they can determine what the hitter

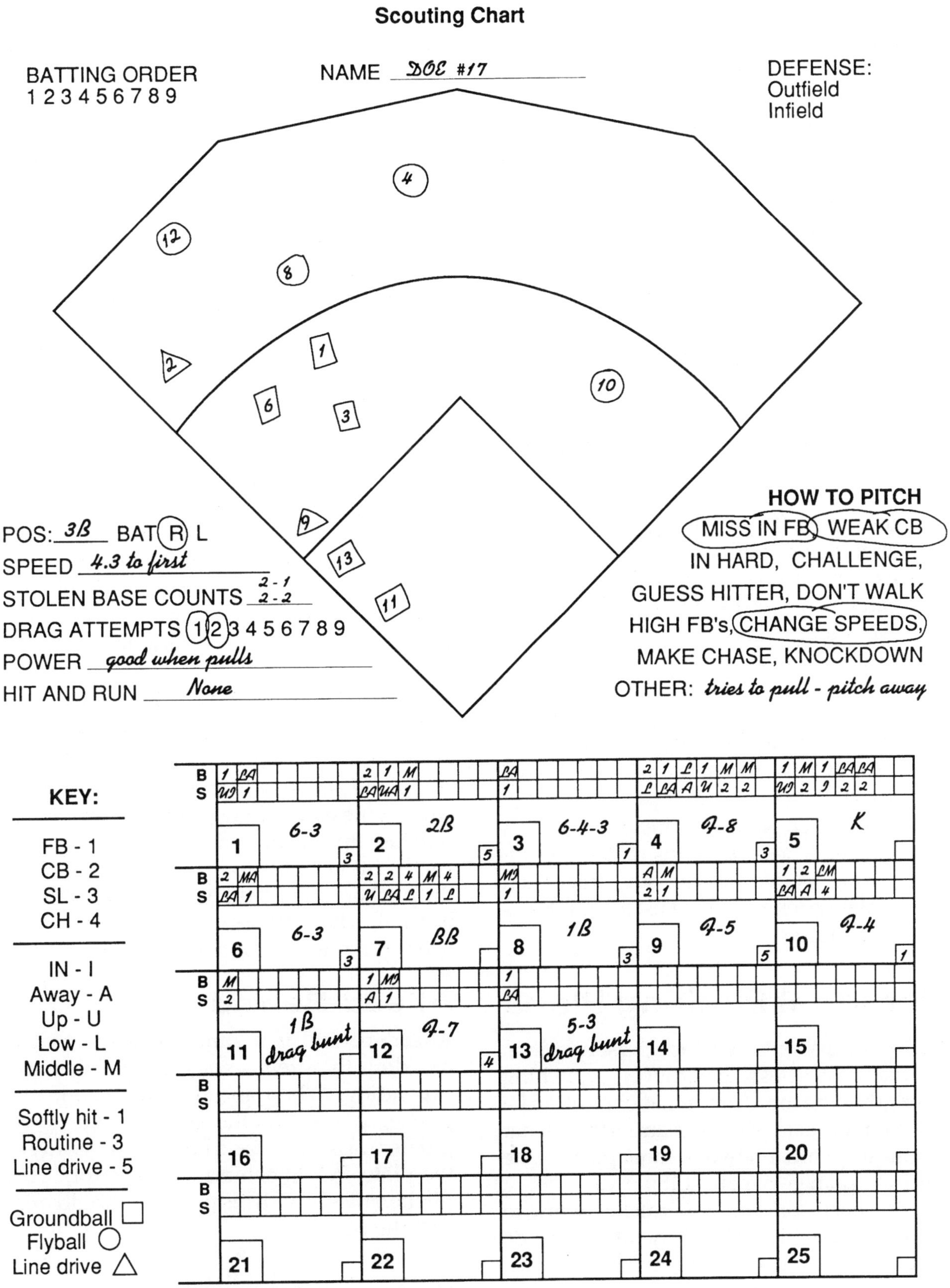

Scouting Chart

BATTING ORDER
1 2 3 4 5 6 7 8 9

NAME _DOE #17_

DEFENSE:
Outfield
Infield

POS: _3B_ BAT (R) L
SPEED _4.3 to first_
STOLEN BASE COUNTS _2-1_ _2-2_
DRAG ATTEMPTS (1)(2) 3 4 5 6 7 8 9
POWER _good when pulls_
HIT AND RUN _None_

HOW TO PITCH
(MISS IN FB) (WEAK CB)
IN HARD, CHALLENGE,
GUESS HITTER, DON'T WALK
HIGH FB's, (CHANGE SPEEDS,)
MAKE CHASE, KNOCKDOWN
OTHER: _tries to pull - pitch away_

KEY:

FB - 1
CB - 2
SL - 3
CH - 4

IN - I
Away - A
Up - U
Low - L
Middle - M

Softly hit - 1
Routine - 3
Line drive - 5

Groundball □
Flyball ○
Line drive △

1 6-3	**2** 2B	**3** 6-4-3	**4** 9-8	**5** K
6 6-3	**7** BB	**8** 1B	**9** 9-5	**10** 9-4
11 1B drag bunt	**12** 9-7	**13** 5-3 drag bunt	**14**	**15**
16	**17**	**18**	**19**	**20**
21	**22**	**23**	**24**	**25**

Figure 7.1 Sample hitting traits chart.

will do in many situations. The more data a team can obtain, the better their odds are of defending against the hitter.

Many teams, particularly college teams and some high school teams, now rely on scouting reports of opposing teams. Scouting reports can give a pitcher a good indication of hitters' strengths and weaknesses. How these reports are used can determine the success or failure of a pitcher.

Teams must consider three factors when using scouting reports:

- The report must be reliable.
- Pitchers must consider their own strengths before considering hitters' weaknesses. Many a game has been lost because the pitcher used his second- or third-best pitches in response to a scouting report. If a pitcher is going to lose, he should lose with his best pitches. For example, the report on a hitter is that he can't hit a high, hard fastball because he has a lunging problem. If a good hard-fastball pitcher is pitching, he should go with the report. If a sinker-ball pitcher is throwing, he ought to pitch his game and not try to throw it by the hitter but stay around the knees and try to get groundballs.
- The coach should consider using a pitcher whose strengths match the opposing team's weaknesses rather than make a pitcher try to adjust to the hitter's weaknesses.

Personal Pitching Plans

Each pitcher should develop a personal pitching plan that is designed around his pitching strengths. The more command of location he has, the more extensive the plan. As the pitcher begins to command two or three pitches, the pitching plan gets more complex.

The coach, pitcher, and catcher work to develop a pitching plan. When they decide on a plan, the pitcher then uses bullpen time, simulated games, and intrasquads to master his strategy. The catcher plays a vital role in this process, especially if he is calling the game. The catcher should spend time in the bullpen with all the pitchers so that he can become familiar with several plans. See figure 7.2 for an example of a personal pitching plan.

As the pitcher matures and adds velocity, movement, or new pitches, his plan will change. This new approach can be worked in when the situation allows.

Simple Strategies

The following are some simple strategies to use when pitching. Many pitchers make the mistake of trying to do too much and never really establish a plan or strategy. What works for one pitcher may not work for another. Each pitcher needs to have a basic idea of what he is trying to accomplish.

As a pitcher develops and can locate two or even three pitches, he can then pitch exclusively to hitters' weaknesses. Each pitcher should use a simple strategy to be effective within the framework of his ability.

Get Ahead and Expand

Getting ahead of the batter with the first pitch is the staple of any strategy. Once ahead in the count, the pitcher will then try to expand the strike zone by working progressively inside, outside, up the ladder, or down the ladder. As the hitter fights to make the adjustment, the pitcher can reverse his direction with the baseball. Many hitters will not adjust but will keep trying to catch up to the pitch.

Ahead–Behind

Ahead–behind is a simple strategy that is based on the premise of getting ahead and expanding. When ahead in the count, the pitcher pitches to the corners; but if the pitcher misses his spot, he should miss *off* of the plate. When behind in the count, if the pitcher misses with his pitch, he should miss *over* the plate.

Movement Plus

A pitcher who has good movement (sink or run) on his fastball should throw low and

Personal Pitching Plan   John Doe (LHP)

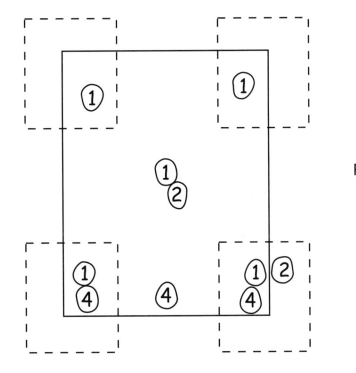

Left-handed batter

Right-handed batter

1 - Fastball
2 - Curveball
3 - Slider/split finger
4 - Change

Figure 7.2   Sample pitching plan.

down the middle early in the count to get ahead. The movement-plus pitcher's advantage is that he will get lots of one- and two-pitch outs by throwing strikes and letting the ball run. The advanced movement-plus pitcher can later learn to pitch outside of the zone and work the ball back over the plate.

Hard In–Soft Away

The majority of hitters can be pitched hard in–soft away. To hit the inside fastball, the hitter has to load early and get the barrel into the hitting zone. To hit the slower pitch on the outside, the hitter must keep his weight back and, more important, keep his hands back. A pitcher who can do both will have his way with most hitters.

Pitchers who use the hard in–soft away strategy must make sure that they do not become predictable; if they become predictable the hitter can make an educated guess about which pitch is thrown. Even the best pitch becomes hittable when the hitter guesses correctly.

Away Early–In Late

This simple strategy is becoming more popular because of the modern hitter's tendency to dive into the plate. Many hitters will look for a pitch on the inner half of the plate that they can drive early in the count. When the pitcher works away early he may get a called strike or a weakly hit ball. With two strikes these same hitters will look for a pitch low and away so as not to strike out by putting the ball in play. When the pitcher sees this adjustment, he can then pitch inside late in the count. Many hitters get frozen and take a called third strike while others get the bat on the ball but get jammed and hit it weakly. Away early–in late works especially well on the middle of the line-up and not as well on contact hitters at the top or bottom of the order.

Pitching Backward

Pitching backward refers to the pitcher's throwing off-speed pitches in fastball counts and throwing fastballs in off-speed counts. Some examples of this are throwing a change/curveball in a three-balls, one-strike count or a two-balls, no-strike count. In these counts the batter is sitting on a fastball and will either take the pitch for a strike or take a poor swing at the pitch, sometimes resulting in an out. The pitcher with pretty good off-speed pitches and a subpar fastball will benefit from this simple strategy.

Another example of pitching backward involves using the fastball in off-speed counts. Many hitters will look away with two strikes in anticipation of the breaking pitch and will be late or completely fooled with a fastball in that situation.

Pitching backward is a great way to pitch against a team that is a good fastball-hitting team. In most cases, pitching backward against a team with slow bats will not be as effective.

chapter 8

Building Pitcher–Catcher Chemistry

A good pitcher–catcher relationship is an important ingredient of any successful baseball team. The majority of this book is geared toward the pitching aspect of this relationship; however, the role of the catcher is just as important and should be discussed at length. Even the best of pitchers will struggle without competent catching.

Many Roles of the Catcher

The catcher wears many hats, among them pitching coach on the field, psychologist, confidence builder, strategist, pitcher–coach liaison, and defensive captain. He is also a big factor in umpire relations. The pitcher, in most cases, works with one and sometimes two catchers over the course of the season. The catcher, on the other hand, may have to fulfill his roles with anywhere from 3 to 12 different pitchers. Each pitcher has a different delivery and different pitches as well as a different mental make-up. Each new game brings a different umpire with his own unique strike zone and personality. The catcher is the glue that makes it all fit together. Catching is a difficult job and is often taken for granted. Pitchers and coaches alike should go out of their way to make catchers feel appreciated.

Catcher As Pitching Coach

One of the roles the catcher assumes when he puts on the gear is that of pitching coach on the field. Coaches should go to great lengths to teach their catchers small adjustments that they can pass on to their pitchers.

In most cases each pitcher will have a recurring problem that he will need to be reminded of during the course of a game. Whether it be to slow down his leg lift or reach out front on his change-up, the catcher should be able to spot these problems and remind the pitcher and save the coach a trip to the mound.

A catcher must listen to the coach when the coach is working with a pitcher in the bullpen. Before a game the coach should discuss that particular pitcher's nuances, including some quick mechanical adjustments for the pitcher.

Catcher As Psychologist

One of the most important roles of the catcher is that of psychologist. Each pitcher has a personality all his own. The catcher's job is to find out which buttons to push to inspire that pitcher to perform at his best.

Some occasions call for a stern look or a finger in the chest, whereas another visit to the mound might require a joke or comment to loosen up the pitcher. Occasionally the catcher must play good cop–bad cop after a coach has visited the mound. For example, if the coach challenges the pitcher or loses his cool, the catcher may have to calm the pitcher down to get back to the business of getting batters out. The pitcher must pitch with con-fidence and not be afraid to make a mistake down in the zone. When catching a bullpen workout, the catcher should practice blocking the ball in the dirt to build confidence in the pitcher. Pitchers who don't have confidence in the catcher's ability to block the ball, especially with a runner on third base, will have a tendency to throw a hanging breaking ball, which has a good chance of being hit hard.

Catcher As Confidence Builder

Regardless of the situation, the catcher must present a confident front when working with pitchers. Obviously when a pitcher is getting

The pitcher and catcher relationship is one of the most important of the game.

hit around or struggling with his control, the catcher needs to encourage with conviction. A confident pitcher is always more successful than a pitcher who lacks confidence.

A catcher's body language is so important when he deals with pitchers. The catcher should give his signs with conviction even when he is unsure of what pitch to call. When the catcher shows even a hint of indecisiveness, that feeling will be passed on to the pitcher. Indecision leads to poor pitches, which lead to poor results.

The pitcher must believe that no matter what happens, the catcher is there for him. A catcher with a positive attitude, confident voice, and body language will inspire his pitcher to be the best he can be on that day.

Catcher As Strategist

The catcher has the vantage point of a pitch and, more than anyone in the park, can determine which pitches work, the pitcher's command, and the umpire's strike zone. He also has a great view of the hitter and where he sets up in the batter's box. As batters make adjustments to the pitcher or the umpire, the catcher is in a position to see these small changes and figure out how to counter these moves.

Regardless of who calls the pitches (coach, catcher, or pitcher), the catcher should be consulted between innings to determine whether the batter is making adjustments during the course of the game. Between innings, the coach and catcher should discuss the batters that are due up in the next inning as well as talk about the current pitcher to determine whether he still has good stuff. The catcher can also be a valuable tool to the coach in determining relief pitchers to use. Having caught the entire staff either in the bullpen or in a game situation, the catcher can suggest to the coach a possible relief pitcher who should have success against a particular batter or team.

The coach and catcher must have an open and honest relationship when discussing a pitcher. Personalities must be put aside for the sake of the team. The catcher, more than anybody else, can determine whether a pitcher is on his game or has lost it altogether. It is good practice to confer with the catcher before talking to the pitcher during a mound visit.

Catcher As Defensive Captain

The catcher has the whole game in front of him; therefore, he is in charge of a large percentage of defensive plays. One of the most important is bunt defense, which concerns the pitcher. When fielding a bunt, the pitcher has his back to the base runners and therefore relies on the catcher to make the appropriate call. Knowing the strengths and weaknesses of each pitcher will help the catcher in determining the proper call. This familiarity can only happen through frequent practice on bunt defense with the pitchers.

Another part of the defense that involves the pitcher and catcher is stopping the running game. Many pitchers will become so focused on the batter that they forget or neglect the base runners. The catcher, with the use of signals, can force the pitcher to hold runners by ordering picks or signaling for a slide step. The pitcher and catcher must practice these signals on a regular basis in the bullpen to avoid confusion in a ball game.

Catcher As Umpire's Ally

Developing a good relationship with the umpire will go a long way toward getting the borderline pitch called a strike. The following are some simple guidelines to help the catcher develop a good working relationship with the umpire.

- Respect the umpire's authority. Do not raise your voice or argue, and do not show up the umpire by looking at him after a missed call. Holding the pitch in question for a long time is just another way of showing him up.

- Do not try to frame a pitch that is an obvious ball. Catch it and get it back to the pitcher as soon as possible.

- Ask the umpire how you can help him see the pitch better. "Am I popping up and blocking you? Do you prefer that I catch the low pitch over or under the ball? Did I take that one out of the zone?"

- Protect the umpire by blocking balls in the dirt. Should an umpire get hit with a foul tip, the catcher should take a trip to the mound to give the umpire time to shake it off.

Umpires are people too and will always respond better to positive talk and encouragement than to confrontations. In the course of a ball game the difference can be those four or five borderline pitches that get called a strike. People make mistakes; umpires will miss one now and then. The good catchers accept this and will move on to the next pitch.

Communication Between Pitcher and Catcher

Unlike many sports, baseball involves very little verbal communication during the game. Most communication takes place with hand and body signals. The pitcher and catcher rely most on these set signals to communicate with each other. Before each pitch, the pitcher and catcher must make several decisions: the type of pitch, the location of the pitch, whether to try to pick off a base runner at first or second, and where the baseball should be thrown if a batted ball goes to either one of them. The pitcher and catcher also need a set of backup signs in case the opposing team figures out the first set of signs.

It is inexcusable to lose a game because of a communication problem. Yet in lower leagues it is common to see a catcher completely miss a called strike because of a mix-up with a pitcher. Perhaps even more common is a pitcher fielding a groundball and throwing to the wrong base, having failed to communicate before the pitch was made.

The following assortment of signs and signals are examples of effective communication that can be used at any level of baseball. Signs must be simple enough to prevent confusion but complex enough to be undecipherable by the opposing team.

Selection of Pitch

A pitcher may have as many as four different pitches in his repertoire. He needs a set of finger signals the catcher can flash to him to determine what the next pitch will be. In this particular set of signals, the catcher holds down his index finger to represent the fastball; the index and the second finger to represent the curveball; the second, third, and fourth fingers to represent the slider; and all four fingers for the change-up.

If the pitcher throws only the fastball, curveball, and change-up, the catcher flashes a 1, 2, or 4 and eliminates the 3 (slider signal). The same applies to a pitcher who throws a slider instead of a curveball, only now the catcher eliminates the 2.

If a pitcher has another pitch, such as a forkball, split-finger, or knuckleball, that pitch can be substituted for one of the original four signals (For example, 1 = fastball, 2 = curveball, 3 = split-finger, 4 = change-up.) Some pitchers and catchers use other systems, but there is really no need to deviate from the basic set (figure 8.1).

Location of Pitch

After the catcher gives a signal for the type of pitch to be thrown, the next signal is for location. The catcher can use two basic systems to relay pitch location information to the pitcher: hand signals and finger signals.

Hand signals. The catcher flashes the number for the desired pitch and then touches either the inside of the left thigh for a pitch on that side of the plate or the inside of the right thigh for a pitch on that side of the plate (figure 8.2). If the catcher wants the pitch up in the strike zone, he motions up with his hand (palm up). When no location sign follows the pitch selection sign, the pitch is to be thrown down the middle.

Finger signals. By establishing a number for a particular location, the catcher can give location by flashing signals with the fingers

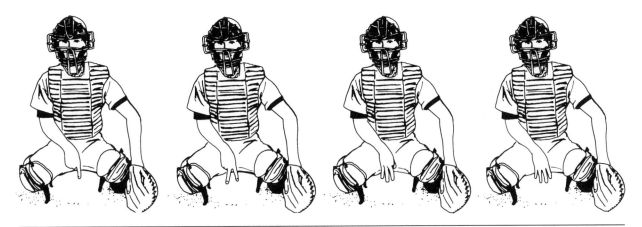

Figure 8.1 Finger signals show pitch selection.

Figure 8.2 The catcher follows a finger signal with a hand signal for pitch location.

(for example, one finger for an inside pitch, two fingers for an outside pitch, three fingers for a high and inside pitch, and four fingers for a pitch down the middle). Using this method, the catcher can flash four finger signals in succession, with the first sign as the pitch selection and the third sign as the location of the pitch (or any other combination).

Miscellaneous Signs

A catcher can give the pitcher several other signs concerning pitch location, pickoffs, and fielding. These common signs are simple to do yet difficult for opposing teams to decipher.

Intentional ball. Sometimes the pitcher wants to throw an intentional ball for the purpose of (a) moving a hitter off the plate,

(b) throwing a pitch just outside of the plate to entice the hitter to swing at a ball, or (c) throwing a pitch above the strike zone to entice the hitter into swinging at a high pitch. A pitcher should never have to throw a pitch more than six inches inside, outside, or high of the strike zone. With this in mind, the catcher can give a sign with his thumb and little finger that means "throw the pitch six inches off the plate." (When the thumb and little finger are spread apart, the distance between them is approximately six inches.) This sign should be flashed between the pitch selection sign and the pitch location sign. For example, if the catcher wants the pitcher to throw a fastball inside at a right-handed hitter's hands, he flashes a 1 (the intentional ball sign, figure 8.3) and taps the inside of the left thigh.

Figure 8.3 Hand signal for intentional ball.

Figure 8.4 Hand signal for pitchout.

Pitchout. The standard sign for a pitchout is a fist (figure 8.4). (In the pitchout the pitcher must not slow down either his wind-up or the pitch.) The catcher flashes the fist, and the pitcher throws a four-seam fastball at the catcher's chest as the catcher steps to the baseball. The catcher steps to a spot 18 inches outside of the plate, away from the hitter.

Intentional walk. The catcher gives the intentional walk sign while standing up behind the plate. While standing, he extends either his glove arm or his throwing arm toward the intended target area (right-handed batter, right side; left-handed batter, left side; figure 8.5). The catcher cannot step out of the catcher's box until the pitcher has started his delivery, or a catcher's balk will be called.

Figure 8.5 Hand signal for intentional walk.

Pickoff attempt at first base. The catcher can also give a sign to make the pitcher throw over to first base in an attempt to pick off a runner or hold a runner close. The catcher might see the base runner take a big lead, or sometimes the catcher will think that the base runner is stealing. The catcher's sign for the pitcher to throw over to first base is to use his thumb to point toward first. The catcher should use no other signals when giving the pickoff sign (figure 8.6).

Figure 8.6   Hand signal for a pickoff attempt at first base.

Signs With a Base Runner on Second Base

Base runners at second base are notorious for trying to steal signs from the catcher and relay them back to the hitter. Pitching is hard enough without the hitter knowing what type of pitch is being thrown. The following sets of signals are examples of sequences a pitcher and catcher can use when a base runner is on second base. These signals must be simple, yet confusing to the opposing team.

Four flashes.   The catcher should always give at least four signals with a base runner on second base. The pitcher and catcher can get together before each inning and decide which of the signals will determine the pitch. (For example, if the catcher flashes a 2-3-1-4, and the predetermined signal is the third sign, then the pitch should be a fastball.) This system is relatively simple and can be decoded by the opposing team if the predetermined signal is not changed every inning. The opposing team will also be tipped off if the pitcher goes into his set immediately after the predetermined signal instead of waiting for all four signals to be flashed.

Outs plus one.   In this system, the catcher again flashes four signals to the pitcher. The pitcher determines the number of outs at that time and adds one to that number. If there are no outs, the signal is the first sign; if there is one out, then the signal is the second sign,

and so on. The beauty of this system is that it changes all the time so that it is tough to decipher.

Touch signals.   In this system, the catcher makes a predetermined touch to some part of his body to designate which of the following four finger signals will be used. A simple system is for the catcher to touch his facemask if he wants the first finger signal, the chest protector if he wants the second signal, the thigh area if he wants the third signal, or the shin guard if he wants the fourth signal.

More systems can be used when a runner is on second base, but usually one of these systems is sufficient. Should someone notice that the runner on second base is stealing signs, then obviously the catcher and the pitcher have to change systems. The catcher can simply call a time-out and go to the mound to put on a new set of signals.

Shake-Off Signs From the Pitcher

As mentioned earlier, the pitcher should throw only the pitch he desires to throw, unless of course the sign comes from the coach. With this in mind, the pitcher needs a sign he can flash to the catcher to change signs. To change the type of pitch, the pitcher can simply shake his head from side to side. The catcher will then flash another sign, and the process is repeated.

Fake Shake-Off Sign

The catcher and the pitcher need a signal for a fake shake-off sign. A fake shake-off sign from the catcher tells the pitcher to shake his head from side to side as if he doesn't want to throw that particular pitch. The fake shake makes the hitter think about what pitch is being thrown. (Any time a hitter starts to guess what pitch is coming, the pitcher has the advantage.) A simple sign for the fake shake is for the catcher to shake his signal hand back and forth.

A fake shake can be used any time in the count, but it is particularly effective when a batter has two strikes. (A good example of when to fake shake is immediately after a swinging strike on a breaking ball to run the count to two balls and two strikes. When the pitcher shakes his head to change pitches, many batters assume that the pitcher will throw another breaking ball. When the pitcher throws a fastball, the hitter will freeze.)

Change-Location Sign

When the pitcher wants to change the location of a pitch, he must have some way of relaying this to the catcher. Obviously the only locations that need to be changed are outside to inside or inside to outside. The pitcher can relay this to the catcher by changing the position of his glove or his throwing hand, whichever one is hanging by his side. The change of position can be a subtle change, just enough for the catcher to know to change locations. If the pitcher holds his hands together when he is getting the sign, perhaps he can move his head up and down to change location.

Fielding Communication

There are several instances when the pitcher and catcher communicate before the pitch about fielding assignments: bunt defense, double-play balls, covering first base, and a wild pitch or passed ball with a runner on third base. See chapter 3 for more information.

chapter 9

Managing the Pitching Staff and Bullpen

Managing individual pitchers and an entire team can make or break a coach. A coach can have all the knowledge in the world, but if he cannot teach and lead individuals, both the players and the coach suffer.

This chapter begins with managing individual pitchers to get the very best performance out of each player. After a coach has established proper mechanical, physical, and mental instruction for each pitcher, he then has the task of managing the entire team, which includes using pitchers properly in the course of a game and a season. Staff composition and establishing rotations are of the utmost importance for using each pitcher's talents to win. Making pitching changes and setting up practice schedules are also important to the winning coach.

Baseball history shows that the coach with the most pitching talent does not always have the best record. Often the top coach is the one who can get the most out of a pitcher's talents and manage his staff effectively.

Managing Pitchers

A pitching staff is composed of several pitchers, all of whom have the same job to do but with different arm angles, velocities, pitches, and degrees of control. Coaches have a general philosophy of pitching, but they have to deal with a host of different pitchers and their different ways of learning. Coaches can accomplish a great deal more if they treat pitchers as individuals and respect their uniqueness. Too many times coaches tend to teach all the pitchers in the same manner: They teach them the same skills, in the same ways, and expect them all to accomplish the same goals. Certainly coaches can't favor certain pitchers over others, because this will have a detrimental effect on the team, but they can remember that each pitcher requires individual attention.

Each pitcher responds in his own way to various teaching methods. Some pitchers can learn just by watching others' examples; others need the coach to guide them through the actions, so that they can feel the movements to learn them. Still others may need to see themselves on film or videotape to fully understand what changes they need to make. The important thing is to realize that pitchers learn in different ways. Experiment with different methods so that all pitchers may learn.

Teaching Methods

Coaches can choose from several different teaching methods to educate players. Different players respond to different methods or combinations of methods.

Audio

This is the most common form of teaching and coaching. The coach describes certain aspects of a movement pattern, and the player transforms the words into mental images. A coach must make good use of the language to be effective in using just the lecture method.

Visual

This method allows the player to see correct movement patterns, and hopefully the player will emulate them. Visual aids can take many forms, such as the coach's example, another player's movements, or a picture. Video equipment lets the player observe his own movements and make corrections. Mirrors and shadows can also work as visual aids to help the player understand correct movement patterns.

Kinesthetic

Many players can understand or visualize the correct movement patterns but have no kinesthetic sense of, or cannot feel, the correct movement. These players must be led through the movement so that they can learn to sense the correct movement. Little Leaguers in particular need this type of instruction.

A player can learn by hearing, seeing, feeling, or any combination of the three. If a player or two cannot grasp what the others have learned through the normal teaching methods, change the methods for their benefit.

Feedback

Many times the only feedback coaches have from their teaching is the player's *performance*. A coach can use other ways to get a player's feedback that will help the coach determine whether what he is teaching is fully understood.

- **Oral.** The pitcher should verbalize the material covered. If the pitcher can explain and demonstrate the material, then he comprehends it.

- **Written.** After a teaching session, the pitcher can write down the material covered; when appropriate, he can also draw diagrams to explain the material.

By using one or both oral and written feedback methods, a coach can find out who is fully understanding the material. Many times players hear things differently and transform the words into completely different mental images than what the coach intended. The oral and written feedback methods ensure that each player is learning properly.

Communication

Communication is the key to successful teaching. The coach who has the most baseball knowledge will not be the greatest teacher if he has trouble communicating. Coaches can use various methods of communicating the content to pitchers.

Use Positive Reinforcement

Human beings respond much better to positive than to negative reinforcement. Sometimes coaches have to look deep to find something good in an athlete's performance, but each athlete always has something good to build on. Even when a coach needs to level with an athlete and tell him several negative things about his performance, he should always end on a positive note. This emphasizes that, as badly as the athlete played, there is still hope.

Something should be said about the effects of positive and negative suggestions on a pitcher's performance. Coaches should communicate with positive statements and avoid negative connotations. The following is an example of positive communication.

Why mention the word *walk* to a pitcher? No pitcher wants to walk a hitter. Yet it is very common for a coach or another player to say to the pitcher, "Don't walk this hitter." If a pitcher is concerned about not walking a hitter, chances are he will end up walking the hitter or making bad pitches. (Anybody who has played golf has experienced this phenomenon. If you're thinking about the lake or the tree while you're swinging, it seems the ball will always find these obstacles.) The coach or fielder should convey his concern about the hitter by being positive and saying, "Make this batter hit the ball." The subconscious cannot differentiate between positive and negative. If the pitcher is thinking about *not walking* the hitter, the subconscious will see to it that the batter is walked. If the pitcher is thinking about making the batter *hit* the ball, then the subconscious will see to it that the pitcher throws strikes.

Pitch selection is another area rich with examples of filling a pitcher's head with unnecessary negative thoughts. Suppose someone says to a pitcher, "Whatever you do, don't throw this hitter a high fastball." Now the pitcher wants to throw a fastball, but he is thinking about not throwing high instead of thinking about keeping it on the knees. Sure enough, the pitcher throws a high fastball.

Instill into pitchers what they need to accomplish and not what they don't want to accomplish. A pitcher should concern himself only with what will be successful and think only positive thoughts.

Be Honest

Speak openly and honestly to your athletes. Honesty may hurt more initially, but the athlete will respect you more for it. Everyone likes to know where they stand so that they can do something about it. If you're honest with your athletes, they'll know exactly what you expected of them and what they need to do. Honesty solves immediate problems and prevents many future problems.

Communicate at the Athlete's Level

Communication is a must in teaching. Sometimes this requires you, the coach, to speak at the athlete's level. Don't be afraid to simplify things so that everyone understands. If you're trying to teach pitching to Little Leaguers, and you use the same approach you would use to teach college pitchers, the Little Leaguers will probably learn very little. On the other hand, one sometimes has to teach college pitchers with the Little Leaguer approach. But anyone can learn if there is communication.

Be Sincere

Athletes can see right through the insincere coach. If the athlete knows that the coach cares about him individually and not just as a tool for the coach's success, the athlete will be more receptive to learning and improving.

Breaking Habits

A habit is an action that has been performed for so long that it feels natural or comfortable. One of the toughest jobs a coach has is breaking habits. When athletes train muscles and nerve endings a certain way for a long time, they find it very difficult to retrain these same muscles and nerve endings. Changing bad habits requires patience and thousands of repetitions performed in the correct manner. In pitching, it is impossible to throw thousands of repetitions, and for this reason throwing-arm habits are the hardest of all to correct. So it is important that each athlete learn the proper arm action when he is very young.

Guidelines for Breaking Habits

When helping a pitcher break bad habits, use the following tactics.

• **Break the skill down into its smallest parts.** Work on each separate movement through countless repetitions. Many of the drills in chapter 4 are examples of breaking down skills into components. When skills are broken down, the pitcher can concentrate on a particular segment of the delivery.

• **Overexaggerate.** Sometimes a pitcher needs to overexaggerate a certain movement for faster learning. An excellent teaching method for changing a bad habit is to overexaggerate the correction for a period of time and then simply tell the pitcher to forget all about it and go back to his original way. The end result is usually a compromise. The athlete feels more comfortable and gains back some confidence. His performance will change, however. Because of the period of overexaggeration, the performance will fall somewhere between the old habit and the overexaggeration (the intent, of course, is to put the performance in the area of the perfect action). The player will be happy because he feels that he is doing it his way, and the coach will be happy because the player has broken the bad habit.

The pitcher who throws across his body provides a good example of the effectiveness of overexaggeration. After countless repetitions of overexaggerating his stridefoot landing to the open side, the pitcher will eventually land on the line to the target. Landing on the line to the target will actually feel very comfortable to him after he has been forced to land on the extreme open side of the line.

• **Have the athlete do countless repetitions of the proper movements.** The athlete will soon feel comfortable with proper movements and uncomfortable with the improper movements. For example, if a pitcher has been breaking his hands at arm's length from his body for several years, this movement will feel very comfortable to him. To break this habit, the pitcher must practice breaking his hands the proper way for thousands of repetitions or until it begins to feel comfortable. The pitcher will have to practice this on a daily basis, both in drills and on the mound. To get the required repetitions, the pitcher will need to break this movement down into drill form so that he will not hurt the arm.

Give Ground to Make Ground

"Give ground to make ground" is the old football adage that means a punt returner should give a little ground so that he may turn the corner, find his wall of blockers, and make a big run. Many times when the athlete is learning something new, his performance suffers for a while, and then it all comes together. After this period of adjustment the performance should be better than ever.

This adjustment time is a delicate time for the athlete and coach. The athlete won't like his subpar performance and will want to revert back to the old habits. It is the coach's duty to make sure the athlete gives the new habit a chance to become effective. A patient and positive coach will help the athlete through these rough learning times.

It takes lots of time to break bad habits and create new mechanics. The older the pitcher is or the longer a pitcher has been pitching, the longer it takes to change a movement pattern. A Little Leaguer who has pitched only for a year or two may be able to change in a matter of days or weeks. A high school pitcher who has been pitching since Little League may require two or three months to change bad habits to good habits.

Remember that when changing a pitcher's mechanics, the coach and pitcher should do all of the drill work in the bullpen. If the pitcher has to pitch in a game before the change is completed, he can't be expected to think about his mechanics during the game; there, he should be thinking only about getting the opposing team out. Many times coaches rush players, force them into the lineup, and expect them to have good mechanics in the game. If the pitcher is busy worrying about his mechanics, he probably will not fare well against the opposition. This can have a detrimental effect on the teaching process, because if the pitcher loses, he might no longer believe in the change.

Give the pitcher time to make the change. Explain to him that his results may suffer somewhat right now but, with continued work, he will be a much better pitcher down the road.

Self-Motivation Through Goal Setting

If all pitchers were self-motivated, the job of coaching them would be much simpler. Coaches can teach the concept of self-motivation through the use of goal setting. Setting goals and using them properly can be very helpful to both the player and the coach.

Coaches often set team goals (number of wins, conference championships, and so on), and these goals definitely have a place in motivation. However, for individual improvement, individual goals should be incorporated. The two varieties of individual goals are *immediate* and *long-range.* Some examples of immediate goals are to increase the number of wins in the upcoming season or to get a higher percentage of breaking balls in for strikes. Some examples of long-range goals are to play professional baseball or to increase the fastball velocity by five miles per hour.

Goals give players self-motivation and direction. When a player is undecided about what he wants to accomplish, he will have trouble accomplishing anything. As Ben Franklin said, "Living without goals is like shooting without a target."

In the goal-setting process, players need to read and think about their set goals on a regular basis. One way to encourage this is to have each player put a copy of his goals on his locker door. Then the player can read them before and after practice. Reading the goals beforehand helps motivate players for practice or a game, and reading the goals after a workout helps to positively reinforce the hard work.

Goal Guidelines

To use goal setting properly, there are certain guidelines to be followed. Goals that are unrealistic or vague only confuse and demoralize players. The coach can lend valuable experience and expertise to help pitchers set realistic and organized goals.

Goals must be attainable. For example, a pitcher's goal is 10 wins. If he gets 10 to 15 starts, then 10 wins will be possible. Of course, the pitcher also has to be in the rotation. If he is not, then his first goal should be to get in the rotation. A better way to state this goal is to say, "10 wins or 80 percent of starts." This still gives the pitcher a chance to achieve his goal even if he has some rainouts or misses a few starts because of injury. It is good to set high goals, but the goals must be within reach.

Goals must be well defined and measurable. For example, a pitcher's goal is to be the best he can be. This goal is abstract and impossible to measure. Another example of a vague goal

is that the pitcher will give 100 percent. Who knows what 100-percent effort is? Goals should be measurable by some standard—total numbers, clear percentages, measurable statistics, or even an amount of time. An example of a clearly defined goal for a pitcher is throwing at least 66 percent strikes. This is measurable; the pitcher can determine his percentage after every inning, game, or season by checking the pitching chart.

Goals must not interfere with team success. For example, a pitcher's goal is a certain number of strikeouts. This goal has many problems. First of all, the pitcher may not be a strikeout pitcher; groundball pitchers who try to be strikeout pitchers generally aren't successful. This type of goal could hurt a team if the pitcher is so concerned with strikeouts that he is too fine with his pitches and walks a lot of batters. A better way to include strikeouts in a goal is to shoot for a certain strikeout-to-walk ratio. The coach must assist players in goal setting so that each player's individual goals will not interfere with a team's success.

Goals must have time limits. To give an athlete direction, goals must be set for a specific completion date so that the coach and pitcher can pursue a legitimate plan. Without a completion date, it is impossible to measure progress or redefine goals. An example of such a time limit is for a pitcher to have a goal he wants to accomplish by his third game or perhaps by the end of the season. When the time limit is up, the pitcher then evaluates his progress and determines whether he needs more time or needs to change his goals.

Goals must be adjustable. Goals should be well defined and measurable, but they must also be adjustable to allow for changes. Some factors that may affect goals are injury, weather, and success or failure. If a pitcher is able to adjust goals, he can keep them attainable through adverse conditions.

The most common example of the nonadjustable goal is to get to the World Series. The team reaches its goal to get there, only to lose the Series because they already reached their goal and didn't have any more direction.

Goals must be written. Writing down the goals is the first commitment that an athlete makes in achieving goals. The process of writing out goals fosters a positive attitude. Merely thinking of goals may be more productive than not thinking of goals, but writing them down is a step in the direction of reaching them. When a goal appears in writing, the goal setter becomes responsible for achieving it. A written statement provides documentation of goals. Without the documentation, there is no proof that a goal was met or that it even existed. Writing down goals is an action, the first step to achieving goals.

Preparing a Goal Sheet

When preparing a goal sheet, athletes must have a plan of action for each goal, be it a long- or short-range goal. Players need to follow this plan if they are to achieve their goals (see figure 9.1). Examples of long- and short-range goals are listed in figures 9.2 and 9.3.

Goals. Goals should be measurable and well defined so that athletes can measure progress toward a goal. Goals should also be realistic; this is where a coach can counsel his players and give them proper direction.

Deadline. Players and coaches should set a date as the time limit for achieving the goal. At that time, either the goal will have been attained or a new goal should be made.

Ingredients. Ingredients of a goal are much like ingredients in a recipe. What will it take to achieve this goal? What is needed, step by step, in a plan of action to achieve this goal? The coach can help players determine what they need to achieve particular goals.

Sacrifices. Goals are not met without some degree of sacrifice. In most cases, the player who has failed to achieve his goal has failed to make the necessary sacrifice. Almost anything is possible if a player will do whatever it takes to achieve his goals. A coach can help define what sacrifices are necessary for achieving a player's particular goal.

Visualization. After a player defines his goal, he must visualize himself achieving his goal. Visualization acts as both a positive reinforcement and a motivational tool. The coach can help the player achieve his goal by encouraging visualization. (All visualization must be positive and successful. Positive visualization builds self-confidence.)

Commitment. After the player has constructed his goal sheet, he must make a commitment to follow the goal-achievement plan. The player signs his name as a symbolic gesture of commitment.

Managing Pitching Staff

After a coach has worked individually with each member of a pitching staff, he must manage the entire staff in an organized and professional way. Individual pitchers win individual games, but the pitching staff wins championships. The coach who can successfully manage a pitching staff has a big edge on the competition.

Throwing: How Much, How Often?

Many times coaches are guilty of throwing pitchers entirely too much and taking a chance of seriously hurting a pitcher's arm. Other times coaches are guilty of not working their pitchers enough, which leads to underdevelopment. Both patterns hurt a pitcher's chance of becoming the best pitcher he can be. In trying to win, coaches tend to overthrow their best pitchers and underthrow the rest of the staff. If a coach sets up a schedule that includes all pitchers and he adheres to it, both types of pitchers will benefit and, as a result, so will the team.

Throwing occurs in long-toss workouts, bullpen work, scrimmage games, and of course, actual game pitching. The coach should carefully monitor the number of pitches thrown in each of these situations.

Long-Toss Work

Long toss has many definitions, and there are many views on what the long toss is supposed to accomplish. All the same, here is a description of a standard long-toss workout. The

GOAL SHEET

Name _____ Date _____

Goal:

Deadline:

Ingredients: 1.

2.

3.

4.

Sacrifices: 1.

2.

3.

4.

5.

6.

Visualization: I can see myself. . . .

I, _____, commit myself to achieving the above goal by following this carefully written guideline to success.

Figure 9.1   When preparing a goal sheet, you must have a plan of action for each goal.

Name _John Doe_   Date _2-3-03_

Goal: To be in the starting rotation by spring of 2003

Deadline: 5-15-03

Ingredients:
1. Be able to throw at least two types of pitches for strikes 75 percent of the time
2. Be in excellent physical condition to be able to pitch seven innings
3. Have a healthy body and arm
4. Field at least .975, and get my release time to 1.35

Sacrifices:
1. Allocate my practice time to work on my mechanics
2. Make every bullpen workout a quality one
3. Work extra hard on wind sprints, flexibility, and strength training
4. Get eight hours of sleep, eat three good meals a day, and take care of my arm
5. Force myself to take a minimum of 25 groundballs a day

Visualization: I can picture myself starting in the conference championship game, winning the game, and having a party on the mound.

I, _John Doe_ , commit myself to achieving the above goal by following this carefully written guideline to success.

Figure 9.2 Sample short-range goal.

Name _John Doe_   Date _2-3-03_

Goal: To increase the speed on my fastball by five miles per hour

Deadline: 2-3-04

Ingredients:
1. Perfect mechanics
2. Healthy arm
3. A bigger, stronger body
4. Increased flexibility

Sacrifices:
1. Allocate time daily to drills and bullpen work to perfect my delivery
2. Work my arm as hard as possible without injury
3. Increase body weight by 15 pounds
4. Increase arm strength by 15 percent, leg strength by 30 percent
5. Increase flexibility by 10 percent
6. Play long toss a minimum of three times per week for a minimum of 50 throws

Visualization: I can see myself winding up and throwing fastballs right by the hitters. I see the pro scouts start to talk among themselves as I light up their ray guns!

I, _John Doe_ , commit myself to achieving the above goal by following this carefully written guideline to success.

Figure 9.3 Sample long-range goal.

pitchers start 50 feet apart and gradually back up to a distance just beyond what they can throw in the air. After 10 throws at the maximum distance, the pitchers work their way back to the 50-foot mark. About 40 to 50 throws are usually adequate to stretch the arm. However, in the off-season, when a pitcher is trying to develop arm strength, more repetitions are required—up to 100, with one third of those at the maximum distance.

Unless he is injured, a pitcher should long-toss at least every other day. During the in-season the pitcher may want to reduce the number of long tosses. Off-season, the pitcher should long-toss only every other day and increase the repetitions to develop arm strength.

Long-tossing, more than anything else a pitcher can do, increases velocity. It also shortens a pitcher's recovery time. Long-tossing the day after pitching a game stretches out the arm and helps with blood circulation in the arm.

Game-Pitch Work

As a general rule, 15 pitches per inning times the number of innings in a regulation game is a good cutoff point. (For example, 15 pitches × 7 innings = 105 pitches, which should be the cutoff point for high school pitchers. For college pitchers, 135 pitches would be the cutoff point.)

When a pitcher reaches this cutoff number, he should be removed to avoid overuse and possible injury. By keeping track of pitches, the coach can look ahead and have a reliever ready to go in when needed. Obviously, a few pitches above the cutoff point probably will not harm the pitcher if the pitcher needs only one out to finish the game. It is estimated that 80 percent of all arm injuries occur after these cutoff points, so the coach must monitor the number of pitches each pitcher has thrown.

Bullpen Work

Monitor the number of pitches each pitcher throws in the bullpen to avoid overuse and to insure that the pitcher will be effective when called on. When counting pitches in the bullpen, it is important to include all throws. Many pitchers will consider those throws to the catcher when he is standing up to be warm-up pitches and think they should not count. *Every* throw in the bullpen should be monitored. The number of pitches a pitcher throws during a bullpen session should always be based on when the pitcher is expected to pitch next in a game.

Between-Starts Work

In a between-starts workout, the pitcher should throw no more than 50 pitches to the catcher. These pitches should be divided equally among the different pitches he throws, with some emphasis on the area he needs to improve.

Relief-Pitcher Work

Coaches who use their bullpen effectively are most often the most successful coaches. A middle- or long-relief pitcher should try to stay on an every-other-day plan. The coach should be able to work the relief pitcher's bullpen to coincide with the schedule.

Short-relief pitchers can throw on a schedule of two days on, one day off, because they seldom throw many pitches. Should the short-relief man throw an excessive number of pitches one day, he should not throw in the bullpen or in a game the following day.

When a relief pitcher throws an excessive number of pitches preparing to go into a ballgame, the coach should keep track of the number of these pitches. A relief pitcher might throw only 15 pitches in a game, but he might have been warming up for five innings if the starting pitcher was constantly in trouble. Many coaches ignore the warm-up pitches and count only the actual game pitches when deciding whether that pitcher is available the next day. By monitoring *all* bullpen work, the coach would realize that the relief pitcher threw 75 pitches in the bullpen plus 15 pitches in the game for a total of 90 pitches. This pitcher should have a day off the following day, not only to prevent overuse but also to ensure effectiveness.

Pitching-Staff Composition

A pitching staff is made up of starting pitchers, long-relievers, middle-relievers, mop-up pitchers, and short-relievers. All have different roles to play, and all have great impact on a season.

Starting pitchers. The starting pitcher starts the game and pitches either until the game ends or until he is removed from the game because of performance, injury, or number of pitches. Starting pitchers usually pitch every fourth or fifth day in a set rotation.

Spot starters. The spot starter is usually the fifth man in a four-man rotation. He occasionally gets to start a game when the schedule gets backed up. The spot starter also doubles as a long-reliever.

Long-relievers. When the starting pitcher gets in trouble early in the game, the long-reliever takes over for him and tries to get the team into the late innings or possibly finish the game.

Middle-relievers. When the starting pitcher goes into the middle innings before he has to be removed, the middle-reliever comes in to either finish the game or at least get into the late innings.

Mop-up pitchers. The mop-up pitcher comes into a game when the game is lopsided one way or the other. The goal of the mop-up man is to go as long as needed to finish the game (and impress the coaches along the way so that he will assume a better role in the future).

Short-relievers. When the preceding pitchers get into the late innings before failing, the short-reliever comes in to try to finish the game.

Selecting Starters and Relievers

Deciding who will be the starting pitchers and who will be relief pitchers is one of the coach's most important responsibilities. The coach should use several criteria (described in the following paragraphs) when making this decision. After using all the criteria and adding a little gut feeling, the coach should be able to come up with various roles for the pitching staff. Of course, performance and injury factors will create some changes in these roles throughout the season.

Once the coach defines the players' roles, he should inform the pitchers of their roles and their requirements to move up in the scheme. When the pitchers know what is expected of them and what they need to do to move up, the rest will take care of itself. The bottom line in deciding the composition of the pitching staff is to have the best pitchers doing most of the pitching.

Ability Levels

Considering that the starting pitcher will be pitching many more innings than the relievers will pitch, it makes good sense that the better pitchers on the staff should be starters. Many games have been lost when a coach saved his best pitcher for the end of the game, only to find that at the end of the game it was too late. The ball should be in the hands of the best pitcher when the game starts. A coach who is blessed with four or five good pitchers of equal ability should make one of them the short-relief man. Going strictly by ability level, the lowest on the staff should be the mop-up pitchers, followed by the middle-relievers, long-relievers, spot starters, short-relievers, and starters.

Experience

Experience plays a big part in determining who should start and who should relieve. If possible, pitchers with more experience need to fill the roles of starter and short-reliever. History shows that most great major league baseball teams have a few experienced starters and an experienced short-reliever. The spot starter, long-reliever, middle-reliever, and mop-up are good roles for younger, more inexperienced pitchers to gain experience. These roles usually do not have as much pressure.

Earl Weaver was excellent at grooming young pitchers by having them work in the spot starter, long-reliever, middle-reliever, and mop-up roles first to get their feet wet and build confidence. As the young, inexperienced pitcher gets more playing time, he can be introduced gradually to the high-pressure positions of starter or short relief. Confidence is a necessity for a successful pitcher, and confidence comes only with successful experiences.

Mental Toughness

Mental toughness plays a large part in determining the pitcher's role. A short-reliever must be extremely tough mentally to be able to pitch in precarious situations in late innings. Mental toughness is not as necessary in the middle-relief and mop-up roles.

Durability

Whether or not a pitcher can pitch every day is an important criterion for deciding who should start or relieve. A pitcher who has a long recovery time between pitching stints may have to be a starter, long-reliever, or middle man. However, if a pitcher can throw a little every day, then the role of the short-reliever might be right for him.

© Jennifer Smith

Ability level, experience, and mental toughness are among the factors a coach considers when choosing starting and relief pitchers.

Number of Pitches Mastered

A starting pitcher should have at least two good pitches, although three would be ideal (fastball, breaking ball, and change-up). A spot starter or long-reliever should also have two or three good pitches he can control. A middle-reliever or short-reliever can get by with one great pitch as long as he uses it correctly. Middle- and short-relievers can get by with one great pitch because they have to face the opposing team's lineup only one time through. Usually the pitcher who has only one pitch gets hit hard the second time through the lineup.

Control

Walks are not desired in any phase of a game, but at certain times they are more acceptable. A starter can sprinkle in a walk or two, and it might not affect the outcome of the game. On the other hand, if the short-reliever comes in with bases loaded in the ninth inning, a walk can be catastrophic. Control is a definite criterion for deciding the role of a pitcher. Short-relievers must have excellent control to be effective.

Left-Handed or Right-Handed Pitcher

Most coaches don't have enough good pitchers to worry about trying to get a balance of left-handers and right-handers. Ideally, though, it would be good to have a couple of each in the rotation as well as a good balance in each of the other roles. A good balance in the different roles should be a coach's goal, but it may be at the bottom of the list as far as criteria for deciding what role each pitcher has.

Setting Up the Rotation

A coach has to make many choices when setting up the rotation of the starting pitchers. The opponents, field, weather, game times, and pitchers' recovery times are all important things to think about when determining which pitcher will pitch against which team.

A coach who can properly set up his pitching rotation can go a long way toward winning more games. Using the available pitcher best suited to the opposing team under the circumstances is a must for winning games.

Many coaches make the mistake of having their pitchers try to change style to fit a game's circumstances. The coach should try to match pitchers and game situations so that each pitcher can achieve the most positive results by pitching the type of game that best suits his style and abilities.

Opponents

When the coach knows the opponents, he can figure out who among the starting pitchers would be the best choice to start in that particular game.

Right-handed and left-handed batters. Whether the opponents have more right-handed or left-handed batters can affect the decision on whom to start. Right-handed batters generally have more trouble with right-handed pitchers, and vice versa. Most hitters will prefer to hit a breaking ball that is breaking toward them instead of a breaking ball that is breaking away from them.

Team speed. When the opponents have great team speed, the coach might choose a left-handed starter to hold the runners better at first base.

Team power. When the opposing team hits a lot of home runs, the choice for a starting pitcher might be a sinker or slider pitcher; this might keep the ball in the ballpark.

Opponents take a lot of pitches. When the opposing team takes a lot of pitches, the starting pitcher obviously should have good control.

Opponents like fastballs. When the opposing team likes to hit fastballs, particularly hard ones, the best choice might be a pitcher who specializes in off-speed pitching.

Opponents have a good hitting team. When an opposing team can just flat-out hit, it might be good to start a down-the-line pitcher who might get them out once around the order. "Bad" pitchers (who are herky-jerky or throw very slowly) often get out good hitters better than some supposedly good pitchers.

Field

The type of field the players perform on may figure in to the rotation. Two things to consider are the surface of the field and the dimensions. Is the field grass or artificial surface? A sinker-ball pitcher may not be the best choice for starter on an Astroturf field, given how many groundballs might be hit. The better choice for turf might be the pitcher who gets a lot of flyball outs; the groundball pitcher may be better suited for grass. In assessing the dimensions of the field, note that a groundball pitcher might be best suited to a short field, just as a flyball pitcher might get the best results on a longer field.

Weather

It's hard to base a rotation on the weather because the weather is often unpredictable, although sometimes it is possible to predict when the weather may be colder or warmer than usual. Some pitchers pitch better in cold weather; some pitch better in warm weather.

Game Times

Different types of pitchers are best suited for day games and night games. High-velocity pitchers might fare better at night, because they probably rely on their fastball. Curveball pitchers might be successful at night because it is hard to pick up the spin of the curveball under the lights. Groundball pitchers might have trouble with night games; the dew that accumulates on the ground makes the ball wet and harder to throw.

Pitcher's Recovery Time

Some pitchers pitch better in a four-day rotation and others in a five-day rotation. The number of pitches a pitcher threw in his previous start will also have some effect on his recovery time. When setting up the rotation, a coach has to know how many days of rest each pitcher needs for recovery.

Making a Pitching Change

Deciding when to make a pitching change is one of the hardest decisions a coach has to make during a game. Coaches who are successful usually have a knack for knowing when to remove a pitcher. But it involves more than a hunch; knowing when to remove a pitcher is a combination of data and gut feeling. The gut feeling is a trait acquired through experience, whereas accumulating data is something that all coaches can do.

Making the right or the wrong pitching move has probably won or lost more games than anything else in baseball strategy. By knowing each pitcher's mechanics and traits, planning ahead, using statistics, and being organized, a coach will make a higher percentage of good moves. When a coach is considering making a pitching change, his first concern is whether he has a pitcher who is ready to come in to pitch.

Anticipate Trouble

Plan to have the relief pitchers within 20 pitches of being able to go in to pitch. When the pitcher in the game is closing in on his allotted number of pitches, the bullpen should start to get ready. A coach can stall a certain amount of time to allow the bullpen to get ready, but these stall tactics are best saved for emergencies when the pitcher in the game suddenly loses it.

Know the Opponents' Batting Order

The coach should know at all times exactly where the opponents are in their batting order. Who are the left-handed batters, right-handed batters, best hitters, power hitters, base stealers, good bunters, and batters who take a lot of pitches? Figure 9.4 shows a chart that can be used for recording hitter information. The decision of replacing a pitcher is often based on this information, and by thinking ahead the coach can have the appropriate pitcher ready (for example, a curveball pitcher to a fastball hitter). An example of this chart filled in is given in chapter 7.

Organize the Bullpen

Keeping the bullpen organized takes a lot of pressure off the coach. The bullpen pitchers should also know the situation and who is coming to bat so that the appropriate pitcher will be physically and mentally ready.

Scouting Chart

NAME _____

BATTING ORDER
1 2 3 4 5 6 7 8 9

DEFENSE:
Outfield
Infield

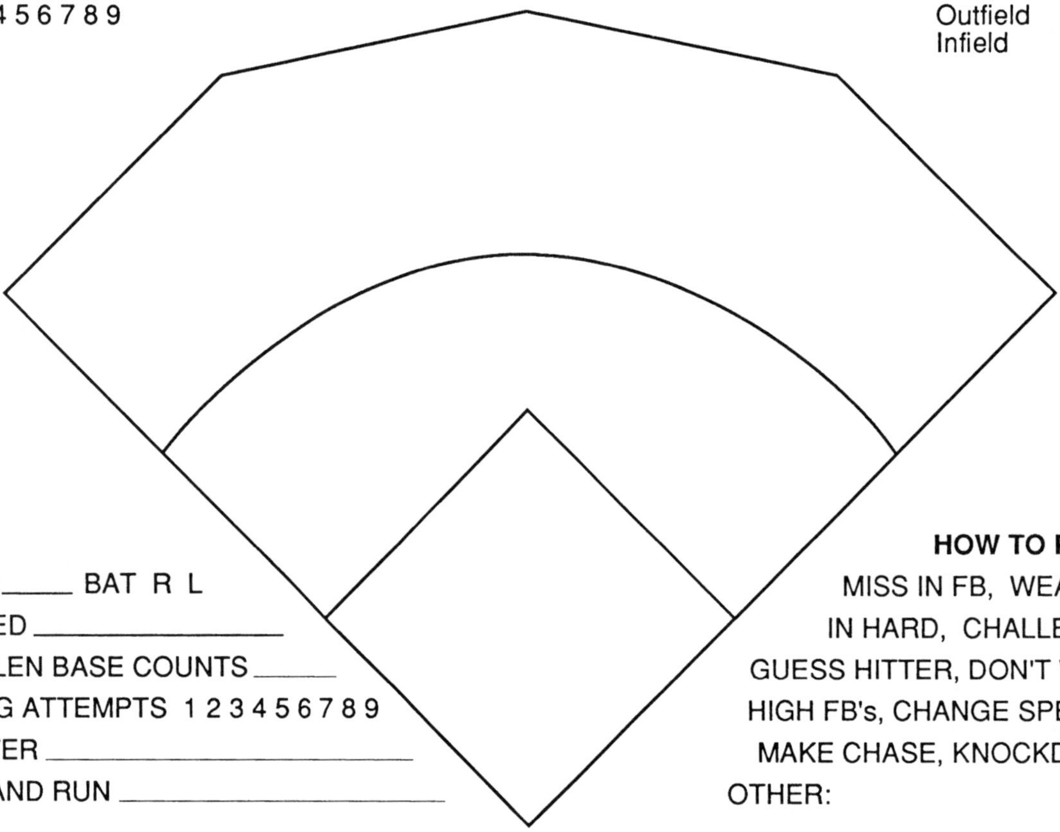

POS:_____ BAT R L
SPEED _____
STOLEN BASE COUNTS _____
DRAG ATTEMPTS 1 2 3 4 5 6 7 8 9
POWER _____
HIT AND RUN _____

HOW TO PITCH
MISS IN FB, WEAK CB
IN HARD, CHALLENGE,
GUESS HITTER, DON'T WALK
HIGH FB's, CHANGE SPEEDS,
MAKE CHASE, KNOCKDOWN
OTHER:

KEY:

FB - 1
CB - 2
SL - 3
CH - 4

IN - I
Away - A
Up - U
Low - L
Middle - M

Softly hit - 1
Routine - 3
Line drive - 5

Groundball ☐
Flyball ○
Line drive △

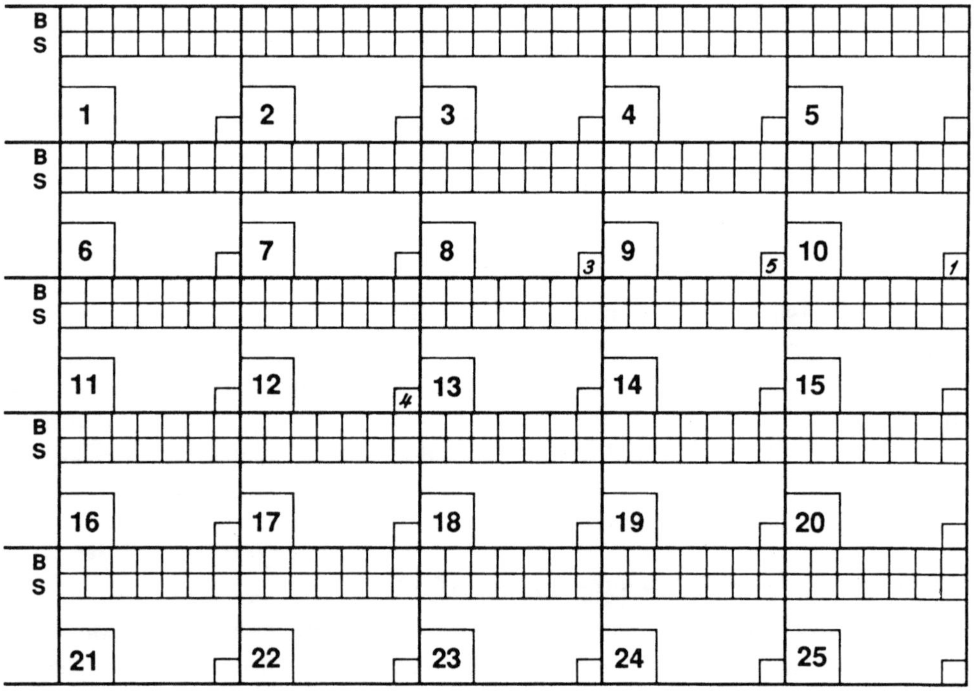

Figure 9.4 Use this chart to record hitter information.

Before the game, the coach should inform his bullpen who is in long relief, short relief, and so on so that the pitchers will be stretched and ready to pitch at a moment's notice. When a relief pitcher doesn't know whether he should be throwing at the start of an inning, a good formula for him to go by is *outs plus one*: The relief pitcher starts getting ready to go in when the situation is no outs plus one base runner, one out plus two base runners, or two outs plus three base runners.

Decide Between Luck and Skill

Often a coach has to decide whether to leave in a pitcher who has been getting hit hard but getting the opponents out or, just the opposite, who is not getting hit hard but is consistently in trouble. An old adage states that it's better to be lucky than good; but baseball is based on percentages, and the percentages say that hard-hit balls have a better chance of being hit than balls that are not well hit. The coach has to use his own discretion, but by playing the percentages the pitcher who is not getting hit hard should have the opportunity to stay in the game longer than the pitcher who is giving up hard-hit outs in great numbers.

Watch for Fatigue

A coach needs to know what to look for to determine whether the pitcher is fatigued and whether he needs to make a pitching change.

- *Number of pitches.* The coach should predict a starting pitcher's fatigue by the pitcher's past performance. If a pitching chart is kept throughout the season, the coach will know at what number of pitches the pitcher gets fatigued. Of course, different pitchers handle fatigue better than others. A pitcher who depends on his high velocity might be affected more by fatigue than a sinker pitcher who uses movement to get hitters out.
- *Change in mechanics.* When a pitcher is fatigued, he consciously or unconsciously changes his pitching mechanics.

Most of these changes in mechanics affect the pitcher's control, and the result is usually higher pitches. Also look for changes in the pitcher's normal routine.

- *Dropped elbow.* One of the first signs of pitcher fatigue is that the throwing-arm elbow drops below shoulder level. This drop results in pushing the ball, making the fastball and change-up stay high and the curveball flat.
- *Overstriding.* The fatigued pitcher tries to use his legs more to compensate for the fatigue in his upper body. The result is that he overstrides and throws the pitch high.
- *Lack of follow-through.* The more fatigued the pitcher gets, the less he follows through. The follow-through protects the arm, and the pitcher who fails to follow through is risking injury.
- *Pitch selection.* A fatigued pitcher sometimes changes his pitch selection to pitches that are easier to throw, usually fastballs.
- *Time between pitches.* Taking more time between pitches is a sure sign of fatigue.

Play the Percentages

Baseball coaches, more than any other coaches, are notorious for playing the percentages. This alone is responsible for many pitching changes. The theory is that a left-handed pitcher is harder for a left-handed batter to hit, and vice versa. Playing the percentages is an excellent method of coaching if there is merit to the system. But those coaches who play by the percentages blindly, without real proof, may be outcoaching themselves.

The coach should keep statistics on the entire pitching staff, showing how each pitcher does against left-handed and right-handed hitters. The coach is then properly armed with data to play the percentages. Depending on what pitches they throw and the arm slot they throw from, some pitchers defy the abstract percentages.

To replace a pitcher strictly to play the percentages, without data to back up the move, is foolish. If you choose to play percentage baseball, then take the time to arm yourself with statistics for your own team to back yourself up.

Watch for Injury

Injury is similar to fatigue in that the pitcher will change his mechanics and mannerisms to compensate for the injury. Little decision making is involved in removing the pitcher when he gets injured—he should be removed immediately. Of course, the rulebook helps here because when an injured pitcher is being replaced, the relief pitcher can take as many warm-up pitches as he needs to get ready.

Setting Up a Practice Schedule

Often some pitchers get ignored when the team practice schedule is set up; they don't get enough work on pitching, pickoffs, and fielding. Structure practice so that the pitchers are working on some phase of their game at least every other day. It is also a good idea to divide the pitchers into two groups; this makes scheduling practices easier.

Table 9.1 Six-Week Preseason Throwing Program

Day	All pitchers	
1	10 minutes (NC)*	
2	10 minutes (NC)	
3	10 minutes (NC)	
4	5 minutes (NC)	
5	5 minutes (NC)—5 minutes (WC)*	
6	Off day	
7	*Divide pitchers in half—groups A and B*	
	Group A—6 minutes (NC), 6 minutes (WC), 6 minutes (NC)	
	Group B—10 minutes (NC)	
8	B—6 (NC), 6 (WC), 6 (NC); A—10 (NC)	
9	A—6 (NC), 6 (WC), 6 (NC); B—10 (NC)	
10	B—6 (NC), 6 (WC), 6 (NC); A—10 (NC)	
11	A—6 (NC), 6 (WC), 6 (NC); B—10 (NC)	
12	B—6 (NC), 6 (WC), 6 (NC); A—10 (NC)	
13	Off day	
14	A—3 innings or 50 pitches; B—15 (NC)	
15	B—3 innings or 50 pitches; A—15 (NC)	

Day	Relief pitchers	Starting pitchers
16	A—15 (NC); B—15 (NC)	A—15 (NC); B—15 (NC)
17	A—6 (NC), 6 (WC), 6 (NC); B—15 (NC)	A—6 (NC), 6 (WC), 6 (NC); B—15 (NC)
18	A—15 (NC); B—6 (NC), 6 (WC), 6 (NC)	A—15 (NC); B—6 (NC), 6 (WC), 6 (NC)
19	A—3 innings—50 pitches; B—15 (NC)	A—5 innings—75 pitches; B—15 (NC)
20	B—3 innings—50 pitches; A—15 (NC)	B—5 innings—75 pitches; A—15 (NC)
21	A—15 (NC); B—15 (NC)	A—15 (NC); B—15 (NC)
22	B—15 (NC); A—6 (NC), 6 (WC), 6 (NC)	B—15 (NC); A—8 (NC), 8 (WC), 8 (NC)
23	A—15 (NC); B—6 (NC), 6 (WC), 6 (NC)	A—15 (NC); B—8 (NC), 8 (WC), 8 (NC)
24	A—3 innings—50 pitches; B—15 (NC)	A—6 innings—90 pitches; B—15 (NC)
25	B—3 innings—50 pitches; A—15 (NC)	B—6 innings—90 pitches; A—15 (NC)

Grouping Pitchers for Practice

The coach should divide the pitching staff into two separate groups (A and B) and have them do the same work on alternate days.

If the coach has an idea about who the starting pitchers are, he should put two starters in each group. This way the coach can start planning practice schedules to complement the rotation as the season gets closer. Table 9.1 shows a preseason practice schedule.

Work Days and Off Days

Because of the nature of the position, pitchers, unlike other players, have work days and off days. This lets the arm rest after a day of strenuous throwing in the bullpen. A work day consists of bullpen or game work, pickoff practice, or fielding practice. An off day consists of light throwing or long toss. Of course, flexibility and conditioning are a part of every practice.

When the team is doing drills on such things as bunt situations, pop-ups, cutoffs,

Day	Relief pitchers	Starting pitchers
26	A—6 (NC), 8 (WC), 6 (NC); B—15 (NC)	A—15 (NC); B—15 (NC)
27	B—6 (NC), 8 (WC), 6 (NC); A—15 (NC)	A—8 (NC), 10 (WC), 8 (NC); B—15 (NC)
28	A—6 (NC), 8 (WC), 6 (NC); B—15 (NC)	B—8 (NC), 10 (WC), 8 (NC); A—15 (NC)
29	B—6 (NC), 8 (WC), 6 (NC); A—15 (NC)	A—7 innings—100 pitches; B—15 (NC)
30	A—3 innings—50 pitches; B—15 (NC)	B—7 innings—100 pitches; A—15 (NC)
31	B—3 innings—50 pitches; A—15 (NC)	A—15 (NC); B—15 (NC)
32	A—6 (NC), 8 (WC), 6 (NC); B—15 (NC)	A—8 (NC), 12 (WC), 8 (NC); B—15 (NC)
33	B—6 (NC), 8 (WC), 6 (NC); A—15 (NC)	B—8 (NC), 12 (WC), 8 (NC); A—15 (NC)
34	A—6 (NC), 8 (WC), 6 (NC); B—15 (NC)	A—7-9 innings—100-120 pitches; B—1 (NC)
35	B—6 (NC), 8 (WC), 6 (NC); A—15 (NC)	B—7-9 innings—100-120 pitches; A—1 (NC)
36	A—3 innings—50 pitches; B—(NC)	A—15 (NC); B—15 (NC)
37	B—3 innings—50 pitches; A—(NC)	A—8 (NC), 15 (WC), 8 (NC); B—15 (NC)
38	A—6 (NC), 10 (WC), 6 (NC); B—15 (NC)	B—8 (NC), 15 (WC), 8 (NC); A—15 (NC)
39	B—6 (NC), 10 (WC), 6 (NC); A—15 (NC)	A—9 innings—125 pitches; B—15 (NC)
40	A—6 (NC), 10 (WC), 6 (NC); B—15 (NC)	B—9 innings—125 pitches; A—15 (NC)
41	B—6 (NC), 10 (WC), 6 (NC); A—15 (NC)	A—15 (NC); B—15 (NC)

* NC = no catcher, WC = with catcher

1. One half of all pitching time should be from the stretch.

2. Fastball and change-ups only, during the first week.

3. All throwing sessions are to be preceded by a warm-up period of stretching and exercising.

4. Pitching batting practice can be incorporated into this workout program by rotating the pitcher from warm-up, to pitching to a catcher, to throwing batting practice (warm-down). Example: 6 (NC), 10 (WC), 6 (BP).

5. On light days of throwing it is advisable to throw long distances to stretch out the arm.

6. Should a weight program be administered during this six-week training program, the following rules should be followed:

   • Start before six-week program, if possible, to give the body time to adapt. The next best thing is to start in conjunction with the program. *Do not start a weight program during the throwing program.*

   • Only lift on heavy workout days. Weight train after the workout. Lifting before could be detrimental to performance, and lifting after may help remove some waste products from the muscles.

7. Pitchers should be advised not to throw too hard too soon. (Many coaches will not let their players use their gloves for the first few days to make sure that there is no overthrowing.) Six weeks is plenty of time to get in shape.

relays, first-and-third situations, rundowns, and pickoffs, the pitchers obviously stay with the team until that part of practice is over. When batting practice begins, the pitchers divide into their two groups.

Suppose this is group A's off day (table 9.2). Then group A is in charge of running batting practice. Their duties include hitting ground-balls to the infielders, retrieving home-run balls, and backing up outfielders (who should be taking balls off the bat; pitchers play behind the outfielders to not interfere). A pitcher also is in charge of the batting-practice ball bucket. Running the entire batting practice is group A's only duty on their off day.

This is a work day for group B, who will report to the bullpen when batting practice starts. In the bullpen area, the pitchers throw to a catcher, work on pickoff moves, or take groundballs.

During the time allotted for batting practice, all of the pitchers in group B should be able to get in a good bullpen workout plus perform many repetitions of pickoff moves and fielding groundballs. (A pitcher can't get enough practice with groundballs, but pickoff work will depend on the condition of the pitcher's arm.)

Pitching Charts

The coach and pitcher can use pitching charts in several ways during the season. The pitching chart gives a pitch-by-pitch statistical analysis of a ball game. It can also be an immediate feedback tool to help pitchers determine how to pitch different hitters during a game. After the game is over, the coach and pitcher can go back over the chart to learn from any strategy successes and failures they had during the game.

The standard pitching chart as shown in figure 9.5 is designed to measure several different statistics during the game. Those listed are some of the most common statistics and uses.

Table 9.2 Team Practice Schedule

Activity	Player breakdown	Time
Prepractice	Pitcher's fielding practice	Unlimited
	Individual hitting work	
	Individual fielding work	
	Individual bunting work	
Stretching and conditioning	Team	30 minutes
Long toss	Team	15 minutes
Team defense	First-and-third defense; rundowns	30-60 minutes
	Pop-up communication; cutoffs and relays	
	Pickoffs; bunt defense	
Batting practice	Group A pitchers—work day	30-60 minutes
or	Group B pitchers—off day (batting practice)	
Scrimmage game	Group B pitchers—work day	
	Group A pitchers—off day (batting practice)	
Conditioning	Hitters: base running, sprints, distance, weights, aerobics, plyometrics	20-30 minutes
	Pitchers: sprints, distance, weights, plyometrics, aerobics, intervals	
Postpractice	Pitcher's fielding practice	Unlimited
	Individual hitting work	
	Individual fielding work	
	Individual bunting work	

Total pitches. The total-pitch number helps in determining whether a pitcher has been struggling (too many pitches), when it may be time to get a relief pitcher (too many pitches), and what kind of shape the pitcher is in (the point in the game when fatigue starts to set in).

Strikes and balls. The number of strikes versus balls the pitcher is throwing is a good statistical tool for determining improvement and effectiveness. A further breakdown will reveal what percentage of each type of pitch is thrown for strikes. This is an excellent tool for determining which pitches players need to work on more in the bullpen.

Getting ahead of the batter. A quick glance at the chart tells the coach what percentage of batters the pitcher gets ahead of in the count. This information also provides data for the next bullpen workout.

Groundballs, line drives, and flyballs. The pitching chart reveals what happened with each batter on batted balls. A pitcher is usually a groundball or flyball pitcher, so the chart can point out any trends developing in this area. If a groundball pitcher is giving up too many flyballs, he has a problem with mechanics or location.

Batter tendencies. A pitching chart reveals information about where the hitter likes to hit the ball, whether he swings or takes on the first pitch frequently, and whether he is weak on a particular pitch or location.

Success against right-handed and left-handed hitters. Compiling pitching charts over the course of a year can reveal valuable information about the pitcher's success against left- and right-handed hitters. Many coaches assume that a right-handed pitcher can get out a right-handed hitter easier than a left-handed pitcher against a right-handed hitter (and vice versa). This is not always the case, as the pitching chart will reveal.

Pitching patterns. The pitching chart reveals whether a pitcher is getting into a pattern with his pitches. For example, a pitcher might get fastball-happy and start out too many batters with a fastball.

Scoring statistics. Of course, the chart reveals all the official scoring statistics, such as innings pitched, hits, runs, earned runs, walks, and strikeouts.

Starting Pitcher's Pregame Routine

The starting pitcher should have a set routine that he follows the day of a game. Table 9.3 on page 176 is an example of a starting pitcher's routine. Coaches should develop a plan with each of the starters so that they will be thoroughly prepared when the game starts.

SAMPLE PITCHING CHART

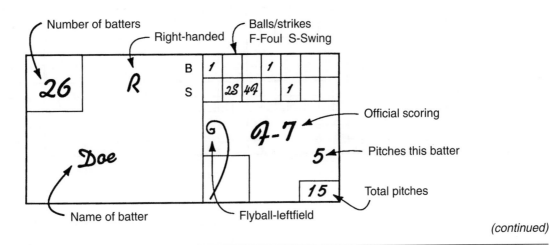

(continued)

Figure 9.5 The standard pitching chart is used to measure several different statistics.

PITCHING CHART

CATCHER _____   PREPARED BY: _____

BATTER

	B					
	S					

F - FOUL BALL   2 - CURVE   5 - SCREWBALL   - - - - - - GROUNDBALL

S - SWING   4 - CHANGE   6 - KNUCKLEBALL   ⌒ FLYBALL

1 - FASTBALL   3 - SLIDER   7 - FORKBALL   ⟶ LINE DRIVE

PITCHER	Left Hand Hitters					Right Hand Hitters				
	AB	H	AVG	SO	BB	AB	H	AVG	SO	BB

PITCHER	Total Batters	1st Pitch Strikes	Percentage	1st Pitch Selection				Total Ground Balls	Total Fly Balls	Total Line Drives
				FB	CB	SL	CH			

PITCHER	IP	H	R	ER	BB	SO		Fast Balls	Curves	Change	Slider	Screw Balls	Knuckle Balls	Fork Balls	TOTALS
							BALLS								
							STRIKES								
							BALLS								
							STRIKES								
							BALLS								
							STRIKES								
							BALLS								
							STRIKES								
							BALLS								
							STRIKES								
							BALLS								
							STRIKES								

COMMENTS: _____

_____

_____

AREAS TO IMPROVE: _____

_____

_____

Figure 9.5 *(continued)*

Table 9.3 Starting Pitcher Pregame Routine

Arrival

1. Check out weather conditions.
2. Check out field conditions.
3. Check out field dimensions, foul territory, and so on.
4. Discuss opponents with coach.
5. Relax and visualize.

Stretching

1. Casually stretch and loosen entire body.
2. Think happy and positive thoughts.
3. Calm the butterflies in the stomach with visualization.

Warm-up

1. Concentrate on individual keys such as rhythm, staying on top, or nose to toes.
2. Develop pitch-by-pitch focus.
3. Think positive-aggressive thoughts such as taking charge, relentlessness.
4. Start with fastball, go to change-up, and then to curveball or slider.
5. Pitch first inning in the bullpen.
6. At five minutes until game time, towel off and get a drink. Have last-minute communication with coach and catcher.

Arrival. Upon arrival the pitcher should gather any data that might be pertinent to his pitching performance. After gathering facts about weather, field conditions, and so on, he should talk with his coach to formalize a plan for the day. He should spend the rest of this time thinking about the opponents and visualizing success.

Stretching. The pitcher should allow himself plenty of time to get loose, stretch, and perform whatever other personal pregame rituals he needs.

Warm-up. The coach should now rejoin the pitcher and be there for the warm-up pitches to offer advice, make positive suggestions, or help with the mechanical aspects of the delivery. Different pitchers take different numbers of warm-up pitches, so it is important to time the end of the warm-ups to coincide with the start of the game. Table 9.4 shows a standard warm-up plan.

Managing the Bullpen

In an ideal world a team's starting pitching would be good enough and healthy enough

that every game would be a complete game. That's obviously not the case. A coach's management of the bullpen, his communication with the bullpen, and close administration of the bullpen can make the difference in many games—especially the close games.

Establishing Roles

Players perform better when they know their roles on the team. Relief pitchers are no exception, and establishing roles helps a relief pitcher to feel a part of the team. It also helps that pitcher to better prepare for his turn on the mound.

Players and coaches establish roles in several ways. Many coaches try to place their top three or four pitchers in the rotation, which makes sense because starting pitchers will throw a large percentage of a team's innings. After the rotation is established, there are several schools of thought about the rest of the pitching staff.

Should the coach have a good starting rotation that goes deep in the game and an offense that will produce leads late in the game, then the next-best pitcher ought to be

Table 9.4 Warm-Up Schedule and Plan

1. **Warm up to start a game or between-game workouts.**

   Jog 2 foul poles.

   Hang 1 minute.

   Stretch entire program.

   Jog 1 foul pole (before picking up baseball).

2. **Begin throwing fastballs to catcher (50 percent in full windup and 50 percent in stretch).**

   Start at 40 feet.

   Work back to 80 feet.

   When loose, go to rubber and start throwing to catcher in a down position. Make sure to throw from the same windup you would use in a game.

   Throw 3 pitches 1 foot outside left side.

   Throw 3 pitches 1 foot outside right side.

   Throw 3 pitches 1 foot outside left side.

   Throw 3 pitches 1 foot outside right side.

   Throw 3 pitches 6 inches outside left side.

   Throw 3 pitches 6 inches outside right side.

   Throw 3 pitches 6 inches outside left side.

   Throw 3 pitches 6 inches outside right side.

   Throw 3 pitches on black, outside right.

   Throw 3 pitches on black, outside left.

   Catcher mix up (in and out).

   Change-ups

   Work both corners (knees or lower).

   Do not quit until it is right.

   Alternate fastball and change-ups.

   Curves, sliders

   Start at 35 feet, spinning to catcher (5 pitches).

   Now at 50, spinning to catcher (5 pitches).

   Use full velocity.

   Alternate with fastballs.

   Catcher calls pitches; mix it up.

   Also throw two pitchouts to each side.

   Also throw two brushbacks to each side.

   Also throw two intentional walk pitches.

   Entire workout is equal to 50 to 60 pitches in 10 to 12 minutes, if 10 seconds between pitches.

   If entering game, put on jacket and go to dugout.

   If between starts, stretch just as before workout (run, then put on jacket or change undershirts).

the closer to protect those leads. On a team with average starting pitching and a suspect offense, perhaps that closer ought to come into a game after the starter to keep it close.

Most coaches agree that young, inexperienced pitchers should be worked in gradually in situations where they have a good chance to succeed. The middle of a game is usually the best time to wean the younger members of the staff. Also, anytime there is plus or minus four or five runs is a good time to get the feet wet. When a coach has several pitchers, all of whom are competent but none who stand out, then the approach would be to mix and match according to the situation, the batter, and so on.

No steadfast rules exist about the roles of relief pitchers, but the coach who studies the strengths and weaknesses of his pitchers as well as communicates daily with his staff will soon be able to discover some patterns.

Practicing Relief Situations

Relief pitchers, like all athletes, will have better success rates when they prepare for unique situations that they may encounter. Many of these situations can be simulated in the bullpen or intrasquads to get the relief pitchers mentally prepared.

Coaches can develop intrasquad games to work on different situations in the preseason to prepare for the upcoming season or midseason if a pitcher hasn't had much work. Coaches and players can set up and repeat any possible situations in an intrasquad for gamelike experience. Here is a situation: Bases are loaded. One out, or runners on second and third base and even runner on third base with no one out. Fielders and hitters benefit from these situation intrasquads as well.

Simulation games are great for pitchers who need work to stay sharp. A great way to keep the bullpen sharp as well as the bench players (who may not be getting a lot of at bats) is to end each practice with a little one-on-one competition. When these players are needed midseason because of a teammate's injury, they will be ready to contribute.

Position Players Who Pitch

It is not uncommon for position players to also pitch, especially in youth league. High schools will usually have one or two players who are two-way players; colleges may also have a couple of players who both pitch and play a position. Coaches need to pay extra attention to the welfare of these players to avoid taxing the players' arms and causing damage through overuse.

Two basic categories of two-way players exist: the starting pitcher who plays another position and the position player who is a relief pitcher.

Starting Pitcher–Position Player

When possible, try to put this player at a position that does not tax the arm, such as first base or the outfield. These positions require throwing but not as much as shortstop, third base, or catcher.

On days this player is a starting pitcher, he should be treated as a starting pitcher. The pregame should be identical to that of a regular starting pitcher and should not include infield or outfield drills in pregame or batting practice. If he is also the designated hitter, he should take batting practice but avoid any throwing except what is necessary for a starting pitcher. Upon removal from the game, the pitcher should not go play in the field; instead, he should do the warm-down and postgame procedure as a regular pitcher would.

On the day after the starting pitcher–position player starts, treat him as a regular starting pitcher; the two-way player should not start in the field. To avoid temptation, the two-way player who starts on the mound should be used in situations where the team does not have a game scheduled the next day. Most high school teams are not allowed to play on Sundays, so when possible the two-way pitcher should pitch on Saturday games. The starter in this situation can be the designated hitter the next day while his arm is resting and he is rehabbing for his next game.

Position Player–Relief Pitcher

Often position players with good arms are asked to come into a game in late innings and be the closer. An inning here and there will not hurt the closer's arm; however, arms can be damaged through overuse when not monitored.

The biggest problems concerning position player–relief pitchers are usually the day after pitching and too little bullpen work through the week. Common sense and good judgment should assist the coach with these decisions.

Treat the position player–relief pitcher as you would a regular pitcher. Should a regular pitcher throw two or three innings in a game, he would not be scheduled to pitch the next day. A position player–relief pitcher should not play the next day if he throws more than one inning in relief. It makes perfect sense to use these players on a day that does not precede a game day. As is the case with regular pitchers, if a two-way player has back-to-back one-inning stints, he should rest on the third day. Rest means not playing; it does not mean simply not pitching.

The position player–relief pitcher needs to throw from a mound between appearances to stay sharp and work on his game. On scheduled bullpen days the two-way player should make fewer throws from the field.

The two-way player can help himself and the team by being honest about the condition of his arm. Players who pitch through pain or have trouble getting loose not only can perform poorly and hurt the team but can also hurt themselves and perhaps their future in baseball.

All position players (with the exception of the catcher) may pitch on occasion. There have not been too many successful pitcher–catchers or catcher–relief pitchers because the throws are different and it's too taxing on the arm to go from one position to the other.

Bullpen–Game Communication

Many coaches do not have the luxury of having a bullpen coach or a phone system to the bullpen to communicate with the bullpen. This can create problems on game day unless a communication system is in place. The following are signs that coaches can use to communicate with the bullpen.

- *Right-hander* and *left-hander*. The coach will raise the appropriate hand and simulate a throwing motion.
- *Get ready* and *get ready ASAP*. A slow circle with the hand tells the pitcher to get ready. A fast circle means to get ready as soon as possible.
- *Ready sign*. The coach tips his hat to the bullpen to ask whether the pitcher is ready. The pitcher tips his hat if he is ready.
- *Number of pitches to get ready*. If the pitcher does not tip his hat, he should indicate so by holding up 5 fingers for 5 pitches or 10 fingers for 10 pitches. (Remember, the pitcher gets 8 more pitches on the game mound. Make sure the bullpen understands to include these 8 pitches in his readiness count.)
- *Sit down*. Sometimes the situation dictates the pitcher to sit down. Other times the coach will use both hands to push down to tell the pitcher to sit until further notice.

When the coach doesn't have an assistant coach or bullpen coach who can go down to the bullpen to monitor the action, then he should assign another player to go to the bullpen to relay information back to the coach.

By thinking ahead, the coach should be able to create some delay tactics to give the relief pitcher the time he needs to get ready. A signal to the catcher or third baseman to go to the mound to talk with the pitcher will allow for some time, especially if the player will wait until the umpire breaks up the talk on the mound. The coach himself can slow down his walk when necessary and wait until the umpire forces the coach to make a decision concerning a change of pitchers.

Pitcher's Bag

The pitcher's bag is fairly small, and one of the pitchers is responsible for bringing it to the bullpen. This bag contains items that the pitcher needs at some point during a game or practice. The pitcher's bag is kept in the bullpen at all times.

Baseballs

The bag should contain six to eight new baseballs that are to be used for bullpen work either in practice or before entering a game. If your team uses a ball that's different from that of other teams, the bag should also contain a few of the opponents' type of baseball so that a pitcher can get used to the seams of the strange ball. Nothing is more frustrating than having a relief pitcher who is supposed to be warming up but is looking for a baseball instead.

Surgical Tubing

Surgical tubing should be in the pitcher's bag so that the pitching staff can prepare for games when on the road. Tubing is a good tool for strengthening the pitcher's rotator cuff muscles, and it serves as a quick warm-up tool for a relief pitcher who may go into the bullpen. A loop should be tied on both ends of a four-foot piece of tubing so that it can be attached to a fence or pole in any situation. See chapter 4 for specific exercises using the tubing.

Roll-Up Home Plate

Unfortunately, many visitor bullpens are not kept up to home-bullpen standards. On occasion, home plate is missing from the visitor bullpen and a substitute is needed. A roll-up home plate can be a piece of carpet, plastic, or rubber cut in the shape of home plate and used in a pinch when needed.

Tape Measure

Some coaches still pull unsportsmanlike tactics to disrupt the opponent's pitchers by placing home plate at the wrong distance. A quick measurement can put home plate in the legal position and at the same time create a comfortable atmosphere for the pitchers.

Many Little Leagues and high school teams play at city parks that have no home plate to begin with. Why leave anything to chance? Measure off the correct distance, throw down a roll-up plate, and get started.

Clip-On Clipboard

A clip-on clipboard can be hung up on a fence in or near the bullpen. This clipboard can be

---

Relief Pitcher Game-Time Rules

1. Always have your spikes on.
2. Know where your glove is at all times.
3. Always have a game ball in your glove.
4. Watch the game to anticipate coaching moves.
5. Exercise and stretch between innings to stay warm.
6. Make sure the catcher is ready to go. The bullpen catcher should keep shin guards on at all times and a face mask close at hand.
7. Use surgical tubing to decrease warm-up time.
8. Be honest about readiness when the coach asks. Going into a game before you're ready does not help the team.
9. When ready, slow down between pitches but do not stop warming up unless coach indicates.
10. Work from the stretch in the bullpen. Chances are you'll be in the stretch when you go in the game.

used for any organizational purposes the coach might need. A coach can list the daily conditioning assignments or the throwing schedule for easy access.

During a game the coach might list who is first up to go into a game or who has the day off. The opponent's lineup card with some statistical information can be used to help the bullpen prepare for when they go in the game. This also allows pitchers to prepare mentally and physically for a situation when they might be needed. (For example, a left-handed player might see that three left-handed batters are coming up next inning, and he might be asked to pitch.).

Potpourri

The pitcher's bag might include a set of strings to use in the visitor bullpen, a two-seam and four-seam training ball to use for practice in staying behind the ball, and even a small dumbbell or two to work the elbow. Players keep a pitcher's bag so that they can be prepared for any situation and at the same time make the visitor's bullpen feel like home.

Evaluating Pitchers

Pitchers can be evaluated in any number of ways. The box score will indicate wins, losses, and saves as well as innings pitched, hits, strikeouts, and walks. This information is useful, but it only tells part of the story of a pitcher's performance.

Performance Statistics

Philosophies vary from coach to coach, but most coaches agree that there is a direct correlation between throwing strikes and winning baseball games. Statistics such as pitches per inning, strike percentage, and first-pitch strike percentage are very valuable to the coach as a teaching tool. Performance statistics do not have to be limited to three statistics. They can include batting averages for right-handed and left-handed batters, percentage of the time the lead-off batter reaches base, and even how often the lead-off batter scores. Percentage of walks that score is also a valuable statistical tool to help young pitchers

learn the importance of making the opposition hit the baseball.

Pitches Per Inning

Pitches per inning is a statistic that is more telling over the course of the season than it is during a single game. Efficient pitchers will find that the defense behind them plays better because they are more mentally prepared than they'd be with less-efficient pitchers. Umpires prefer pitchers who throw strikes and make things happen early in the count. Fewer pitches per inning also allow the pitcher to go deeper in the game, which saves on bullpen wear and tear.

Over the course of a season, pitchers who have a high pitch-per-inning statistic will need more recovery time between appearances and are more susceptible to injury. Obviously, strikeout pitchers will always have a higher pitch-per-inning count than a pitcher without strikeout ability.

Strike Percentage

At any level, the pitcher who throws strikes will prove to be more successful over the course of a season. A goal of 66 percent (2 of 3 pitches as strikes) is very achievable and can be used as a minimum standard depending on the level. Use of the strike percentage as an indicator of success teaches long-term pitching values. Because of the nature of the game, many external factors that are out of the pitcher's control affect the pitcher's performance. Strike percentage statistics encourage the pitcher to take charge of his efforts as well as take responsibility for the results of those efforts.

Getting Ahead

Getting ahead of the batter is the most significant of all pitching statistics. No other statistic correlates into individual and team success as the pitcher getting ahead of the batter. At any level an emphasis should be placed on getting that first pitch over the plate.

Getting ahead with the first pitch sets the tone for the at-bat. The mental implications alone make throwing the first pitch in there for a strike. The batter is in the hole and becomes more defensive, whereas the pitcher has many more options and can afford to be in a more relaxed frame of mind.

Batters who are first-pitch hitters will not be nearly as successful as those who work the count. The pitcher who can throw two or more pitches consistently over the plate will get a high percentage of one-pitch outs and keep his pitch count down in the process.

Pitcher's Diary

Many successful pitchers in the major leagues admit to keeping a notebook, journal, or diary of their performances. This is an excellent method of determining many things about themselves as pitchers. To be successful over the long run, a pitcher has to pay attention to all the details leading up to a performance so that he can make adjustments and improve on each performance along the way. A pitching diary can help a pitcher identify patterns and solve technical and mental problems, which will assist him in his preparation for his next appearance. The pitcher's goal is to be physically and mentally prepared to pitch. Keeping a daily diary of activities helps a pitcher realize just what will give him the opportunity for a peak performance.

Grading System

A grading system helps both the coach and the pitcher to evaluate performance and determine how the arm feels at any given moment; a grading system also fosters communication among all parties involved.

The letter grade system is simple and something all pitchers and coaches are familiar with. After prepractice stretching, conditioning, and perhaps even an easy long toss, the pitcher will report to the coach a letter grade indicating how his arm feels that day. This letter grade will then determine the rest of the practice for that pitcher. It is so important for the pitcher to be completely honest in his dealings with the coach so that the coach is able to help the pitcher.

The goal is to keep the arm in the *A* to *B* range as much as possible, especially on days when the pitcher is scheduled to pitch. Throwing routines, conditioning, drill work, and even weight training should be monitored with this in mind.

The A Arm

The pitcher's arm feels as good as it possibly can. An *A* arm means a good work day at practice. Coaches should be wary of the *A* arm if it is that pitcher's turn to pitch in a game. The pitcher who feels too good has a tendency to overthrow. The pitcher who reports an *A* arm on game day should probably do a little more conditioning before the game or perhaps throw a few more pitches in the bullpen before taking the field. The exception to this might be the overpowering relief pitcher who will enter a game throwing ultimate fastballs.

The B Arm

The pitcher with the *B* arm is feeling pretty good and can do a fair amount of work in practice. The majority of pitchers pitch their best games when they are in the *B* to *B*-plus range. They don't try to overthrow, and they have a tendency to locate their pitches. Coaches should prepare their pitchers throughout the week before pitching just enough to keep the arms in the *B* to *B*-plus range for game day.

The C Arm

The pitcher with the *C* arm has a tired arm and sore arm muscles. This soreness is the result of either a hard training day (such as a hard long-toss session) or a heavy bullpen, or perhaps the pitcher recently pitched in a game and is in the recovery stage. The pitcher with the *C* arm needs to do little throwing but a lot of stretching and conditioning in an effort to freely recover.

A starting pitcher who pitched the day before should have a *C* arm. A relief pitcher who threw more than 25 pitches the day before may also have a *C* arm. Remember that bullpen warm-up pitches also play a factor in arm care. A relief pitcher who was up in the bullpen off and on throughout the game will need special consideration.

The D Arm

The pitcher with the *D* arm is not only sore and tired but is feeling pain either in the elbow or the shoulder and should be monitored very closely. The pitcher should consult the trainer or even a doctor when he reports a *D* arm.

The cause of the *D* arm needs to be determined. The coach should review this pitcher's mechanics as well as the possibility of overuse. The *D* arm will need more recovery time than the *A*, *B*, or *C* arm requires; if the problem persists, it may be best to give this pitcher an extended period of rest.

The F Arm

The pitcher with the *F* arm is feeling acute pain and should be on the shelf until a physician determines the cause of his pain. After consultation with the physician, a plan of action can be developed.

PITCHER'S ASSIGNMENT SHEET

Date _____   Opponent _____

Pregame BP   **INF/OF**

Ball bucket _____   Back up   1B _____

Fungo   1B _____   3B _____

              2B _____   Plate _____

              SS _____   OF fungo _____

              3B _____   _____

Over the fence (RF) _____

Over the fence (LF) _____

Charts

Pitching chart _____   Running times _____

Spray chart _____   Radar gun _____

Get-ahead chart _____   Pitcher's bag _____

Foul balls _____

                    _____

                    _____

                    _____

Starting pitcher _____

Long relief _____

                    _____

Short relief _____

                    _____

Pregame conditioning _____

_____

_____

Announcements _____

_____

PITCHER'S EVALUATION CHART

1. Fill out all charts accordingly.

2. Counts

   A. # 0-1 - _____

   B. # 0-2 - _____

   C. # 1-2 - _____

   D. # 2-2 - _____

   E. # 1-0 - _____

   F. # 1-1 - _____

   G. # 2-0 - _____

   H. # 2-1 - _____

   I. # 3-0 - _____

   J. # 3-1 - _____

   K. # 3-2 - _____

   Add up A-D and E-K. A-D are advantage pitching counts. How many did you achieve?

   _____

3. Number of times ball was put into play in three pitches or less? _____

4. Areas to improve _____

   _____

   _____

   _____

   _____

   _____

   _____

   _____

5. Additional comments _____

   _____

   _____

   _____

   _____

   _____

   _____

   _____

   _____

Pitching Evaluation Sheet

Date _____

Name _____ Height _____ Weight _____

Top velocity _____ Working velocity _____ Future velocity _____

Types of pitches and grades (5 is college average)

FB	Movement	1	2	3	4	5	6	7	8	9	10
	Velocity	1	2	3	4	5	6	7	8	9	10
	Control	1	2	3	4	5	6	7	8	9	10

When and how to use _____

_____

_____

CB	Break	1	2	3	4	5	6	7	8	9	10
	Control	1	2	3	4	5	6	7	8	9	10
	Velocity	1	2	3	4	5	6	7	8	9	10

When and how to use _____

_____

_____

SL	Break	1	2	3	4	5	6	7	8	9	10
	Control	1	2	3	4	5	6	7	8	9	10
	Velocity	1	2	3	4	5	6	7	8	9	10

When and how to use _____

_____

_____

SP	Break	1	2	3	4	5	6	7	8	9	10
	Control	1	2	3	4	5	6	7	8	9	10
	Velocity	1	2	3	4	5	6	7	8	9	10

When and how to use _____

_____

_____

CH	Break	1	2	3	4	5	6	7	8	9	10
	Control	1	2	3	4	5	6	7	8	9	10
	Velocity	1	2	3	4	5	6	7	8	9	10

When and how to use _____

_____

_____

(continued)

MECHANICS

Full windup	1	2	3	4	5	6	7	8	9	10

Areas of concern _____

_____

Stretch	1	2	3	4	5	6	7	8	9	10

Areas of concern _____

_____

HOLDING RUNNERS

Pick to first	1	2	3	4	5	6	7	8	9	10
Release time	1.0	1.1	1.2	1.3	1.4	1.5	1.6	1.7		
Pick to second	1	2	3	4	5	6	7	8	9	10
Release time	1.0	1.1	1.2	1.3	1.4	1.5	1.6	1.7		

DEFENSIVE SKILLS

1-3 play	1	2	3	4	5	6	7	8	9	10
1-6-3 play	1	2	3	4	5	6	7	8	9	10
3-1 play	1	2	3	4	5	6	7	8	9	10
1-2 play	1	2	3	4	5	6	7	8	9	10
Bunt defense	1	2	3	4	5	6	7	8	9	10
Backing up bases	1	2	3	4	5	6	7	8	9	10
Range	1	2	3	4	5	6	7	8	9	10

MENTAL TOUGHNESS

Handles inclement weather	1	2	3	4	5	6	7	8	9	10
Degree that errors affect performance	1	2	3	4	5	6	7	8	9	10
Degree that missed calls affect performance	1	2	3	4	5	6	7	8	9	10
Pitching with runners in scoring position	1	2	3	4	5	6	7	8	9	10

PHYSICAL CONDITION

Health of arm	1	2	3	4	5	6	7	8	9	10
Cardiovascular	1	2	3	4	5	6	7	8	9	10
Leg strength	1	2	3	4	5	6	7	8	9	10
Abdominal strength	1	2	3	4	5	6	7	8	9	10
Flexibility	1	2	3	4	5	6	7	8	9	10
Weight	1	2	3	4	5	6	7	8	9	10

PERSONAL PITCHING STRATEGY _____

_____

_____

_____

Personal Pitching Plan

Name _____ R or L

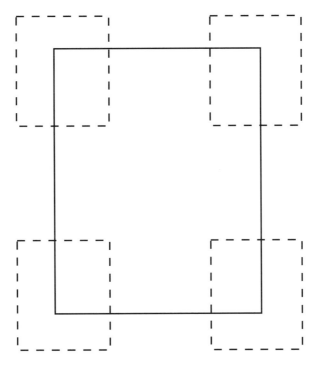

Left-handed
batter

Right-handed
batter

1 - Fastball
2 - Curveball
3 - Slider/split finger
4 - Change

about the author

Joe "Spanky" McFarland is the head baseball coach at James Madison University. He started his coaching career in 1977 and has coached at Florida State, Georgia Tech, South Florida, and Northern Illinois University before taking over at JMU in 1998. McFarland has coached 55 pitchers who have signed professional contracts. In 2002, he was named the Colonial Athletic Conference's Baseball Coach of the Year.